For Sharon & Mack

I hope You enjoyed
reading this book
as much I did
writing it.

29
Jan 30. 2019

THE FORESTER'S SON

The Forester's Son

One Man's Journey from Communist
Poland to the American Dream

By George R. Swiderski
with Aleksandra Corwin

ISBN 13: 978-1-4951-8032-3

Library of Congress Cataloging-in-Publication Data has been applied for

The Forester's Son

One Man's Journey
from Communist Poland
to the American Dream

George R. Swiderski
with ALEKSANDRA CORWIN

DEDICATION

In loving memory of my parents, who made me who I am today. For my mother, who instilled in me an appreciation for the beauty created by both God and men. For my father, who by example taught me the value of discipline, responsibility, and respect to others, and who also ignited in me a love of nature and the sport of hunting.

To my wife Sława—for her tireless work and valuable contributions throughout the process of writing this book. For reading my handwriting, for helping me recall my stories, and for her insightful viewpoints at every stage of the manuscript. But most of all, for the continued inspiration she has been to me for over fifty years of marriage.

And finally, to my biggest treasure—our daughter Krystyna, whom I love dearly, and for whom I wish to leave the story of my life.

You only live once.
If you do it right—
Once is enough.

PRESENT DAY POLAND

LOCATION OF VILLAGE

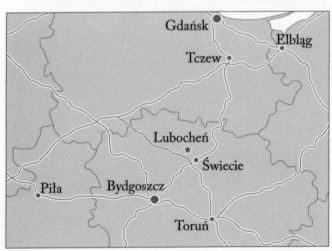

INDEPENDENT POLAND, 1920-39

CONTINENT OF AFRICA

CONTENTS

PART III. AFRICA, ART, AND THE AMERICAN DREAM 359

PREFACE

T HE VAST FORESTS OF RICH TIMBERLAND ALONG
Poland's Baltic shore have served as a staging ground for
hundreds of years of turmoil in modern European history. The
fortunes of Poland's people have risen and fallen at the whims
of its more powerful neighbors to the east and west—which in
alternating centuries stormed across the central European plain,
waging fierce battles back and forth.

These vulnerable borderlands are where I call home, and everything I am today has its roots in the troubled geography of the
place I was born. Thousands of years ago glaciers carved out the
rolling hills that frame the southern end of the grand Tuchola
Forest in northwest Poland. This pristine countryside is home
to thousand-year-old oak trees, and nestled among them is my
ancestral village, Lubocheń.

The bewitching landscapes that I loved as a boy exist today
only as a faint shadow of their former selves. The trauma of the
Second World War and a half century of Communist brutality
ripped apart the social fabric that had created the magical place
of my youth. Today you can go and visit those fields and those
homes, but they are not the same. They have been broken down
by history and war, divided by government, and painted over
by bureaucracy. Despite all the decades that have passed, I still

remember the grandeur of that place, and the harmony that existed for so many years. Neighbors were free to treat each other with honor and dignity, something the latter half of the twentieth century would rob them of.

My tale begins with two families, the Polish Swiderskis and the German Plehns, who should have been enemies, but instead were friends through one of the darkest periods in European history. It first unfolds over two hundred years ago in the twilight years of Poland's golden age in Europe.

Long before the wandering Germanic tribes of the central European plains were organized into anything resembling a nation-state, Poland was already a great and powerful country. The Polish-Lithuanian commonwealth was one of the largest and most populous of European countries from the mid-fourteenth century until the eighteenth century, when they were the predominant power on the European continent. The Polish commonwealth had a track record of progressive ideas, including religious tolerance and representative government. Unfortunately, and perhaps because they were in fact too progressive, their central government was weak. The elected monarchs they installed had little power over the landed gentry, and the requirement for unanimous votes in parliament meant constant legislative gridlock and inaction. Foreign actors with an eye on Poland's territory filled the power vacuum, and they were willing to pay large bribes to instill chaos and strife. By the late 1700s, Poland was disorganized and vulnerable to overthrow. In three waves, starting in 1772, Poland began to disappear from the map of Europe, first when Prussia annexed a large chunk of Poland's western edge, including Lubocheń.

Simultaneously, Austria-Hungary occupied the southwest provinces of Poland and the Russians moved in from the east. Poland lost about 30 percent of its landmass during these invasions.

Twenty years later, what remained of Poland was still in disarray, but in 1791 a new constitution was signed that was modeled on the historic American constitution, which had just been adopted in 1787. It represented new ideas of egalitarianism and democracy, and Poland's neighbors saw it as a threat because it could signify a Polish resurgence. The second partition came almost as soon as the new constitution was adopted, and in 1792 Russia and Prussia annexed another two-thirds of what remained of Poland. Skirmishes and Polish unrest increased, and in 1795 Russia, Prussia, and Austria-Hungary decided to do away with Poland entirely and divided up what remained among themselves. The Polish king was forced to abdicate the throne, and Polish citizens ceased to be represented on the map of Europe for the next 123 years.

This was a time of an ascendant Prussian Empire, what today we would think of as Germany. At this time the German Empire was encouraging the mass colonization of these areas of Poland, and hundreds of thousands of Germans moved into traditionally Polish lands. They were expanding, and they wanted Poland's fields, forests, and seaports in the north. The Plehn family rose to prominence around the time of Poland's partitions, and many quickly settled in the region I come from. In 1812, Napoleon's army marched through these regions en route to their disastrous invasion of Russia. History has recorded that the French developed a saying, "Cette plaine est pleine de Plehn" (The plain is full of Plehns)—a testament to this family's prominence and power.

The manor I was born in was an old stone building with massive brick cellars built deep into the ground, and had belonged to the Plehn family for nearly one hundred years. It resembled the architecture of the mid-nineteenth century, with its massive peaked roof and stucco walls, but legend had it that the original building dated to the 1600s and had been a convent for knights of the Teutonic Order. Growing up I heard stories about how the knights had occupied this region until about 1850, but that the convent had been neglected and had fallen into disrepair when support from Rome started flagging. There were rumors that a nun had been encased inside a brick wall in the cellar, alive, for having an affair with a knight. I was never completely sure if the stories were true, but it added to the allure and mystery of this place. The mid-1800s was the perfect historical moment for a Prussian gentleman to strike out on his own and explore the new frontiers of this country, and this is exactly what Anton Plehn did in 1850.

It was here, in what was then known as West Prussia, in 1865 that Rose Plehn, the youngest daughter of Anton Plehn, was born in the same estate that I would be born in seventy-five years later. After her parents died in the 1880s, she was the only one of the five Plehn children who continued living on and managing her family's land. She was the family anchor for her siblings, all of whom were prominent scientists, doctors, and professors and who would often visit Lubocheń.

The Plehn children were the movers and shakers of their day—their names are written down in the history books and science journals of the times. They published papers on original research in their fields, they agitated for rights of the oppressed, and Rose's paintings were collected by German galleries. They were fair and honest employers, and when Rose took the helm of her family's estate, it created a renaissance for the local Polish village because she employed almost every able-bodied person in town. They were respected and beloved by all who knew and worked for them.

While the Treaty of Versailles restored Poland as an independent state in 1919, sovereignty was short lived, because the Nazis would terrorize the land beginning in 1939. After six years of Nazi occupation, the final trauma of World War II swept through Lubocheń in the guise of the Russian front. Through all this, three generations of my family worked there, starting when my grandfather came into the employ of the wealthy German gentleman farmer Anton Plehn. Later on, my father would come to occupy a high position in the Plehn family estate as head forester for their valuable timberland. In the end, it was my father who was the last advisor, confidant, and employee of the Plehn household when it and its inhabitants were destroyed in 1945. He alone would bury the last of the Plehn heirs.

The Swiderskis and the Plehns enjoyed type of a unique harmony that is not often remembered in modern society, especially when we think of the Poles and Germans in this region of the world. That we treated each other with a fundamental respect for human dignity reflected the values of a bygone era. This was a time when a man was only as good as his word, and when nationalities and religious affiliation did not matter as much as honor and decency. When I was going through it, I didn't even realize what an extraordinary and powerful example my parents set for me amidst the horrors of World War II and the imposed Communism that followed. Being a young boy in those troubled times was all I had ever known. In many ways it wasn't until I was finally able to escape from behind the Iron Curtain and travel to America that I was able to completely grasp the magnitude of what I had experienced in the first twenty years of my life. From that point on, my life was dedicated to the great American values of life, liberty, and the pursuit of happiness. America has allowed this immigrant an opportunity to find himself and find a new place to put down roots in an adopted homeland. I have been lucky enough to fall in love along the way with an extraordinary woman who shared my values and dreams, Sława. Our lives have taken us on such a remarkable journey that we could not have imagined it in the sometimes-bleak moments of history we faced in our youth. Our story is a testament to what can happen when dreams and hard work meet in the place that nurtures them best, America.

PART I
The Last Heiress

CHAPTER 1

The Plehn Family

IF THERE WERE A SINGLE PLACE IN POLAND THAT captured all the facets of nature's bounty in one simple snapshot, it would be here. Lubocheń's wholesome, effortless beauty entranced all who visited there. The fields of natural wildflowers rolled on for miles, and the meadows were rich with fragrant grasses and fertile soil. The hilly banks of the Wda River, which locals called the Black Water River, and the gorges that shaped its various tributaries were lined with wildflowers that looked as though they were planted by some ancient creator purely for our enjoyment. This whole scene was planted beneath powerful oak and linden trees that would take a grown man thirty paces to walk all the way around. It bewitched all who set eyes upon it.

Anton Plehn was the youngest of the seven sons of Julius Reinhold Plehn, a wealthy German landowner and descendant of a long line of successful Prussian merchants and farmers. While most of Anton's siblings were entering the world of academia, Anton followed his heart and his love for nature. He was a man who loved the land, just like I did, and he had a talent for bringing forth life from the black soil. He chose Luboheń to settle in because few places could compare in terms of sheer beauty. Here nature showed off all of her possibilities in the bounty that erupted from every corner.

The Black Water River was the lifeblood that churned through these hills, connecting many of the ancient glacial lakes throughout the region. The water was perfectly clean, but when it flowed under the leafy canopy of the dense forest, and poured over the dark soil, it looked black. Many treasured days of my youth were spent fishing and swimming in the Black Water River, and catching frogs that huddled on its shores. The Baltic Sea was just beyond Luboheń, a little over eighty miles away, and it permeated the air we breathed. It provided a moderating effect on the weather, and enriched the soil with its salty essence. The wildflowers thrived on this fresh breeze, and the oak trees survived for hundreds of years, with some rumored to still be healthy and strong at over one thousand years old.

The earliest historical texts ever written about Poland date to approximately AD 1112 and were written in Latin by an ancient historian known today only as Gallus Anonymous. Gallus is thought to have been a highly educated French monk traveling in Poland at this time, and his manuscripts were the first written accounts of the history and rulers of Poland. All Polish children learn about these texts in grade school, but they were especially notable to me because they specifically document battles that happened right in my backyard. His texts are some of the most precious manuscripts in existence on medieval Europe, and in them Gallus names certain towns, like Drzycim, which were less than an hour's walk from my home, and which were the site of important battles between Polish soldiers and pagan Germanic tribesmen. Gallus was writing about the frontiers of Europe at the time, and my neighborhood featured prominently. Growing up I would play in the Wda River and often envision the troops that must have stormed across it hundreds of years ago in full battle dress.

Growing up I assumed, as did everyone I knew, that the massive building at the center of Lubocheń was in fact a remnant from the Middle Ages. Old stories swirled about the days when the Teutonic knights, a German military order, roamed this land, forcibly converting pagan Prussians to Christianity, at the order of the Holy Roman Empire. It was essentially a grand three-story brick mansion, with several levels of large basements that in places revealed walls that were four feet thick. It had been abandoned by the knights when they lost power and fell out of favor in the German Empire in the early 1800s. Anton Plehn would buy this property, and the surrounding fifteen thousand acres, and make this his home in 1858.

When Anton Plehn settled here, Poland was not a traditional feudal society, and people did not belong to their lords. A landowner could buy a village, but he did not own its people. Residents were compensated for their labor and for their time spent working the owner's land. The Lubocheń estate was divided evenly between mature virgin timberland and agricultural land that Anton was eager to cultivate, employing virtually all the people in the village.

Anton had finished his agricultural studies in Germany, where he met and married Johanna Maercker. They settled in Lubocheń in 1860 and thus began an era of prosperity that would build a meaningful foundation for the next generation of Plehns. My maternal grandfather was already working for Anton Plehn at this time, and he was one of the only members of my family to meet (and therefore remember) the Plehn patriarch before his untimely death from illness in 1887.

The first child of Anton and Johanna Plehn, Albert, was born in 1861, and the younger daughter, Rose, who would save my father's life more than once, was born in 1865. This was a period of prosperity and happiness for the Plehns. Anton Plehn traveled to the illustrious World's Fairs in London and Paris—essential and important trips for any serious and worldly person of the times. The World's Fair was a place of new ideas and inventions that were essential to the progress of his generation. They were not primarily for entertainment value. Anton would bring back cutting-edge agricultural ideas to implement at home. While he was a gentleman and a landowner, he was first and foremost a dedicated naturalist. In addition to farming, Anton also set up a distillery and a kiln for making bricks—as these two were actually more profitable for him at the time than farming. The family had many sources of income and prospered.

In 1868 the Plehns built a large addition to the house and were dutifully raising their five children. Until now the family had been living in the old manor, with cellars that looked like they were built in medieval times. Now Anton Plehn invested in an expanded living section adjoined to the older portion to house his growing family. Most of the rooms in the manor featured grand twelve-foot-high ceilings that were common in Europe at the time. The height made everything look all the more spectacular. The entire home was lined with massive, ornate crown moldings made out of dark wood. Some rooms, such as the library, were lined with wood paneling from floor to ceiling, while the rest of the house was covered in ornate, shimmery wallpaper. In the central entryway there was an immense spiral staircase that stretched four stories—from the basement to the top floor of the house. It had elaborate carved railings and carpeted stairs and was an imposing presence to all who entered.

After completing studies at the local high school, the Plehn children were sent to universities either in Germany or throughout Europe. Unfortunately, tragedy struck the family when the youngest daughter, Ilse, died at age ten in 1880. Johanna Plehn fell into a deep depression from which she would never truly recover. During this time the farming economy also experienced a depression, and by 1888 both Plehn parents had succumbed to illness and infirmity within a few months of each other. Rose Plehn was only twenty-three at this time, and all five of the remaining Plehn children were in various universities in Germany. The Lubocheń estate would surely have been lost if it were not for Anton's brother Bernhard Plehn who lived nearby, and who stepped in to manage the property. In doing so he also ensured the children's educations were financed and completed. Much of the land had to be sold off to pay for the children's education, but Uncle Bernhard was a blessing to the still inexperienced Plehn heirs.

It's worth noting how unusual it was for the family of a gentleman farmer to invest so heavily in the educations of all their children—including the girls. There were two doctors, two professors, and another child with a PhD, all of which was highly uncommon for this day and age. There were of course many wealthy, landed families in the region, but they generally sent their children to finish some sort of agricultural studies in local schools, and that was the extent of it. The Plehn children meanwhile developed a social circle of illustrious figures, mainly revolving around German intellectuals such as Friedrich Nietzsche and Ricarda Huch.

The Plehn children were taken with the possibilities of travel, and all of them would go on to lead adventurous lives. All three brothers pursued distinguished careers in academia. The two oldest, Albert and Friedrich, both became medical doctors who traveled the world with German and Dutch expeditionary forces and made enormous strides in battling tropical diseases. They became famous in Bavaria as lecturers and authors on the subject of exotic illnesses. Albert Plehn first ventured to the Far East as a ship's surgeon with the Dutch military in the Dutch East Indies, today known as Indonesia. Later on, just five years after Cameroon became a German colony in 1884, both brothers, doctors with a desire to see the world and alleviate what suffering they could, set off for the unexplored African wilderness.

At the time, Africa was known mainly as the "white man's graveyard" because of the rampant malaria for which there was no reliable treatment. Both brothers would spend a large part of the next decade working on and researching these tropical diseases, at great peril to their own health, in these uncharted lands. They were able to make major breakthroughs in the application of quinine as a treatment for malaria, which saved countless lives of both locals and Europeans. As they began their research, a common and horrible side effect of treating malaria with quinine was known as the blackwater fever, named after the telltale symptoms of fever and black urine, and which often resulted in death. The Plehn brothers were able to devise an application of quinine that was effective against malaria but not dangerous to the patient. They were therefore also able to halt the progression of the blackwater fever. Albert and Friedrich Plehn thus paved the way for further European exploration of the African continent, which was one of the most significant medical advances of that era. They both published works that became the bible for all Europeans wishing to survive Africa, and became in-demand lecturers and experts on these subjects. They were arguably the most famous doctors in Bavaria at this time.

The youngest brother, Rudolph, was also taken with high adventure while he simultaneously pursued higher education. He joined the German army, and in 1895 became their representative at the outpost in Misahoehe, Togo. He earned his doctorate in 1898 after spending several years studying the ethnology of the various tribes of Togo while with the German colonial forces there. His pioneering work was the first major German book to describe the relationships of the tribes in these regions. He took after his father and later studied his first true love, which was nature and dendrology, or the study of trees. In 1899, Dr. Rudolph Plehn, also an officer in the German army, organized an exploratory expedition on the Ngong River, where he would serve as resident expert on forestry and plant life. Unfortunately, the unit was ambushed, and Dr. Plehn met his end while fighting valiantly. He was shot in the right side of his ribs with a poisoned arrow. Before he collapsed he was able to yank the arrow out of his side, and continued to calmly lead the battle charge over the ridge to overtake the fortress the locals were hiding behind. Once he and his men were inside the newly captured fortress, Rudolf sat down on a bench, and died. His sergeant later wrote an emotional account of the battle, describing the heroics of Dr. Plehn in leading the charge, despite his soldiers' pleas to keep his head down.

The Plehn brothers certainly had their share of adventure and excitement, but it was actually the oldest sister, Marianne, born in 1863, who achieved perhaps the most fame and success over her long career. Marianne Plehn dedicated her life to science, and never married. Even given her highly educated and progressive family, it was unheard of for a woman to declare that she would pursue a career in academia, like her brothers. This was all the more unusual since they had grown up in the country and not in a big city. This only spoke more of her determination and strong will, traits which were clearly a part of all the Plehn children. Her pioneering work in zoology with a specialization in fish pathology helped keep Germany's lakes and streams healthy and bountiful. Like any woman of those times, Marianne constantly faced the obstacles placed before women in obtaining a higher education. No university in Germany would accept her, and so instead she pursued her studies in Switzerland, where she received her doctorate in zoology in 1893. By 1898 she was already a renowned expert in her field, and is today considered one of the founders of the field of fish pathology. She spent thirty years on the faculty of the prestigious Royal Veterinary College in Munich, where she consistently published groundbreaking research on the study of diseases affecting life in the water. She traveled all over the German Empire whenever there was an epidemic among fish and other cold-blooded species, which were her specialty. She battled the odds, and pursued her love of the study of animals and fish, along with the health of the various bodies of water that supported them.

Perhaps most telling of all, she was truly accepted into the brotherhood of her fellow scientists. In 1914, she became the first woman in history awarded the title of Royal Professor by the king of Bavaria, which was an enormous honor. When she retired in 1929, her colleagues at the University of Munich published an article highlighting the fact that it was a woman who had made such an enormous contribution to this field of study, despite having all the odds stacked against her. They praised her illustrious career and admitted that despite being an uncommon phenomenon at the time, Dr. Marianne Plehn was in fact "the embodiment of collegiality" in their department. Even though she could have retired to a life of leisure, she maintained an office and lectured at the university until her death in 1946.

Their causes and passions flung this family far and wide, and it was Rose, the younger daughter and the artist of the family, who held them all together. While I certainly share her brothers' thirst for adventure, it was Rose's life choices that speak to me the most. While no one in my family was an artist, I felt I had grown up with Rose Plehn's example before me. Like Rose, I went to art school, and like her, I filled my home with paintings, and exotic artifacts from around the world. I believe that the wonders that filled her house inspired me from my earliest memories with an appreciation for the importance of surrounding myself with elements that appealed to my visual sense. It would forever influence the course my life took.

After Rose finished her primary schooling she knew instinctively that she wanted to dedicate her life to art. From a very young age she exhibited a natural talent for drawing. She studied art in Dresden and Berlin at several different conservatories, working under various prominent master artists. In 1890 she moved to Munich where she studied under the illustrious German artist Ludwig Herterich at the Academy of Fine Arts in Munich. He was one of her greatest artistic influences, and his realism and attention to detail was reflected in her equally lifelike works. It was during this time of living in a big city that she developed friendships with prominent thinkers and intellectuals of her day. She would later credit her friends such as poet Friedrich Huch and philosopher Ludwig Klages with inspiring her work. Klages in particular was known for his involvement in the Munich Cosmic Circle—a group of progressive thinkers and writers who met at the turn of the century to discuss philosophy and mysticism. Rose held many exhibitions of her work in Munich and other prominent European cities. They were well reviewed and the pieces were collected by her fellow society members. Her paintings were saturated with themes of spirituality and nature. She also painted massive landscapes of West Prussia—her home, and my home.

When it came time for Rose to pick a place to make her residence after she finished her studies in 1905, it was easy for her to decide on Lubocheń. She became the sole owner and heir of the estate while her surviving family members roamed the globe. She would be the anchor that would hold them all together, and for years the Plehn family would reunite for the summers at the Lubocheń estate. At the time that Rose moved back permanently, it had been many years since any member of the Plehn family had lived there year-round. She created a sort of renaissance for the village, because her lands employed all of the roughly 130 people who lived in Lubocheń. In addition, there were large barracks adjoining the fields which would house the hundred or so migrant workers that arrived for each harvest season from central Poland. This was once again a time of plenty and productivity in Lubocheń.

Along with her siblings, Rose's friends from her time at university enjoyed soaking in the relaxing atmosphere of country life in Lubocheń when they needed a break from the big cities in Germany. Some of her friends were prominent personalities of the times, such as Ricarda Huch—one of the first women to receive a doctorate from Zurich University, and who was a famous poet and historian—and Käthe Kollwitz, considered one of the most important German artists of the twentieth century. Rose and Käthe studied art together at the University of Munich in the late 1880s under Ludwig Herterich. Käthe was a talented draftsman and sculptress, and agitated for the working class. She also criticized the Nazi regime, as did most of the German elite, but was able to get away with it thanks to her fame. Rose's social circle reflected her status in life; the people who surrounded her were aristocrats and intellectuals, and like the majority of the German elite at this time, they hated Hitler and the Nazis. They saw Nazi populism as an appeal to the lowest common denominators of society—a set of values that would set out to destroy the cultural and intellectual accomplishments of civilization. In conversations with my parents Rose would reveal her opinion of the Nazis as an uncouth horde, which rejected God, common decency, and human dignity. This was her position before the worst of what the Nazis did was even known. Like any educated woman of her day, she was involved in the events of the time, and my parents remembered her constantly coming and going, attending meetings and lending her support to important causes. By nature of her high education and interests, she was involved in the European Bohemian movement, and was one of the artists producing work during this restless period in European history.

Rose Plehn's manor was full of exotic collections representing different cultures from all over the world. For decades the family had amassed a library that was full of thousands of rare books and priceless manuscripts. The walls were hung with leather tapestries and mounts of exotic animals, mainly from Africa. Her brothers had also collected a variety of primitive weapons during their expeditions, and never-before-seen costumes and masks rounded out this collection. The Plehn manor was an extraordinary museum that could have rivaled any at the time in Poland. This was the house I would soon be born in.

My mother's father, Jan Mackowski, was at this point the manager of the agricultural workers who farmed the land. He would ring a large gong that stood on the edge of the field to symbolize when the workday started and ended, and was in charge of all personnel issues in the fields. My father, born in 1900, was still a young man at the time, but he too would soon start to work in Rose Plehn's forests.

It was in the twilight of these peaceful years in Lubocheń that my parents would come into her direct employ. My brother Henry was fifteen years old when I was born, and my sister Henrietta was twelve. They were already teenagers when the darkest period in Lubocheń began to unfold. While I didn't arrive on the scene until 1941, the events to come would soak themselves into the fabric of the Swiderski family, and the storm that arrived would shape the course of my life for good. The peace was about to be broken.

CHAPTER 2

My Forefathers

MY MOTHER WAS BORN IN LUBOCHEŃ IN 1903, while my father was born in Kromplewice, later moving with his family to a nearby village called Bedlenki. My paternal grandfather worked in a sawmill there, just over two miles away from Lubocheń. My parents and grandparents were raised in a world where Poland had not existed for over one hundred years, and yet they always considered themselves Polish to the core. They attended Prussian schools and took lessons in German, but they spoke Polish at home and attended Polish mass. Both of my parents completed middle school in German, and for the rest of their lives could read and write Polish and German with equal fluency. Most Polish families in this region were peasants who worked the land—they had little social status and rented a small plot for cultivating from the landowner, to whom they paid rents. It was rare for a family to insist on educating their children past grammar school, and yet my grandparents did it for my parents, and my parents did it for us. That my parents grew up fluent in the language of their occupiers, the Prussians, would later prove to be a mixed blessing. While it is surely one of the reasons my father was able to make a name for himself in this region, it also earned him many enemies and made our lives difficult when disgruntled locals assumed that anyone who spoke German had questionable loyalties. As the war was coming to a close, and it was clear the Germans would be on the losing end, my father's life was in grave danger because of these very facts.

My father was the oldest of seven children, and when his father died suddenly, he became the man of the house at the age of fourteen. He quickly earned a reputation for being strong and tough, despite being only five foot six. More importantly, he had a well-deserved reputation as a man who was fearless and didn't shy away from throwing a punch if someone deserved it.

It was the same year that the First World War began, and my father, born in 1900, was just coming of age. In 1914, Poland was divided among the Prussians (or Germans), Austro-Hungarians, and Russians. The Prussians and Austro-Hungarians were the aggressors in the war, and would stand to lose much of their land as it became clear they were facing defeat. Thousands of Polish soldiers joined the Allied forces against Germany because they knew there was a possibility that as World War I came to a close, Poland might again have a chance at independence. After nearly five years of bloodshed, Poland would be reconstituted as an independent nation at the end of 1918.

There was a sizable Polish contingent of about one hundred thousand soldiers that fought with France during WWI, against the Germans. There were even an estimated twenty-five thousand volunteers from America, mostly recent Polish immigrants, who crossed the ocean just to join the cause of Polish independence. Renowned Polish General Józef Haller led this group of enthusiastic expats across Europe. In 1916 he became the commander of the Polish Legion in France, which was the name for the Polish army abroad, and which would later go on to fight its way across Poland, and against the Bolsheviks on the eastern front.

General Haller's volunteer Polish army fought against the Germans in Poland in the final months of the war, and he was able to seize the important port city of Gdańsk in 1920. My father was finally of legal age and he joined the Polish volunteers pushing the Germans out of our region as soon as he could. He eventually joined the cavalry and served on horseback for two years with Haller's Army in Poland before he returned home. At the time, the formation of Haller's Army was an event of massive significance for the Polish people. They were pushing the Germans out of the last Polish lands they still held on to. More importantly however, for the first time in 123 years a Polish army came into existence, complete with a Polish uniform and Polish flag. The fervor of patriotism and joy that swept across the nation at this time was immense. It was the first time in anybody's memory that the Polish nation again took its place alongside the countries of Europe.

In February of 1920, just after the last of the Germans had been forced out, General Haller conducted an important ceremony in the town of Puck, near Gdańsk. The event was called Poland's "Wedding to the Sea" and symbolized Poland's renewed access to the Baltic Sea, which had been lost since 1792. My father was present on the shore as General Haller threw a platinum ring into the water, representing Poland's fidelity and union in perpetuity with the ocean. Bruno Swiderski, my father, was nineteen years old as he witnessed the rebirth of Poland, and his dedication to a free Poland never wavered from that moment on.

Later that year, in August 1920, the Bolsheviks invaded Poland from the east, and the newly formed Polish army was called again to fight foreign invaders. My father was with the forces of General Haller's army as they held the northern front in fighting off the Reds. The Communists, led by Lenin, had just seized power in Russia, had killed the last Tsar, and believed it was the perfect moment to try to seize as much land as they could in a Europe that was still reeling from WWI. Their goal was to bring their Communist ideology all the way to the shores of Britain. The Polish army, led by General Józef Piłsudski and commanded in the various regions by his senior leaders, among them General Haller, participated in the epic Battle for Warsaw of 1920, known as the "Miracle on the Vistula River." Despite being vastly outnumbered, the Polish army was able to outmaneuver the Communist forces and push them back to their border. My father fought as far as Kiev under General Haller before returning home.

This was a happy and exuberant time for Poles—they were once again living in a free country! The German schools were disbanded, and there was a newfound joy and energy in Polish people everywhere. The Germans were still the primary landholders in our region of northwest Poland, and they were allowed to keep ownership of their land, under the condition that they take on Polish citizenship after 1919. Poland was not feudal at this time because while lords could own the land, they did not own the people who lived on it. Peasants were paid wages for working the land, and were required to provide a certain amount of goods to their landlords in return for their private parcels. My father came back from the war and went to work in the local village. It was the Roaring Twenties, and in his spare time he also became a drummer in a local band, a true renaissance man of his times. Most importantly he began courting my mother.

He liked to tell the story of how he would walk the four kilometers to her village once a week, in his only suit, to visit with her. Once when he was leaving Bedlenki on his way to visit my mother, Waleria, he passed by a house in Dolsk that was on fire, and a full bucket brigade was out front tossing water onto the flames to put out the blaze. A fat policeman was standing in the middle of the scene directing able-bodied men to pick up a bucket and start helping. He tried to force my father to participate in the bucket brigade, but my father wasn't about to ruin his only suit, which he needed to wear when he courted his girlfriend, Waleria. Basically, he just punched the policeman, knocking him to the ground, tossed the policeman's gun into the bushes, and ran off. That was my father—tough and strong willed, both traits that would serve him well during the coming difficult phases of his life.

He and my mother were married in 1923, and they settled in the nearby village of Dolsk. My oldest sister, Halina, was born in 1924, followed by Henry in 1926, Henrietta in 1929, and Casey in 1931. By the early 1930s my father was working as a logger in the vast Tuchola Forest, a large portion of which was owned by the Plehn family. This time in his life was also when he first encountered a man named Ernst Niehoff, a figure who would play prominently in my family's future.

After WWI, Lady Rose was in her late fifties and wanted to slow down the pace of her life and focus as much on painting as she could. She decided to issue a long-term lease on her land to a local German man starting in the 1920s. This man was the troublesome Herr Niehoff. It was an unusual move for a landed gentry woman such as herself to lease her lands to a stranger, but Rose had her own ideas about how she preferred to spend her time. She was well liked and respected by her neighbors and community members, so while people might have shaken their heads at her methods, they understood her desire to want to focus her energies elsewhere.

Her land was truly gorgeous. The forests were filled with pine, spruce, and many varieties of hardwood evergreens. There were also oak and linden trees in abundance, many of which were hundreds of years old. This was virgin forest that had never been touched, and provided a rich source of timber for the surrounding areas. All the forests were filled with ravines and low rolling hills, and it was a lush, leafy, and tranquil place that my father worked in.

While my father had worked on the Plehn lands from a young age, Herr Niehoff was the man who first hired him. His job was to cut down specific sections of the massive pinewoods and float the logs down the river to where they could be loaded onto trains at a dock. This was the only economical way to move the timber, and it was considered a very dangerous job because it was a fast-moving river and if the logs came apart you could easily get crushed between them, as happened to many men in those days. From there he proved himself as a tough and able-bodied young man, and started to work his way up. However, there was trouble with Niehoff almost from the start. My father was a meticulous man and kept records of his daily activities, including how many trees were cut, from which sections, what was replanted, and so on. Within a relatively short amount of time he realized Niehoff was lying to Lady Rose about the figures, and severely underreporting to her the actual amounts he was harvesting. My father was shrewd and honest, and felt he had to report to the lady of the manor what was happening, and that Niehoff was cheating her out of large amounts of money.

Soon enough my father had enough undeniable proof in his records, and he went to Lady Rose with his findings. She was devastated at the news, and on the strength of my father's records, took Niehoff to court. She sued him for damages, and asked the judge to break the lease she had signed with him for the timberland, as she now wanted it back in her possession. Based on the meticulous detail of my father's notes, the judge awarded Lady Rose control of her timberlands, and ended Niehoff's leasehold in that region. While he still retained the roughly two thousand acres of agricultural land, the two thousand acres of Tuchola forests returned to Lady Rose's sole control. My father, meanwhile, had made a dangerous enemy for life out of Niehoff, and their clashes would lead to many sleepless nights in our family.

After this, Lady Rose realized that Niehoff was basically a scoundrel. It was soon apparent that he was cheating her in other dealings as well. For the term of the lease they had signed, Niehoff was supposed to provide a certain amount of money and goods to Lady Rose. He was always coming up short, and had myriad excuses for why he couldn't provide the amount of eggs, milk, pigs, or other goods that he had agreed to. At the time, the man running the forests was another German by the name of Rajkowski. He had not been an employee of Lady Rose's for long, but had taken over after Niehoff had gotten kicked out. The truth was that this new forester, Rajkowski, was in cahoots with Niehoff all along. In 1933 the term of Niehoff's lease on the agricultural land was supposed to expire, and Lady Rose was looking forward to that day that she would be free of the dreaded Niehoff for good. She had by then realized what a terrible mistake it was for her to lease out the lands. Rajkowski, at the behest of Niehoff, had asked Lady Rose to sign a document, as she undoubtedly had to sign many official papers in the course of her timber business. Unbeknownst to her, Rajkowski had actually put a ten-year extension on the lease in front of her, and she had unwittingly signed it. Niehoff was filled with glee that he had a legal document entitling him to ten more years of exploitation, and it was actually my father who broke the news to Lady Rose of what they had tricked her into doing. By this time she was sixty-eight years old, and of course she relied on her advisors and employees to help her run her estate. When she realized what she had done, she collapsed and remained in her room for a full day without getting out of bed. The entire family was terribly worried about her, and my sister Henrietta remembers the eerie hush that fell on the house that day when Rose fell ill from this betrayal.

This was the moment when Rose finally realized that the only person she could trust was her Polish logger, my father. She fired the German forester Rajkowski immediately, but there was no legal recourse for her to take beyond that or against Niehoff, as she had signed a legally binding document. Niehoff had been a thorn in her side from the moment she decided to lease him her family's land. From 1933 forward, my father became her chief forester and trusted advisor in all the business matters of her estate. My father would protect her from those sorts of mistakes in the future, and from all those who would try to take advantage of an elderly lady's trust.

Over the subsequent years my father became her chief champion and advisor. As sharp as Lady Rose was, she was nonetheless an aging woman, without any of her family around her, and she was trying to run a huge estate on her own. She increasingly leaned on my father for advice. The Polish peasants in the area generally didn't speak German, and so my father's fluency in both languages was in great demand. Thus began a period of flourishing for our family. However, the most serious consequence of this period was that my father made an enemy of Niehoff, and this would later put his life in great danger when the Second World War came and the Germans occupied the whole region.

Still, these years witnessed the beginning of what would be a beautiful friendship between our family and Rose. For the next six years, our family would enjoy a period of relative peace and prosperity. My father was gainfully employed, and his children were healthy and growing, enjoying their rich surroundings and attending Polish schools. The best part about coming into Lady

Rose's confidence was that our family now helped maintain her private thirty-acre park, which was directly adjacent to the manor. This was land set aside for her own private cultivation and enjoyment, and it was rich with fruits, flowers, and rows of plump vegetables. That our family could work in Rose's private garden, instead of toiling all day in the fields for Niehoff's gain like most of the other Poles in the region, was an enormous blessing.

Life at the Plehn estate hummed, and the four oldest Swiderski children enjoyed the prosperity and calm that came with living under the auspices of a kind German lady in a newly established Poland.

CHAPTER 3

Life at the Estate
of Lady Rose

LADY PLEHN, AS I CALLED HER AS A BOY, WAS A KIND
and impressive figure. She was the last of the Plehns to live
and die in Poland. In my later years, as I realized my home in
America increasingly resembled the Plehn manor of my youth, I
would often think back on this illustrious figure I was fortunate
to know. She was a fair-minded woman, an activist, and an artist.
What I remember most about Lady Plehn was how tall she was:
taller than my father, probably close to five foot ten in height. She
was always attired in layers of Victorian-era dresses, even though
they might have been considered old-fashioned by the 1930s. She
never left her private apartment with a thread out of place, and
her long white hair was always tied in a neat bun at the base of her
neck. On her left arm there was always a small woven basket that
held in it a large ring of more than a dozen large metal keys that
unlocked various storerooms and buildings on the property. She
was very slender, and with a spine as straight as a candlestick and
her strongly tailored attire, she was always an imposing figure.

As long as Lady Rose's remaining siblings were alive they would continue to visit their family home, especially during the summer. Although her brothers Friedrich and Rudolph had died tragically at the turn of the century, her oldest brother, Albert, continued to summer here and visited regularly until his death in 1935. She was also close with her older sister, Marianne, who would visit frequently until her death in 1946. Her siblings would bring with them their friends and members of their social circles from the big cities in which they resided. These prominent European personalities were often making appearances in Luboche\'n. In 1917, famous German artist and activist Käthe Kollwitz recorded in her journal an account of her time in Luboche\'n, where she spent time working on important posters and sculptures that agitated on behalf of equal rights for the working class. Many prominent personalities from Germany found relaxation and refreshment among Luboche\'n's charms.

Lady Rose would entertain lavishly throughout the years before WWI, and immediately after as well. The dining room was massive and had a table that could easily seat fifty people. She lavished guests with elaborate feasts whenever they came to visit. This was the heyday of prosperity on the farm; Rose was in charge of managing all the land, and she was still full of vigor and energy. My parents remembered how she would host large dances in the meadows on her property for everyone in Luboche\'n, providing food and drink for all to enjoy. She would give a gift to everybody who worked for her, and was generally loved and appreciated by everyone in the town. As she grew older however, she increasingly retreated into her art. By the time WWII was on the horizon, she spent most of her free time painting rather than entertaining. She increasingly preferred smaller, more intimate gatherings, and stopped hosting as many big parties.

The place where she entertained most often was the salon. There were rich hardwood floors with colorful exotic rugs overlaid on top of them. The centerpiece here was the prominent portrait she had painted of her parents, which hung in the center of the main wall above the fireplace—opposite the row of windows, which looked out onto the garden. The room was tastefully decorated with a selection of precious antiques, and a large grand piano resided prominently in one corner. She had it tuned every year by a blind German man to ensure the utmost quality of its sound.

Up until WWII broke out, Lady Rose was always attending meetings in town for a cause, or traveling abroad for rendezvous with prominent intellectuals and artists. Later on, I watched her life as she came and went, not truly understanding what it meant but knowing that I, too, wanted to have such a meaningful and rich life. Even today I can still hear the clatter of her handsome coach approaching on the cobblestone drive in front of the house, pulled by two shiny black horses and attended by a finely polished coachman in white gloves and a top hat.

In her later years, Rose spent more and more time in her art studio, which was a separate building on her estate, dedicated just to making art. She painted beautifully, but her topics at times could be serious and dark. Her themes were often religious, and I remember the enormous canvasses she painted that depicted scenes from the Bible and other prominent religious figures. There was one scene of St. Francis surrounded by animals in a barn, and was at least two by three meters in size. The cows and donkey were fully life-size. They were painted in a very specific Italian medieval style—very dark with only parts of the faces shown in the light. I remember these paintings well because my father persuaded her to donate them to our local Catholic church, where they hung for the next twenty years. They had to send their largest hay wagon to pick them up. Most Germans in those regions were Protestant and were at best suspicious of Catholicism, and saw Polish Catholicism as backward compared to their religion, but Rose wasn't like that at all. She had her own opinions and judged everyone around her based on their merits.

The truth is, Rose was not very politically or religiously motivated. She had good relationships with almost everyone she came in contact with, and as she grew older, what she wanted most of all was time alone to paint. Decades later, sitting in the garden enjoying the sunshine at my home in Palatine, my mother would fondly recall how Rose painted her portrait when she was a little girl. When my mother was ten years old, Lady Rose, then about forty-five, positioned her half reclining on a park bench, resting her cheek on her forearm. Rose took down my mother's long blonde hair and positioned it cascading down her back and partially covering one side of her face. My mother wore a flowing summer dress, and remembered that Rose asked her to pull one side of the dress down to reveal her shoulder! This would have been around 1913, but my mother did it gladly and sat as still as she could for hours while Rose painted her. My mother said that the painting looked like a photograph, and she had it in her possession until the Russians destroyed everything in 1945.

By the fall of 1937 my father was heavily involved in managing all aspects of her home, estate, and forestlands. He was also her most trusted advisor and confidant. At that time, the winds of war were already blowing through the region. Hitler was on the rise, and like most German elite at the time, Lady Rose despised him and everything his regime represented. She decided she wanted to repay my father for his hard work and loyalty, and so she invited him to move into the forester's manor, which stood empty on her land. It was a large, impressive house with several bedrooms and fireplaces, situated on a picturesque ridge over a bend in the Wda River. This was truly a luxurious setting for my family, and quickly engendered jealousy among Niehoff and his cronies. They continued harassing my father and even making death threats against him for what they considered as meddling in their affairs. Niehoff's partner in crime, Rajkowski, was sore that he had lost the forester position and believed the forester's house should have been his. The land that Niehoff managed was also bustling with activity. Farm operations required a stable full of animals including about seventy horses, forty oxen, and sixty cows. Niehoff and my father tried to make sure their paths did not cross in order to maintain the tenuous peace there was between them. The agricultural land adjoined a railroad track where there was a dedicated ramp to load crops onto cars for export to markets around Poland. This, and the timber, was where most of the Plehn income came from. There was also a distillery on part of the land, and several acres of potatoes, which would be turned into fine spirits.

Within a year, Lady Rose made the unprecedented move to invite my family to live at her home with her. Both because of harassment from Niehoff and because she wanted us nearby, she decided having us living directly under the same roof would be for the best. Every time my father interfered with one of Niehoff's latest dishonest schemes, he would tell my father that the day would come when he would put a bullet through his head. With the drumbeats of war on the horizon, we knew Germany might try once again to invade Poland, so these were not idle threats. It seemed Lady Rose had it in mind already that she would have to protect our family from her own people.

Rose spent several weeks preparing an apartment in the large mansion for us. Our family would occupy what today would be considered a half basement, with high windows that were at ground level. There had to be a new entrance constructed to this garden-level apartment for our use, and wood floors had to be put down over the dirt foundations. My brother Henry remembers those glorious few weeks when they were actually allowed to live upstairs on the second floor of her home, in one of her lavishly appointed guest rooms. It was one of the few times he ever saw the inside of one. There was a full crocodile mounted at the head of the bed in the room he shared with my three other siblings. On the opposite wall there was an enormous Cape buffalo head staring down at them. It was a fantastic place for a bunch of children to wander about.

It was during this time that our entire family truly started bonding with Lady Rose. I think she missed the idea of having a family life, and enjoyed all the children who filled the house with laughter and noise. She always treated children as though they were just tiny adults, and didn't act like a patronizing aristocrat, which one might have expected. During those years she would often come down to our apartment and just sit for hours visiting with us, and talking with my parents late into the night.

At that time, it was not uncommon for a Polish family, oftentimes with seven or more children, to live in a simple one-room cottage furnished with little more than a stove, one bed, and no running water. By comparison, our family's accommodations were luxurious, and we lived in a world apart from our Polish countrymen. Because the old mansion was originally built hundreds of years before, likely in the sixteenth century, it had deep and massive foundations. There were several levels of basements and subbasements with thick brick walls. The whole manor was full of history, mystery, and marvels—a little kid's wonderland.

The lights were all kerosene and there was no electricity, but the house did have running water from early on. There was a huge water tank on the third floor, and every day we would lead a pair of horses around a pump outside that would pump the clear water from a nearby pond up to the tank. This created a gravity-fed water system throughout the house that would supply the kitchen, and Rose Plehn's private quarters. In addition, the house had an ingenious plumbing system where the water for her bathroom was run through pipes in the kitchen first, so that it was heated by the stove. Rose could take warm baths in her upstairs apartment whenever she liked, a true luxury at the time.

My siblings Henry and Henrietta are both fond of recalling this era of manor living. All of our family members had to work, but as Henrietta explained, it was pleasant to pick fruit, weed the vegetables, and tend to the flowers in Lady Rose's private garden. Compared to the average local citizen who toiled in the fields under the watchful eye of the stern Herr Niehoff, we were incredibly blessed. We also had our own small barn next to the house where there were cows, pigs, chickens, and ducks that needed to be fed and tended to every day, and this was a task usually assigned to my oldest siblings.

While everyone called it her private "garden," it was in truth a thirty-acre parcel of land dedicated mostly to growing vegetables for the consumption of the residents of the main house and her direct employees. At the time, Lady Rose also employed a cook, a maid, and a coachman to drive her carriage. Our family did the rest of the work around the house. We grew every kind of vegetable imaginable: asparagus, cabbage, wheat, sugar beets, and potatoes being the most predominant. Every morning the gravel pathways that wound amongst the tall linden trees were swept clean, the grass neatly trimmed. This area of lush natural beauty was kept so pristine that it looked like a Japanese Zen garden where even the dirt was raked into neat, pleasing rows. The large pond nearby, almost two acres in size, was full of fish and frogs. The summer evenings were always filled with the loud and beautiful singsong of nightingales, along with the hum of the frogs' serenades. When the frogs dropped their eggs in the springtime, the water close to shore would be thick with a kind of jelly that held the eggs, and you could wade out to your waist surrounded by this floating gelatinous mass. When all of these eggs would hatch at the same time during the early days of summer, the sound of these thousands of frogs in chorus was a deafening noise you would never forget.

The pond and nearby river were also full of fish—mainly karaś fish, a type of golden-colored carp that was a specialty in Poland. In the US, carp is considered a throwaway fish, but in Poland the carp is different and good. It is particularly a traditional meal for all Polish families on Christmas Eve. Approximately once a year my father would set large nets across the river and catch hundreds of fish at a time—probably close to three hundred pounds of fish at once—for us and the neighboring community. Usually he would do this when the hydropower dam that was downstream was closed and the river would come to a halt and flood, filling pools along the riverbanks with fish that had been migrating downstream. This was a perfect time to easily catch the fish, and my dad built a rowboat that he would use to scare the fish and corral them into the big nets waiting on the other side of the pools. Occasionally the river would also provide huge, twenty- to twenty-five-pound northern pike, and huge brown trout, which were considered a major delicacy.

At the center of Lady Rose's park were three massive oak trees, rumored to be close to one thousand years old. There were also dozens of mature fruit trees and bushes. We enjoyed apples, pears, blackberries, red currants, gooseberries, and several varieties of cherries. There was also a greenhouse that would provide fresh herbs and vegetables through the winter. Outside were fields of wildflowers, but inside our little compound were rows of gorgeous flowers, mostly exotic roses and fragrant lilacs for Lady Rose's enjoyment. She would venture into her garden most mornings and bring in fresh bouquets for the salon and living room, so the house always smelled fresh and sweet in the summer. Nonetheless, Henrietta remembers being out in the fields while growing up, and says that she would always collect a bouquet of wildflowers to bring back for Lady Rose, who always clasped her hands in delight and thanked Henrietta graciously for thinking of her.

Father once spotted a pigeon's nest with fresh hatchlings near the house, and made Henry climb the tall linden tree to fetch the small delicacies for Rose. "She'll be delighted with these little treats," my dad said to himself as he carried them inside for her. Indeed she was, and she often returned the favor. Rose would have to pass by our lower-level apartment whenever she headed to her cellars to retrieve something, and she usually stopped and knocked on our door on her way back. She always had a sweet treat in her pocket, or an apple she just fetched to hand to us children. She cared about us, and treated us like her family, perhaps because we were the closest thing to family that she had at the time. We were content, but more importantly, it was the safest place for us to be, as we would see when the war came.

All of this teeming activity was surrounded by a tall redbrick wall about two feet thick, so that it was truly our private garden. Everyone in our family loved that garden like it was our own. It presented a picture of perfect harmony and sumptuous abundance for anybody who saw it. It was an unbelievable image for most people who walked in for the first time. We were completely self-sufficient, and usually had a little left over of our exotic harvest to sell to neighboring estates. Even throughout the darkest days of the war we always had enough to eat, enough firewood to keep warm, and a generous employer who provided for us as if we were her kin. Along with the few other employees she kept on at the mansion, we made that house hum, and were like one big happy family taking care of her property. What was most amazing about all of this was that for the most part she was able to maintain that calm, order, and beauty right up until the final days of the war.

Lady Rose was good friends with a Polish priest from the local Catholic parish, who, like my parents, spoke fluent German. His name was Jerzy Pietrek, and he would often join her for dinner at the Lubocheń estate. Afterwards they would retire to the salon to take their tea and dessert. They liked to sit side by side on the piano bench and play together in harmony, all four hands on the keys at once. In our youth we would hear the tinkle of the piano keys and singing from our apartment several nights a week. She was a tremendous musician, and truly loved to play. The Swiderski children would often fall asleep to the faint music drifting down the stairs into our bedroom.

My brother Henry likes to tell the story of their first Christmas in the manor, in the winter of 1937. Our mother had taught her four children to sing "Silent Night" in German as a special treat for Lady Rose. While Rose was entertaining guests in her salon on Christmas Day, the four Swiderski children filed into the elegant room to perform "Stille Nacht" for Rose's guests. My siblings delighted the guests with the German rendition, and each one was lucky enough to receive a gift. To this day Henry remembers the precious pocketknife he received that first Christmas. It had an elegant carved bone handle, and was unlike anything he had ever seen. It was one of his most precious possessions and would serve him well for many years to come.

When Rose was entertaining guests in her dining room, we would usually take our dinner downstairs. The Polish winters are notoriously long and hard, with massive snowdrifts and endless weeks of subzero temperatures. Luckily for us, the house had a massive, glazed stove in the cellar that would keep the entire house warm in the winter months. We were especially toasty in our basement apartment, and we were of the fortunate few Polish families who always had enough wood to burn during the winter.

The highest holiday in any Polish home is Christmas Eve, called *wigilia*, which means "vigil." This is the day children anxiously await all year. Once the first star appears in the sky, the evening festivities can begin—starting with a dinner that is traditionally shared only by one's closest family members. Each person receives their own thin wafer, called *oplatek*, made of flour and water, made to represent the host, which is given out during mass. We would break off small pieces and exchange holiday wishes for the coming year with each person at the table in turn, with lots of hugs and kisses. This is always followed by a special dinner that consists of twelve specific traditional courses of soup, fish, vegetables, pierogi, and dessert. It is a joyful occasion for Poles as the family celebrates the coming arrival of Jesus Christ on Christmas Day.

Rose would invite her staff into the dining room to celebrate on this holy day with them. Even though she was a Protestant and the Poles who worked for her were Roman Catholic, it was no issue for her. We were all Christian in her eyes, and considering how close the world was to WWII, it was rather unusual for her to have this attitude. She would provide a beautiful dinner spread for my family, the likes of which we had never before seen. The Christmas Day feast was especially opulent—the staple was various kinds of *Bündner Teller*, a traditional German dish stacked with thinly sliced dried meats and cheeses, all arranged in an artistic spread. Most importantly for us kids, she always had chocolate, an almost impossible luxury during the war. To this day I'm not sure how she had access to these fantastic German dishes, or how she managed to continue importing such delicacies when so many in Poland were going without.

On these special evenings our family would join her as guests in the salon where she played and sang beautifully for us the rest of the evening. My parents and those who spoke German would sing along, and it was a very happy and festive atmosphere. Amazingly, we were able to keep this sacred tradition throughout the war. We maintained a sense of normalcy through this dark period in Poland's history thanks to the fact that she was German and had access to resources that Polish people would never have access to. Because she had no husband or children, we were her surrogate family in her twilight years.

The most sacred holiday for Polish people, after Christmas, is Easter. The traditions around Easter were geared towards fun and entertainment for little kids, just like they are in the US. In

Lubocheń, children would build little nests and place them at various points around Lady Rose's garden. It was somewhat similar to a modern-day Easter egg hunt, but in reverse. Children would build baskets, and then the Easter bunny would find them and fill them with treats. Rose always made sure each child had a sweet in his or her basket. It was such a delight for us to come running back out into the garden after Easter dinner and find our baskets filled with treats.

One of the greatest joys of my childhood was exploring the halls of her large manor. The walls were hung with exotic heads of animals I had never before seen. Her brothers would return from hunts in far away lands, bearing treasures my young eyes could barely comprehend. In the summertime, she kept a black African leopard on the veranda. The majestic animal was mounted, sitting erect and alert on a pedestal—and was a startling sight! Visitors would marvel at his beauty and sparkling eyes, and he always looked like he was ready to pounce. While many of the trophy rooms remained locked, there were times, during spring cleaning for instance, when I was able to see inside. Her library was full of books about far-flung places, and the artifacts in her house rivaled any museum of that time. That I wandered these halls as a child would influence the entire trajectory of my life. I would collect those same African trophies and place them on pedestals and hang them on my walls in my American home, only later realizing I was recreating the fantastic and beloved scenes from my youth.

Lady Rose did allow us to play with some of her imported toys, like, for instance, a jack-in-the-box. This was such a treat for me as a child. I would turn the handle slowly on the side of the colorful box, and squeal with delight when the brightly colored clown jumped out. She also had a device that created a magical, colorful world when you looked through it, and only later did I learn it was called a kaleidoscope. These were considered modern marvels in Poland back then! Rose had spent much time in Italy as part of her art studies, and brought back many Italian traditions. A few times she tried to teach us a strange game that resembled billiards, but was played by throwing shiny metal balls at other balls on the grass. We had never heard of bocce ball, and as much as she tried, the Poles never really took to it. I know none of the local Polish kids had access to any of this kind of entertainment. We were lucky we lived in this bubble of happiness and prosperity thanks to the basic human connection and respect that existed between Lady Rose and my father.

In the last few peaceful years before the war, my oldest brother Henry would attend school in town. Sometimes he would catch a ride back with the milkman, but usually he walked or rode his bike for the two miles to the schoolhouse, even through the winter. Oftentimes he would walk home with the local boys, and there was always a moment when he would turn down the pristine lane that led to the manor, carefully lined with beautiful small pebbles, waving goodbye to his classmates, who lived in a different world. The local boys, most of whom lived in one-room cottages, sometimes looked longingly after Henry as he strode to the imposing iron gate in front of the manor. Henry knew the secret method of opening the locks our father had designed to keep strangers out, and would let himself in. It's true that we were a bit isolated, as we couldn't play with the local children, but our lives were filled with so much activity on our little island that we didn't mind too much. Now when I look back on it, the only reason our family had any sort of better circumstances compared to the average people at the time was thanks to my father's quick wit, hard work, and honesty.

I am now the same age Rose was when I was a boy. If someone had told that boy that he too would one day have a large house of his own, filled with exotic trophies he collected from a lifetime of traveling around the world, I never would have believed it. When I think about it now, it all started with those early memories in this extraordinary palace in the Polish countryside. Today only rubble and weeds remain of that gorgeous oasis. The three massive oaks that were its centerpiece were cut down in the years after the war by locals scavenging for resources to keep them warm. The Russians drove their tanks through the elegant brick walls in 1945, and what remained in the rubble was picked over by looters. In the 1990s several of the oldest remaining trees were designated as historical landmarks, and one man received six years in prison for chopping one down. Finally in 2010, the Tuchola Forest was designated a UNESCO World Heritage Site, proving to the world that this was a special place, unique in its natural beauty and wonder.

At the time I was born, in 1941, Rose Plehn also employed my mother's brother, who worked as an administrator over a portion of her timberland. That year, my four siblings ranged in age from ten to seventeen years old. I think it's fair to say I came as a surprise to my parents. Henrietta remembers, when she was twelve, sitting with our mother, who was crying tears of sadness and frustration in her room. To have a child born in the middle of a war was no doubt a fearful event for any mother. Henrietta remembered that just at that moment Lady Rose came in to comfort her.

"There, there now, don't cry," she said, patting my mother on the back.

"This is a joyful occasion. You just wait and see—no doubt this will be your most beloved child yet. The youngest always is."

She cheered my mother up and told her not to worry. Henrietta says her premonition did come true, and that as the baby of the family I was always favored. Lady Rose, who never married, loved children and I think she enjoyed having a houseful of little ones, even if they weren't her own. She was undoubtedly a great source of comfort to my mother at that time. I arrived in the world on January 30th, 1941, in the middle of the harsh second winter of the long war. I was the first and the last of the Swiderski family to be born in the actual home of the Plehn family.

We were so close with Rose that by the time the war came, my father had a special power of attorney to manage all the affairs of the manor in her absence. She often told my father that he would inherit part of the land in her will. They would stroll through the timberlands while doing surveys, and she described to him exactly which parts would be his. Of course, in the chaos at the end of the war, and thanks to the Communist fist that seized everything in Poland, this never came to fruition. However, one day several years after the war ended, my father ran into Rose Plehn's personal attorney in town. They had not seen each other for many years, but the man confirmed to my father that she had indeed left a will that named my father as heir to part of her estate. By then most documents had been destroyed and the Communists had nationalized almost everything they could, so it didn't matter. It was simply a matter of pride for my father that he had earned her trust and confidence to such a degree. It turned out that even in the moment when her family abandoned her, we were there for her to the very end.

CHAPTER 4

The Nazis Arrive at Our Gate

M Y FAMILY WITNESSED WITH THEIR OWN EYES THE first moments of World War II. On September 1, 1939, the war officially began, and on that very day the first German units rolled into our town. Lubocheń was only thirty miles from the German border, so it happened very suddenly. People in town heard there was a battle going on in Warsaw, but I'm not sure that anybody truly understood what was happening until the Nazis were upon us. Their polished and shiny trucks rumbled through town in waves during those first few days, carrying the mechanized infantry units to battlefields further down the line.

When the German army arrived, it was not terrifying, at least not at first. Henrietta was eleven years old at the time, and was weeding in the garden when she lifted her head to see a large truck filled with soldiers stopped in front of the gate. Her heart started beating faster when one of the officers got down from the front of the truck and started walking towards her, motioning with his hand for her to come. He stood outside the garden gate and asked her if he could have a tomato. She could see all the soldiers with perfectly pressed uniforms and shiny black boots seated inside the truck bed. They were intimidating, but polite. She ripped a few tomatoes off the vine and passed them through the bars of the gate. In return he gave her a piece of chocolate, patted her on the head, and returned to the truck. At first she was afraid to eat the chocolate because she thought it might be poisoned, but it looked too good to let it go to waste. The German army didn't stop in Lubocheń for long. They did a thorough search of every inch of the property for stowaway Polish soldiers, but satisfied that we weren't hiding any, they continued on. They didn't touch or destroy anybody's belongings. We were the employees of a highborn German lady, so we were left alone.

The invasion struck close to home for us in one big way—my father had to leave town immediately. He was still a sworn soldier of the Polish army, and took the oath he had made in General Haller's service seriously. He was a member of the reserve unit in a town called Grudziadz, which was about twenty-five miles away. There was an agreement with the local garrison that all soldiers would rendezvous there in the event of a national catastrophe. Those early days of the war were filled with such chaos that many soldiers were never able to report for service. My father felt it was his duty and a matter of honor to keep his promise to defend his country. If my father gave you his word, it was better than money—and he would go through his entire life living by that honorable principle. Our family was devastated, and my older siblings were especially frightened by the prospect of his departure. My mother cried and begged him to stay. He was not a man who would compromise on a matter of honor, and so he left and rode the twenty-five miles on his bike to report for duty.

Needless to say, when he arrived, the garrison was in chaos. About half of the soldiers couldn't be found, and the commanding officers could scarcely organize an effective counterattack. Everything happened so fast in those first few days that few units were ready and capable of fighting the German war machine. The few soldiers who were present decided to make their way towards Warsaw, to see if they could be of assistance there. My father and a small group of soldiers covered the 130 miles to our nation's capital on foot and bicycle over the next several days. He made it as far as the small town of Kampinos, which was just twenty-five miles west of Warsaw. The town was situated on a hill, and from there he had a view of the city, which to his dismay was completely on fire. Bombs were falling and flames were shooting out of all the tall buildings. It was a devastating sight, and he knew that Warsaw was lost. Poland was again occupied by its more powerful neighbor to the west.

My father was also now an outlaw, because he wore the Polish uniform. He had to carefully make his way back to Lubocheń, hiding in the woods and traveling at night. He arrived back in Lubocheń in the dead of night, around three o'clock in the morning, about two and a half months after the war had begun. Before my mother could feel any relief at my father's return, someone informed Niehoff that my father was back. That someone was Rajkowski, the same scoundrel who had gotten Rose to unwittingly sign the lease in 1933. Rose had fired him, but Niehoff kept him around as his special informant, and he was always pestering us. He considered it his special duty to remain informed on all the comings and goings of the Swiderski family, and my father's late-night arrival was big news for Niehoff. We all knew that the greatest threat to any Poles at that time would be the local Germans, many of whom were high-ranking reservists in the German military, and who were now members of the Nazi Party. At the beginning, the German army had largely left Polish citizens alone, as long as they weren't part of an armed resistance. However, the local Germans we worked with day to day had different ideas. Ernst Niehoff had directly threatened to put a bullet through my father's head once the war began. Everyone knew that now that the German officials were in charge of law enforcement in town, the German citizens could basically do whatever they wanted. It was a terrifying time, and thousands of Poles in the region died not at the hands of the invading army but at the hands of the local Germans they had lived alongside for years.

Germans knew the war was coming, and many from this area, fearing that they would be drafted into the Polish army, fled to Germany, even though they might have lived in this region their whole lives. Because this was such a unique region of Poland, with both German and Polish roots, the Germans were leaving in droves to return to their homeland. Some were then drafted into the German army, and would return to these same regions of Poland they grew up in, now wearing a German uniform and acting like they were the lords of the land.

In the summer before the war began, some local Germans started feeling a sense of superiority because they heard the German drumbeats in the distance. That summer, Niehoff would ride around town on his horse and yell at the Polish people that they should all start learning German, because he assured them it would soon be their official language. His haughty attitude angered my father, who reported him to the Polish authorities. To my father it was a matter of principle—he hadn't fought for a free Poland so that an arrogant German leaseholder could intimidate his Polish countrymen. It only increased the tension between the two men, and the whole relationship would soon come to a boil.

There quickly developed a blacklist and my father was one of the first names on it. It took two Germans to officially denounce a Pole and place him on this list, after which he could be murdered with impunity. If the German army didn't kill my father for being a Polish soldier, Niehoff wanted to make sure he could finish him off in another way. This dangerous period of lawlessness lasted for about three months, and so at the time my father returned to Lubocheń at three o'clock in the morning, the region was just barely recovering from this period of criminality and denunciations. My father had never shown any fear at Niehoff's crazy threats. He had always stood his ground. That night, however, the rules of the game had changed and Poland was no longer a free country. He knew he had to obey, and go report to Niehoff, who now considered himself a lord over all the Polish people on his farm, and was in charge of the local German armed militia. My father walked out the door to see Niehoff almost as soon as he got back, and my mother was sure she would never see him again.

To this day we are not exactly sure why Niehoff didn't kill him that night. Our family assumed Rose had somehow managed to intervene and have his life spared. But it's also true that about a month into the war, the official German army had caught wind of the mad behavior of local German militias and began implementing martial law administered by German army officers. German martial law brought some stability to the region after the months of chaos and murder at the hands of the local militias. The month of mayhem under the German militia's rule was one of the most horrible periods for the Polish people of the region, who lived in constant terror. It lasted until October, and at that time, perhaps because the German army was also horrified at the murder of so many civilians in cold blood, Berlin sent representatives to be in charge of local administration. Things calmed down. Even Niehoff was subject to their rules, and my father returned home a little while later saying he had just been given a stern warning. It was no minor miracle to my mother to see him alive again.

What had actually transpired at the time was that the Polish region of Pomerania, which we lived in, had been annexed by Germany. Because Pomerania had strong ties in German history Berlin officially announced that they were annexing Pomerania into the Third Reich. This meant martial law no longer prevailed, and all of our towns and villages were theoretically incorporated into the administration of the German government. However, since there were of course no German civilian authorities on the ground, the German reservists who lived in our neighborhoods effectively were in power. Thus began a new phase of terror for the Polish people of Pomerania, because the local Germans formed what was essentially a police militia, and they suddenly were endowed with the power of enforcing laws and enacting punishments. It was well known among the local Poles that the German reservists who lived among us kept lists of Poles they wanted to kill. Before the war began, Berlin had urged local Germans to keep lists of people who could be considered "enemies of the state"—people who were at odds with Germany, or who were political activists, intellectuals, doctors, and other types of community leaders that were likely to oppose the annexation of that part of Poland into Germany. They had been talking of it for months, warning locals who got on their bad side that their name was on a list, and that their time would come when the war began. These people knew well ahead of time that they were considered a threat to the German government, and my father was one of them.

By October 15, 1939, the mass arrests began. Polish people who had been placed on this blacklist were rounded up and arrested under the guise of being "enemies of the state"—the state of Germany and Hitler's Third Reich. In reality, it was a way for local Germans to get even with Poles they didn't like—they were settling personal vendettas over even the pettiest of issues, with murder that was now ostensibly sanctioned by the central governing body.

Local German militia groups were holding kangaroo courts, which often consisted of a five-minute "trial" in which a German reservist would testify that this person was an enemy of the state and then the Pole would be shot. The trials were a charade, and based on fabricated charges; they were essentially just a notification after the accused had been rounded up that he would be put to death. After the representatives from Berlin were in place about a month later, and perhaps because many of those who had been blacklisted were already dead, most of the mass executions were halted. Instead, the Germans continued to round up Poles they considered enemies of the state, but now they were sent to German labor camps. In truth, however, a German who was even simply jealous of his Polish neighbors could make up any excuse and shoot the man with impunity. If neighbors had a simple quarrel, the Polish people would often disappear.

It's important to remember that at the beginning of the war, the Germans were not yet specifically targeting Jews and were not killing Jews or anybody else in mass executions. The German army certainly wasn't murdering civilians—at first. When, in early October of 1939, the local militia rounded up 120 Jews in the nearby town of Świecie, including women and children, and shot them all in the town square in front of dozens of onlookers, the German officers present wrote letters of complaint to Hitler, discussing the abominable behavior of the local German militia. There was even an investigation into this shooting, because Germany wanted to preserve some semblance of law and lawfulness in what they were doing, which was—theoretically—reclaiming German lands lost in WWI. It was in the months following this period of chaos under the local militias that the mass murders were halted, and prisoners and enemies of the state were sent to labor camps in Germany instead. Now that our region of Poland was considered a part of Germany, the Polish language was forbidden. Suddenly, children would attend school, but all classes would be in German (much to the dismay of the children, most of whom knew no German). This was the reality of Poles in Pomerania at the start of the war.

The very next morning, my mother and my oldest brother, Henry—thirteen at the time—went to see the most senior general of the German forces. My mother asked for a meeting with this general and then pleaded the case for her husband. She explained she had a brother who had died fighting with Germany in WWI (he had been conscripted against his will in what was then West Prussia), and this old general who had also fought in WWI took pity on her. He told her he would not sanction the murder of our father, and so for the time being, he was safe.

In the first year of the war a new character entered on the scene who would play a big role in our lives. His name was Kurt Paesler. He was a strikingly tall, blond man who bore a strong resemblance to Rose. She introduced him as her nephew. He lived in a neighboring town where he was also a wealthy landowner, and what we came to realize once the war started was that he was also a high-ranking SS official. As a matter of fact, his title was "Oberführer," which meant he was the senior leader for the paramilitary units in the entire region. It was the equivalent of being a general, and he was the man in charge of all the local units once this phase of the initial invasion passed. After the war began, he would come and visit his Aunt Rose more frequently, and we would see her anxiously pacing the veranda in anticipation of his arrival on the days he was scheduled to visit. He would ride up the tree-lined lane to the manor on his impressive black stallion, and she would smother him with hugs and kisses while we peeked out from behind window curtains to see who this curious object of her affection was. During the war, he was the only family member of hers we would see.

We didn't discover until after the war that Kurt Paesler was actually Rose Plehn's illegitimate son, but of course it all made sense in hindsight. He looked just like her. It turned out that Rose had given birth to a son out of wedlock in the 1890s, but nobody knew the exact date because it was a scandal that was carefully covered up at the time. She had left Luboche at that time and returned to her mother's ancestral village in Germany to have the child. She came back a year later but without the child, having apparently left him to be raised by distant relatives of hers. She told my father stories about the man she had planned to marry—that he had been a friend of her brother Rudolph, and that he had died along with him on safari in Africa, soon after their relationship began. Of course she never mentioned her son at that time. After the war, one of the few jobs my father could obtain was as a juror in the local court. It was in his work there that he found documents proving that Kurt Paesler was her son, and which indicated that at one point early in the war she had listed him as the heir to her estate. Strangely enough, I don't believe Paesler ever knew that Rose was really his mother.

The Paesler family, whom Rose had left her son with, lived approximately fifteen miles west of Luboche, but we had never seen Kurt growing up. Apparently in 1918, when Poland became an independent nation again and these lands became part of Poland, the Paeslers didn't want to become citizens of Poland, and so they moved back to Germany at that time. For the next twenty years it's likely that Rose was not able to see her son very frequently, but the war reunited them in a way, when he came back not only to claim his family's prewar estate but also to administer the military units in the region.

She was our employer, but we lived with her almost like one family. Lady Rose was very aware of what a dangerous time this was for Poles, and for our family in particular. She also hated Niehoff, and my brother overheard her telling Niehoff one day that if he harmed a hair on my father's head, he would have to answer to her. She had no real authority over him, but she certainly had a kind of moral authority, and people wouldn't cross her lightly. A few months into the war, once Kurt Paesler was established as the senior officer of the reservists, she asked him to intervene on my father's behalf, and tell Niehoff to stand down with his death threats. For whatever reason, Paesler sided with his elderly "aunt" and became my father's protector for the next few years. Niehoff dared not touch him once he knew about the relationship between Rose and Paesler.

At first the family was deeply relieved and happy that this senior SS officer was willing to protect us. That feeling was very short lived however, and soon enough we saw what Paesler was really made of. In the next year's harvest season, the farm was drastically shorthanded. Usually several hundred migrant workers would travel from central Poland and arrive in the fall for seasonal harvest work. Because of the war raging in other parts of the country, this was not possible. Paesler and a few of his junior officers rounded up all high school and college-aged children in the neighboring villages and ordered them to work in the fields around Lubocheń, bringing in the harvest. They trucked in these kids on wagons and ordered them to get to work. There was one boy, probably around nineteen years old, who simply refused. He sat down under a large chestnut tree next to the field and said he would not be forced to work for a German.

What happened next was one of the most horrifying scenes my family saw throughout the war. Paesler dragged the boy over to the middle of the village and pounded on all the doors to get the women and children to come outside and watch. Once he was satisfied that everyone was out of their houses and looking at him, he turned his attention to the boy, whom his junior officers were holding. He pulled out his pistol, but instead of shooting the boy, he turned it around and smashed the boy across the top of the head with the heavy butt of his gun. The boy fell to the ground and Paesler and one of his soldiers proceeded to beat the boy with the butts of their guns, smashing his face and body. They didn't stop until the boy's face was a mound of bloodied pulp. They had also broken all of his ribs, his collarbone, and his arms, so that when they went to drag his lifeless body away, it appeared like a soft rag doll, because his skeleton had been crushed. They dragged him behind the barn and shot him through the head to stop his moaning. They left the mutilated body under the tree and prohibited anyone from burying it for weeks.

Henry and Henrietta both witnessed the horror of this scene at close range. Henrietta ran back into the house, terrified. She sat in a corner of the kitchen trembling when Herr Paesler, his uniform splattered with blood, calmly walked in to wash the blood off his hands. Henrietta said she barely breathed and stood there frozen staring at the monster in her kitchen. If Lady Rose had been home, she would have never let this happen. She was out of town, and when she returned from her business trip, she was furious and confronted Paesler about it, screaming at him that he was not allowed to touch anyone who lived on her land. Rose and Paesler became estranged, and after that there were no more warm visits between the two. We would find out later from her attorney that at this moment she also completely disinherited him from her will. In her mind, she wanted nothing to do with him.

By the end of the war, Herr Paesler had the blood of thousands of Poles on his hands, and I know of only one that he saved—and that was my father. Even though my father became off-limits to Niehoff because of Rose's agreement with Paesler, in truth Niehoff and Paesler had become partners and comrades in their horrible crimes. They roamed the countryside on their black stallions and terrorized the Polish peasants everywhere they went. They treated Poles as their own personal slaves, and rounded up any people they wanted to put to work on whatever tasks they saw fit. They imagined themselves as kings of these dominions, and our family had a measure of safety only because this great German lady stood by to protect us. Our family and Rose Plehn came to rely on each other more and more as the war grew worse, and resources grew scarce. We were increasingly isolated, and few people came to visit. We were lucky we were able to sustain ourselves through our garden and our small number of livestock. Rose, even though she was German, was also alone during this time because her values dictated she could not go along with the attitudes of the Germans around her.

Rose helped many Poles throughout the war. At several points the Germans were rounding up the able-bodied men and putting them on trains to be shipped off to German labor camps, and Rose would go to help those she could and pull people off those transports, claiming she needed them to work her land. But, of course, she couldn't save everyone. During this period after the announcement of annexation, Polish families who owned large farms were frequently resettled. The Germans wanted to consolidate all the German families that lived in the far-flung reaches of the old German Empire—namely, places like Lithuania and Estonia in the northeast and Moldova and Romania in the southeast. The resettlement was in full effect by the winter of 1940, and all the most desirable farms in our region were confiscated. German soldiers would arrive at a Polish family's house in the middle of the night and tell the Polish family they had an hour to pack up their most essential belongings, and then they were required to drive their wagon to the nearest train station. There, a German family freshly arrived from the outer reaches of the former German Empire would be ready to take the wagon and go back to the Polish house, while the Polish family would board the train and be taken to labor camps in Germany.

By 1941, Nazi Germany had turned on Soviet Russia, and the Germans were facing large offensives on their eastern front as well, which they weren't expecting. Now the Germans needed more soldiers for their army, and so they began giving temporary citizenship to Polish families of Pomerania, valid for ten years, mainly so that they could draft the Polish sons into the war. If you were Polish, but your family had lived in Pomerania, or what had been West Prussia before the First World War, you were granted this temporary citizenship of the German Empire. This played to the German idea that these lands were more German than they were Polish, and it was a clever way to make the Poles available as conscripts into the German army. Therefore, the Swiderskis were made temporary citizens of Germany, as were most of the Poles in the region. It was a technicality, but it would prove significant in the future when the German army was in dire need of soldiers to send to the front line. Niehoff was happy about this because he was sure it would mean my father would get drafted and sent to the front lines.

What I didn't find out until recent years was that the Polish underground resistance received a decree from the Polish government in exile, now operating out of London, not to oppose this new German rule. They encouraged Poles who would be subjected to this rule to go along with it, and urged them to become German citizens, because they believed it would help ensure their survival. The reasons, I believe, were twofold. First of all, if you opposed, you were sent to a concentration camp. Secondly, it would mean a Pole essentially could become a kind of "insider" against the Germans—and this temporary citizenship provided a way for us to infiltrate the enemy. Most Poles quietly agreed to accept this German citizenship, because in truth they didn't have much of a choice (as the alternative of resisting would likely be death). In fact, it did lead to the survival of many Poles. Thousands of young men who were drafted against their will to fight with the Nazi army would later find their way to the Allied side in battle, and live to see the end of the war.

Several times during the war, the Germans tried to draft my father into the German army. Niehoff was especially eager to see my father sent off, because it was assumed that being drafted was basically a death sentence. Each time his number came up, Rose would petition on his behalf, and argue that he was an indispensable employee of hers who absolutely could not be sent away. I don't know how she managed it, but she kept my father at home for the duration of the war, when most other able-bodied men in the region were either drafted or sent to concentration camps. Eventually the tide started turning against the German army and they became truly desperate for able-bodied men. To his surprise, Niehoff himself was drafted and sent to the front lines in Russia in 1943. This was the worst possible scenario for a soldier in those days. We would never see him again.

By 1943 my oldest sister, Halina, was nineteen years old. She was drafted into a German forced-labor camp that year, and I would not see her again for seventeen years. My brother Henry had a similar story, and I would not get to know him, either, until I was an adult and we were both living in America. Halina was attending a school in nearby Drzycim when the Germans finally took her. She was drafted into a labor camp on a German military base, where she would actually work as a dentist's assistant. This was actually among the best type of work you could hope for, as some labor camps had brutal working conditions. She was really only about fifteen miles from Lubocheń, but she would not be able to come home again for the duration of the war. When the war was ending, the dentist Halina worked for was sent to the front lines to fight, and he was sure he would die there. He was a kind and honest person, and Halina had even grown fond of him during the years she was forced to work for him. She parted ways with him with tears in her eyes and was now on her own—she had no contact with Polish people, and so she fled along with the Germans who were clearing out in advance of the Russian front. She was sure she would be killed too, found working alongside these Germans, and so she did the only thing she thought would keep her alive. The rumors that were spreading ahead of the Russian front were horrible—that the Russians were raping each and every woman, even if she wasn't German, because to them this was German land. Halina caught a train to Germany, but it came under heavy bombing in Szczecin, Poland. While on a bridge crossing a river, the train was bombed, probably by British bombers based out of the UK, and came off the tracks, hanging precariously by a few cars over the river. Halina barely survived. She and a girlfriend managed to climb through several train cars and out of the wreckage, and to hide in the nearby fields, eating frozen potatoes to survive.

Halina eventually made it to Germany and looked up a distant uncle that we had there, who had been a German citizen for over twenty years. She found the uncle, and he did take her in. Once there, Halina confided to him that she had a small bag of gold scraps that she was carrying for the German dentist she had been working for. She had grown fond of the man, and considered him a good and decent person. He had entrusted her with it when they fled, knowing she would have a better chance of escaping and finding his family in Germany. He asked her to deliver this gold to his family for him. For the several years she was forced to work for him, the German dentist grew to treat her like his own daughter, even though he had his own wife and family back in Germany. After all the running and bombing and surviving in the fields, she had never lost the small sack of gold the dentist had entrusted to her.

Now Halina told this uncle that she wanted to find the family, and deliver the small but valuable parcel to them. Unfortunately, the uncle started to try to coerce her to forget about it, telling her it wouldn't be possible to find this man's family. We always knew he was cheap and greedy, but at one point he tried to steal Halina's gold, and she managed to catch him in the act. After this, a neighbor tipped her off that the uncle was going to report her to the police for carrying the gold, which was considered contraband. She could get in big trouble, so she flushed it down the toilet, and ran away.

The war was coming to an end and there was a lot of commotion in Germany. She joined a group of Polish refugees who directed her to a refugee camp for Poles in West Germany. It was here that Halina settled and lived for the next three years. The camp was full of former Polish POWs and other displaced Polish persons. Halina met a major in the Polish army and fell in love and married him. In 1948 they journeyed together to America and settled in Chicago.

The same year that Halina was drafted to forced labor, my oldest brother, Henry, faced a similar fate. In 1943 Henry was sixteen years old, and he was drafted into a sort of training camp for young soldiers in the German army. Lady Rose was not able to save him, although my mother surely begged her to try. The way they drafted Polish soldiers into the German army was to threaten them with the death of their entire family if they deserted or even if they failed to cooperate. They had killed the families of other Polish soldiers who deserted the German army once they were on the battlefield, and it was a terrifying prospect for young boys. Henry spent that winter in Germany building airstrips for German fighter planes, and training to be a soldier. It was an impossible task to ask a young Polish conscript to shoot at his fellow Polish countrymen across the battlefield. Most, like my brother, feigned incompetence and purposely failed all their marksmanship tests so that they would never have to directly face their Polish brothers on the field. Henry was assigned to the signal corps, and became a radioman and expert in Morse code, which was just fine with him.

Henry turned seventeen in the fall of 1943, and in early 1944 he was shipped to the front lines in the south of France. His constant thoughts were of how to escape the German army—without getting caught as a defector and putting his family at risk. He would see the Allied army or French resistance fighting on the other side of the fields, and he longed to join them, but it was impossible. If he ran off by himself into the woods, he would either be shot by the Germans he was running from, or be shot by the soldiers he was running to—because of his German uniform. Those were dangerous times in the south of France for the German army as well. Germany had occupied France since 1940, but by 1944 their grip was slipping. French underground resistance fighters were everywhere in the woods. German soldiers would even go to the bathroom in pairs, because of one incident where a soldier walked a few hundred yards away to relieve himself, and was found fifteen minutes later facedown with a knife in his back. No one had heard a sound. Henry wanted to join the resistance fighters, but he didn't speak French and couldn't figure out how he would communicate with them before they would undoubtedly try to kill him. The solution presented itself when his unit was captured by the British after just three months on the front lines. My brother immediately went to the commanding officer and explained through an interpreter that he was Polish and wanted to fight with the Polish army. Within a week he was sworn in as a Polish soldier and proudly wearing the British uniform of the Polish soldier in exile.

In March of 1944 my brother was shipped to Monte Cassino in Italy, along with three hundred other Polish refugee soldiers, to reinforce the army of General Anders. This was an army of Polish refugees that had been deported to the Siberian gulags in the first two years of the war, when Stalin and Hitler were still allies. When Hitler turned on Stalin and invaded Soviet Russia in 1941, Stalin quickly switched sides and declared that he was with the Allies after all. As part of his agreement to join the Allied powers and start receiving reinforcements from the US and British sides, he was to release all of the 1.5 million Polish POWs he was holding in gulags throughout his country. Of course, this was all just a show, and in truth very few Polish POWs were able to escape the Soviet Union. The few that did walked for hundreds of miles, and nearly starved before they reached the Red Cross ships that were waiting for them at the Caspian Sea to transport them to refugee camps in nearby Persia (what is today Iran).

General Anders was the highest-ranking officer among the POWs, and he quickly organized a unit that grew to about twenty-five thousand Polish soldiers. They would travel from Persia to the Mediterranean Sea and join the Allied offensive in southern Europe. Since early 1944 the Allies had been engaged in an epic battle for the German stronghold at Monte Cassino, Italy, and it was to this theater of war that my brother Henry went to fight. He went to reinforce the famed Third Carpathian Division of Anders' Army, which fell under the larger organization of the British Eighth Army. Finally, as a Polish soldier, he had something to fight for, and he could use his considerable marksmanship skills against the Germans, who were now trying to kill him, and who were occupying his homeland. In May of 1944 the Polish army made the fourth Allied attempt to overtake the fortifications at Monte Cassino, and they succeeded. It was a tremendous victory and a turning point in the southern front of the war. Unfortunately, my brother had stepped on a land mine in the first few days of the battle and had to be evacuated. The first time he was ever on a plane was as a casualty of war. He recuperated in a Polish military hospital in Italy, where newly available pharmaceuticals, like penicillin saved his life. He lost half his foot, but he would live to tell the tale. He was terribly disheartened to have to leave his Polish brothers-in-arms. They assumed that the entire Polish corps would keep pushing north and would eventually enter Poland together to push out the Russians. Of course the Allied leaders—namely, Churchill and Roosevelt—had other plans, and they knew all along that they would leave Poland in the hands of the Soviets. It was a very sad time, and up until the end, every Polish person hoped that a free Poland would again emerge at the end of the war. By early 1945 the European chapter of the war would come to a close, and in early 1946 all the Polish soldiers who had participated in the Allied European campaign were shipped to Polish resettlement camps in England. In 1950 the American Congress passed legislation inviting these twenty-thousand Polish soldiers to settle in the US, and this is exactly what my brother Henry would do. We of course didn't know it at the time, but Halina had also escaped from the German labor camp and was settled in America as well. In June 1951, King George of England paid for the ticket for my brother Henry to travel across the sea and start his new life in a free land.

Meanwhile, back in Lubocheń, things were also beginning to change in 1943. By this time most of the German aristocracy was aware that Germany was losing the war. Wealthy German families in Poland started shipping their treasures west, back to Germany. They anticipated a Russian front moving in from the east and wanted to preserve as much of their wealth as possible. Niehoff's wife and children were busy shipping crates of their things to Germany, and many Germans were beginning to flee west. There was a general sense of chaos, and resources became increasingly scarce, even for us. One day in the last fall before the war ended, Henrietta and Casey discovered three men hiding in the bushes behind one of the farmhouses. My siblings were scared at the sight of the strangers and called my father, who came to investigate. It turned out they were Jewish Belgian prisoners who had escaped from a German transport train that was destined for a concentration camp. The men were emaciated and nearly frozen to death, but helping a Jew in Nazi-occupied Poland carried a death sentence for the entire family. Nonetheless, I don't think my father thought twice about it, and he hid the men in the attic of one of the barns, where hundreds of sheep were sheltered during the winter. Every day my sister Henrietta would pretend she was going to collect eggs from the adjacent chicken coop, and she would bring food and water to the Belgian men. My family hid and cared for these men until the springtime. After the war ended, my father escorted them to the train station and they left for Belgium. Unfortunately, one died during the journey, but the other two wrote letters of gratitude and sent gift packages to my family for their kind treatment. I specifically remember my older sister Henrietta being delighted at the perfumes and chocolates the men sent to us in 1948 from Belgium, when such luxuries were completely unavailable in Poland.

My father often jeopardized his position by giving people in Lubocheń extra firewood to heat their homes, and extra food so they would not starve. The meal rations that were designated by the Nazis were not sufficient to keep a typical Polish family alive. My father would often bring extras from our cellar to share with the local peasants. If the Nazis had caught him in the act, there would have been nothing even Lady Rose could do to save his life. Of course, his position also engendered a certain sense of envy among the local Poles, who saw that Bruno Swiderski was close with a German family and always had enough to eat. Towards the end of the war, as the Germans were rapidly losing power, my father had to leave Lubocheń for his own protection; that is, protection against those Poles that might turn on him and accuse him of being some sort of Nazi conspirator. Of course, nothing could be further from the truth, because Rose hated the Nazis as much as the Poles did. Still, envy will do strange and terrible things, even to kinsmen.

Even Lady Rose had disowned members of her own family over their vile behavior, and there certainly were other distant relatives of hers that had terrible reputations. A distant uncle of hers, Arnhold von Plehn, lived in the nearby estate of Kopytkowo, and was notorious for his collaboration with the Nazis. Hundreds of Poles died at his hands, and the Nazis carried out massacres at his very estate, with his assistance. This distant Plehn relative managed to escape back to Germany before the war ended, but his name lived on in infamy in the region he was from. The Poles there never forgot the von Plehn who helped the Nazis murder Poles, and to this day a memorial plaque exists on the spot where Arnhold von Plehn sentenced hundreds of Poles to their deaths.

The truth is that during the war, we were incredibly fortunate that we never starved, like many Poles did during those years. The vast storehouses of Rose's cellars kept us fed, and my father was always her watchful advisor and caretaker. I remember those cellars well—they were very deep, and were cool, dry, and an ideal place to store fresh vegetables buried in huge piles of sand, which would perfectly preserve them for the winter. Along with the cans of fruit preserves, sauerkraut, and other pickled delicacies, we had enough to share with those less fortunate. Apples would be stored on massive shelves in between layers of hay that would keep them crisp and fresh for almost the entire winter. In this manner, we thought we would survive the war and be able to resume our normal lives after the Nazis left, but this was not to be.

Those long, dark years of the war brought horrible times to Poland, and yet our family was somewhat insulated from the Nazi terrors thanks to one German woman who hated the Nazis as much as we did, if not more. As the war was coming to an end and the German army was retreating, we thought the worst was over. The truth is, the worst horrors of the war were just beginning—and these horrors, under the guise of the Russian liberating front, would soon be brought to our very doorstep.

CHAPTER 5

The Russian Terror

B Y THE END OF 1944 EVERYONE KNEW THE WAR WAS ending. Every day there were train cars full of Germans and their loot passing through Lubocheń on their way west to Germany. Most of the Germans, especially the prominent officers at the time, had fled. We knew the Russians were coming, and Poland's long and twisted history with Russia meant we anticipated the arrival of this "liberating army" with an unsure mixture of hope and skepticism. Russia had occupied large portions of Poland for a majority of the last 150 years, and had tried to invade as recently as 1920. At that time very few people knew the full extent of the 1.5 million Poles that had been deported to the Russian gulags in the first two years of the war. We knew that the Soviets and Nazis had been allies at first, and had made a pact (the Molotov-Ribbentrop Pact) in 1939 to divide Poland. Still, we hoped for the best. Now that the Russians were fighting alongside the Americans and British, maybe they could be restrained from taking hold of our country once again.

Everyone in the neighborhood, including my father, urged Lady Rose to leave along with all of her German neighbors. She had the money and resources to do so, but she simply didn't want to leave her home. She specifically told my father that she had never done anybody harm, and that no one would want to hurt her. In a normal world she would have been right, but in the crazed chaos of 1945, it was not the case. When the Nazis turned on the Soviets in a surprise attack in 1941, they made mortal enemies out of all Russian citizens, and the Russian army would show no mercy to any German. At this late stage in the game, all conventions of war and shreds of decency had been cast aside.

With Henry and Halina gone, Henrietta—at age fifteen—was now the oldest. She is now eighty-four years old, and to this day, she says the night the Russian army arrived in Lubocheń was the most terrifying night of her life. It was January 1945, and everybody knew they were close—within a day or so of arriving. My father sent our family to stay at the one-room cottage of my uncle, who had served as supervisor of all agricultural employees since my grandfather's death before the war. Here, along with my maternal uncle's wife and children and fourteen other employees from the farm, I took shelter with my mother and my brother Casey while we waited for the Russians to arrive and "liberate" us.

It was now dangerous for us to stay in a house owned by a German family, and Lady Rose knew this when we left. To the very end she believed that her basic humanity would help her prevail against any would-be aggressors. Only my sister and father stayed in the manor with Lady Rose that night, along with the maid and housekeeper; they were all working quickly to finish up some loose ends, and my sister and father planned to join us at the cottage when they were done. In those few hours that our family was separated, and before my father and Henrietta were able to join us, Russian units started arriving through the dark forest in the middle of the night.

They were a ragtag bunch; most of them didn't even have shoes but had instead tied rags around their feet for warmth. Their rifles were tied around their necks with a piece of twine. The Russian soldiers were starving, disheveled, and terrifying. They had already discovered the brewery on the property, and many were now dangerously drunk. The Germans had specifically left this alcohol behind because they knew the Russians would not be able to resist consuming it and that their drunkenness would slow them down. When Henrietta looked out the window and saw the forest around the house filling with hundreds of Russians, she was paralyzed with fear at the sight; it looked like hundreds of undead lurching towards her home. They had no vehicles, and most were on foot. A few had horses, but overall they looked like a band of dirty, homeless thugs, rather than an army that was going to set us "free" from our lives under the Germans. They were everywhere all at once, overrunning the property. They immediately went for the livestock, and began to slaughter several pigs. As they were drunk and surely hadn't eaten in days, they didn't know what they were doing and began butchering the poor animals while they were still alive. Henrietta heard the horrifying squeals from the house. They lit enormous hay bales on fire for warmth, and the scene out the window quickly became one of blood and mayhem attended to by a senseless, drunken, and malnourished horde. Our moment of "liberation" had come.

The Russians immediately commanded my father to show them the direction the Germans had disappeared in. The Germans had a stronghold in the forest that was within a few hours' march, and the Russians were expecting battle to erupt at any minute. A light, fresh snow had just fallen and the German tracks were easy to follow—German soldiers had a unique footprint marked by studs in the bottoms of their shoes, and my father explained this to the Russians as they were tracking them through the snow. My father disappeared in the middle of the night amidst a dangerous-looking patrol of Russian soldiers, and I'm pretty sure he thought he would never come home again. He had no choice, and did his best to cooperate with the Russians in hopes of preserving his life.

My father would later explain that at one point they came upon a large clearing in the woods and that the Germans, in that moment, caught them completely unprepared. German machine-gun fire opened up on them from maybe five hundred yards away, and the Russians scattered, diving behind whatever trees or stumps they could, for cover. There were railroad tracks that ran through one side of the clearing, and there was a tall ramp built next to them for loading goods. My father yelled at the Russians to get behind the ramp and take shelter there. He made it to the ramp along with a few Russian soldiers, who, though they were shooting at the Germans, were so drunk that they were having no effect—exactly as the Germans had predicted. My father kept urging the men next to him to keep their heads down, but given the state they were in, they were in no shape to comprehend what he was saying. The leader of the Russians foolishly jumped up and yelled "Napierod!" (Forward!) to his men, but before he even finished the sentence, he had a bullet between the eyes and fell on top of my father, who remained motionless. My father was lucky that the dead body kept him warm for several hours until the mayhem died down, and by the early morning hours he was able to crawl away and run back into the woods toward our house. Thus ended the first night of the Russians' arrival.

While the Germans may have won that small skirmish, in truth, they were surrounded by Russian forces, and it's likely that none of those German units made it out of the woods alive. There was shelling and artillery fire going on for the next week right in our backyard as the Russians and Germans skirmished, but eventually all the Germans were vanquished.

In preparation for the arrival of the Russians, almost all women dressed themselves in rags and tried to make themselves look as haggard as possible. Henrietta covered her face in mud, and walked hunched over like an old maid, as did almost all the women in the region—all except Rose. She maintained her sense of propriety, and emerged from her bedroom to face the Russians dressed as she always was: in her layers of elegant, formal dress, and with her hair tied neatly at the back of her head.

At first daybreak the Red Army forced their way into the house, where my sister and the maid huddled in terror in the kitchen. The Russian soldiers immediately went room by room, destroying everything that seemed of value. It was pure destructive chaos perpetrated by drunken lowlifes. They smashed the dozens of hand-carved wooden chairs that had been in the Plehn family for generations. They broke all the glasses and plates, smashing each and every piece of fine china and crystal against the floors. They tore all the art off the walls and burned the tapestries. Everything that was precious and beautiful in that house was systematically destroyed. When she begged them to stop they just spat in her direction and used derogatory Russian terms for "German." Rose Plehn, in her seventy-ninth year of life, watched all the possessions of her life be destroyed. Of course, everybody was completely robbed, including the Poles. By the time the Russians left, we had not even a single fork among us.

Absolutely everybody, except for Lady Rose, cowered out of their way. With their tanks the Soviets bulldozed through the beautiful redbrick walls that surrounded her garden, and completely destroyed the years of hard work that had gone into laying the neat foundations of this oasis. They lay waste to a land that had been beautifully preserved and cared for during all these horrible years of the war.

That first morning, while they were drunk and ravaging the house, Lady Rose made a last stand in front of her bedroom. Rose always carried a small woven basket in her left hand that had on it a large ring of keys that opened up the most valuable doors on the property, like those to her stocks of food and to her library. She refused to hand over the key to her bedroom. She stood her ground in front of the door and said that this was her room, filled with her personal items, and they had no business going in. One of the Russian soldiers, dressed in tatters and drunk, simply pulled out his rifle and shot her in the leg to get her out of the way. Henrietta watched the dreadful ordeal unfold before her eyes. Rose was strong, even in her advanced years. She stumbled, but didn't fall, and the soldiers pushed past her, shooting the lock on the door to barge into her personal quarters.

Lady Rose had been shot through the thigh, but luckily the bullet had missed the bone and any large arteries. Nonetheless, she needed medical attention. My father was powerless to help her against the Russians, as we all were. Her maid helped her limp to the nearby cottage of a family that lived on her property and had no children and, therefore, had room to take her in. By this time in the war all the medical supplies were gone. Her maid tore a bedsheet to make bandages and dressed Rose's wounds every day while she recovered. Henrietta and the maid would come to the cottage daily, bringing her food and news of what the Russians were doing in the house. The senior Russian leaders had taken up residence in the manor, making it their staff headquarters. Most of the food stores had been pillaged within the first few days of their arrival, and the Russians were enjoying all they could eat and drink thanks to our months of hard work.

Roughly two weeks passed and Rose was recovering well. She managed to limp around the grounds, but stayed away from the main house for her own safety. Her home was thoroughly destroyed by then, and everything that was precious had been completely desecrated. All the valuable and exotic treasures, the rare manuscripts and art that had been collected over the past one hundred years from the far reaches of the world—it was all smashed, torn apart, broken, and burned. It was devastating to think about so much beauty and value being destroyed.

One day the Russian leadership summoned her to the house, but we didn't know why. She was brave and went ahead by herself, limping up to her old majestic doors where a Russian horde now presided. Rose never returned to the cottage that night, and we all suspected the worst. In the morning her maid found her lying among some bales of hay in the stable adjacent to the house. She was incoherent and moaning. The maid ran to fetch my sister Henrietta, and together the two women tried to bring some comfort to Lady Rose. She had clearly been attacked and brutally beaten. She was completely disheveled and unintelligible. She was drifting in and out of consciousness, moaning in pain. The one thing they could understand was that she kept asking for her small basket with the keys, over and over again, even though she had not carried it for weeks now. My sister and the maid did the best they could to make Lady Rose comfortable in what would be her final hours on earth. They arranged the straw under her head, and brought her sips of water. There was not much else they could do to ease her pain.

During that same night, in the early hours of that morning, Rose's personal maid, who was staying closer to the town, told us that as she was walking to the house, she had had an encounter with a young Polish couple that had been making their way through the woods, and who told her what they had seen. They were escaping from the Germans and were moving east, hiding in the forest and scavenging for food. They had come upon the house last night and had drawn in closer, looking for food. They had been startled by the shocking scene and screaming that was coming from inside the house. They said they saw Rose being beaten and raped by a gang of drunken Russian soldiers. They had been petrified at the evil scene and ran off to hide in the nearby woods.

It was in this abused and injured state that the maid and Henrietta found Rose in at first light. Rose was lying in the barracks that were near the house and generally reserved for the seasonal migrant workers. A few hours later, perhaps because they couldn't stand the sounds of her moaning, or maybe because they wanted to eliminate the evidence of what they had done to the lady of the manor, a couple of young Russian soldiers dragged her out of the barracks and shot her in the head. They threw her body in the manure compost pile. At the last moment, one of the soldiers ripped off the golden locket Rose always wore around her neck, which held a picture of her parents. There was nothing anybody could do; they forbade anybody from touching the body.

In the months that followed, our family was in agony over what had happened to Lady Rose. We had no idea of the whereabouts of my oldest brother, Henry, or my oldest sister, Halina. It felt like our world was falling apart. My father asked permission to give Rose a proper burial, but the Russians wouldn't allow it. By May of that year, the Germans officially surrendered and the war in Europe was over. Poland was a completely devastated country—a shell of its former self. Thousands of Poles from nearby villages had lost their lives. Most landowners had disappeared. The democratic Polish government, which had been functioning in exile in London since the German occupation, now lost all hope of returning to Warsaw. They realized that the Allies had made a deal with Stalin to let him install a Communist regime in our country. Churchill and Roosevelt had essentially sold out Poland to appease Stalin. Overnight, the government administrations in both London and Washington, DC, stopped receiving the Polish representatives they had been working alongside for the past six years. They now gave formal diplomatic recognition to the new Communist government installed in Warsaw by the Soviets. It was a devastating blow for all Poles. We were aware of the shocking developments that were happening on the world stage, but we were also just trying to survive in our own devastated part of the world. For the first time, we were truly in danger of not having enough to eat. All of the stores, crops, and livestock had been consumed by the Russians, and we had very little to go on. We scraped by with what little we could find.

My father wanted to give Rose a proper burial, but of course the Russians wouldn't allow it. It wasn't until almost ten months later, just before Christmas, that he was finally able to exhume her body. It had been constantly on my father's mind, and he had never stopped trying to obtain permission from the local authorities. As we settled into this new normal, with provincial government officials running the show, there was a bit of a thaw just before Christmas of 1945. My father finally had the permission he wanted, and he immediately went to the town to buy some wooden planks with which to fashion a rudimentary coffin. It wasn't possible to get a real coffin at that time, as Poland had been stripped completely bare of everything, first by the Germans and then by the Russian invading army. I remember very clearly how my father worked on building this simple box of wooden planks for several days, pounding and sanding for hours. He was serious and focused—the matter of burying his dear friend weighed heavily on his mind. Finally everything was ready, and on Christmas Eve 1945 he took my fourteen-year-old brother, Casey, with him and, with the help of the local blacksmith who had worked for Lady Rose for years, dug her body out of the manure pile, where it had lain for ten months. She was almost completely decomposed, but her bones and hair were still there. She was held together mostly by her elaborate Victorian dress. The delicate gold chain that had held her precious locket was still there, even though the locket was gone. I was still too young to help, but my father and brother wrapped her remains in a blanket, and placed her gently in the makeshift coffin. They slowly pulled the small wagon which carried the coffin, as there were no horses left, over to the Plehn family plot, where Rose's parents had been buried in 1888. The five members of our family and the blacksmith were the only ones present as my father said a quiet prayer and we laid her to rest. Sadly, most of the Plehn family cemetery plot had been looted already. Local people had taken whatever gravestones they could use as material to rebuild their homes. My father found a very large rock, which he laid over the grave; it took several men to move it into place. Today even that huge boulder is gone, probably looted by someone who thought they had a better purpose for it. To this day Rose still rests in the place my father buried her, next to her parents and the siblings who had died before the war.

In February of 1945, four of my father's siblings, two aunts and two uncles, ended up in the Siberian gulags. Our entire family was in danger because we had been made temporary citizens of the German Empire a few years earlier, when the Germans needed a larger pool for conscripts. Despite the fact that the Swiderskis were obviously Polish and had been for generations, the Russians chose to deport anybody who seemed to have any ties to Germany. Deporting Poles to the gulags was a common event at the time, as the Russians wanted nothing more than to enslave all Polish people and squeeze as much forced labor out of them as they could before they succumbed to death. My father narrowly escaped the transports himself on more than one occasion. At one point he had already been rounded up onto a truck to be taken to the nearest train station for transport. Old grievances certainly played a role, and certainly some Poles liked to point to people like my father and say, "He was a big shot here during the German days"—and that sealed his fate as a so-called German collaborator and condemned him to death. Never mind that this was far from the truth and that it was only old jealousies that made some people point fingers at my dad. Luckily my father had more friends than enemies, and he spoke some Russian thanks to his time with General Haller's army in 1920 on the Russian front. There was one Russian soldier among the occupying force in Lubocheń who was from the Polish city of Lwów, which is now a part of Ukraine but was part of Poland before WWII. He identified himself as a Pole, even though he was in the Russian army, and he tried to help some Polish families by warning them not only of upcoming roundups but also of which Russian soldiers to steer clear of. My father said this Russian soldier, who was raised in Poland, was responsible for the transport of this group to the train station. For some reason he stopped, threw the transport orders into the mud and stomped on them, and told all the men in the back of the truck to run. That was the story of one miraculous escape my father made from a trip to the gulags. Somehow, my father always seemed to manage escaping from the jaws of death at just the last moment. It was clear that God was also looking out for him, now that Lady Rose was gone.

Compared to his siblings, my father was lucky that he had managed to escape the transport to Siberia. One of my uncles never returned, while the other died shortly after his return from two years of imprisonment. He lost any health he may have once enjoyed on those long train rides into the land of bitter cold, malnourishment, and slavery. My two aunts fared a bit better. After two years in the Russian gulags, they returned to Poland, malnourished and ill, but with the strength needed to regain their health. Fortunately, they both reached old age.

My father's trouble did not end there though. Our entire family was thrown out of my uncle's cabin, where we had been staying, because the Russians wanted to set up a radio station there. The Russians treated Poles as their personal slaves. It was a terrible irony for Poles to be living in their now "liberated" country, free of Nazis, but under the thumb of the brutish Russian soldiers. Life was in some ways more tenuous now than it had been for the duration of the war.

The Russians engaged in theft on a wide scale, and were drunk whenever possible. They had an obsession with watches—to these soldiers with rags tied to their feet, they were a sign of status and wealth. They would open up their shaggy coats and proudly display rows of watches on safety pins that they had looted. One time a Russian walked up to my father and asked, "Skolko vremya?" (What time is it?)—and when my father pulled out his pocket watch, the soldier grabbed it out of his hand and ran off.

On one occasion, a few months after Rose had died, my father was carrying me piggyback through the fields. My mother and father and I were taking a shortcut from the next village, where we had been staying at my aunt's cottage. Suddenly, a Russian soldier heard us approaching; he stood up from where he had been hiding, behind some tall reeds, and was immediately upon us. He was alone, drunk, and kept grabbing his holster as if he was going to draw in our direction. It was a terrifying sight for me, but my parents tried to remain calm. The Russian was staggering back and forth, and waving his arms around and muttering obscenities and threats.

"I don't care, I will shoot everybody!" he yelled, while we just tried to keep walking. My mother instinctively took me from my father's back and carried me in her arms. She whispered a prayer over and over, "Holy Mother, save us", as my father tried to prevent the Russian from making any fast moves. My father walked half a step behind us, keeping an eye on the drunken Russian stumbling to our right, prepared to pounce if the man opened the flap that covered his gun. To this day I still remember his unshaven face with snot covering his beard. This tense stroll through the field lasted for a few hundred yards, with no signs of an easy resolution.

To the soundtrack of those prayers, two Russian officers thundered into the field on horseback at a full gallop. I saw them approaching from my right side, and we all froze. My father quickly explained that this soldier had been threatening to shoot us.The Russian leaders knew they had to maintain the pretense that they were an Allied and "liberating" force to some degree, in order to prevent a complete Polish revolt and to keep the Allies satisfied, at least for the time being. This did little to protect the average citizen, as many continued to suffer under the Russians just as they had under the Germans, but nonetheless, the Russians would for the most part restrain themselves from mindlessly executing innocent Polish civilians in broad daylight. Clearly, the soldier knew he was in trouble, and circled behind us as if to hide from his officers. They barely hesitated as they quickly captured the soldier, each one of them grabbing an arm. They tied his left arm to one horse, and his right arm to the other, and took off at a gallop, dragging him between them. Years later, when I was grown up and was talking to my mother about that experience, she told me that while she was praying, I too had repeated a prayer, a small child's prayer, right along with hers, as she held me to her chest. It was the only one I knew at the tender age of four, and I barely remember saying it. She explained to me that when my father handed me to her, he had been ready to jump on the Russian soldier and seize his revolver. If those two officers had arrived just a few minutes later, and knowing my father's fearless temper, he would likely have been accused of murdering a Russian soldier, and the situation would have ended tragically for all three of us. Such was the touch-and-go nature of life under the Russians.

After the war ended, most families in Poland began the desperate search to reunite with their families. We had not spoken to Henry and Halina in almost two years, and we had no idea where they might be. A few months after the German retreat, we finally received a letter from Halina. She was alive and in a Polish refugee camp in Germany. Not too long after that, in the fall of 1945, we received a letter from Henry with news that he was alive and well and living in the Polish army barracks in the UK. We were overjoyed with the news—when the letters came, both my mother and sister burst into tears. We were amazed at Henry's story that he had become a Polish soldier and had been wounded in Italy. With the arrival of this news, my father and mother could finally breathe a sigh of relief. All five of their children—Halina, Henry, Henrietta, Casey, and I— had made it through the war alive. The only member of our immediate "family" who had not was Rose.

In the 1960s, when I was living in Chicago with my parents, a distant relative of Rose Plehn's came to Lubocheń looking for information about Rose. My sister Henrietta, who was still living nearby, provided this gentleman with my father's address in Chicago. This man, Rudolf Maercker, wrote a sickeningly sweet letter to my father, which opened with an account reminding him that they had met before the war, as he was Lady Rose's closest living relative and had cared deeply for her. He wrote in gushing words about how he knew that my father was fully deserving of Rose's loyalty and trust, because she would certainly have been lost without him. Unfortunately, he was writing because he needed my father to provide a notarized statement attesting to the date of Rose's death, as it was necessary in a matter of inheritance and reparations that her extended German family was dealing with at the time. At the same time, Mr. Maercker was sending care packages to my sister Henrietta to thank her for helping to put him in touch with my father. He included things like butter and chocolate—precious goods that were nearly impossible to obtain in 1963 Poland.

My father was deeply saddened and angered by this letter, and the circumstances under which it was written. He furiously picked up his pen and dashed off a scathing letter to Maercker, detailing how Rose died. I don't think I fully realized how beautifully my father wrote in German until I had those letters translated into Polish, years after his death. His letter began by saying that for eighteen years he had hoped someone from the Plehn family would come looking for her, and how much it saddened him that it only happened when there was a matter of an inheritance to be sorted out.

He continued in a sharply worded message to this German cousin by saying he should feel ashamed that no one came to look for Rose after the end of the war. He then went into detail about how the Russians arrived and looted the house. He spared no detail, and told of how they shot her in the leg when she tried to stand up to them. He described how the Bolshevik horde dragged her out of the temporary migrant-worker housing, terrorized her, and finally shot her in the head.

"Believe me when I tell you, Mr. Maercker, that when I saw Lady Plehn's lifeless body, I had tears in my eyes," my father wrote.

"In that moment I decided I would immediately bury her in her family plot, . . . but the moment I began I was arrested by a Russian soldier and held in a cell for several days," he continued. "Despite my best efforts I was unable to obtain permission to bury Lady Plehn in her family's tomb." He expressed how he, with great difficulty, tried for the better part of a year to get permission, build a coffin, and bury her beside her parents.

"I am terribly saddened that I was not able to save Lady Plehn and that she died in such a horrible manner," he concluded. "This is all the more true because she saved my life first, in 1939, when Niehoff had placed my name on the blacklist of people who were to be murdered. I will never forget those days between 1939 and 1945," he signed off.

I have in my possession an original notarized statement of her death that my father made at that time, and to this day I don't know whether there was a second copy he mailed to Mr. Maercker, or whether he never sent it at all. I never got to ask him about this detail before he died. His letter was raw, and even though eighteen years had passed since the events he described, I realized that he had probably thought about them every day since they had happened.

It is very heartbreaking that the life of such a virtuous and decent woman could end so tragically. Lubocheń was a unique place in Europe at that time—it had equally strong Polish and German heritage, and Rose felt incredibly devoted to this place and its Prussian history in the same way we felt devoted to its Polish history, and that's part of why she willingly became a citizen of Poland in 1918. Her family had contributed much to humanity, just as she had contributed with her art, and with her kindness. That her life ended in such an undignified and appalling way was an indication of the horrible milieu that was to come. The system of governance that descended on Poland at the end of World War II would tear apart our society from the inside. It would rob people of their basic dignity by implementing a system where the role of individual responsibility and honor was diminished, and loyalty to a state that promised to take care of all its people was prized above all else.

For those of us who lived it, the Communist system destroyed individuals and tore at the very glue that had held societies together for centuries: honor, decency, and humanity. The Soviets were no liberators; they were just another set of aggressors who installed an oppressive regime in our country. According to socialist theory, the Plehns and the Swiderskis had every reason to be enemies. They were rich landlords, and while we were just regular, poor working class, we never felt demeaned or exploited. The Plehn family we knew were fair and honest, and they recognized and rewarded those who did good work. Those who went the extra mile, like my father, were singled out for advancement; it was a simple matter of effort and achievement, not corruption or exploitation.

This may seem like a very basic idea in a free and democratic system like we have here in America. Rewarding people based on merit was a founding American principle. However, when the Iron Curtain fell over Europe, the theory that each man should be treated as exactly equal, regardless of his skills, education, or motivation, suddenly became a mantra that was shoved down our throats. It may have sounded good in theory, but it quickly became apparent that the main purpose of this new socialist system was to enrich the chosen few leaders. The Communists tried to make us hate the noble and successful people around us, and tried to rewrite the history of those rich yet decent people like the

Plehns—spreading propaganda that any man who owned capital was evil and wanted to oppress those less fortunate. We all knew from experience that this was simply not true. During the next fifteen years of living under Communist rule, I would get a clear view of what were truly the forces of good and evil in the world, and by the time I landed in America, I knew that freedom to live my life as I saw fit was the only thing worth fighting for.

CHAPTER 6

The War is Over and Starvation Sets In

AFTER ROSE PASSED AWAY AND THE IMMEDIATE trauma of the Russian occupation was over, our family moved into the Niehoff family's old house. At the war's end, whoever was left was just scrambling for food and shelter, grasping at whatever they could get their hands on. The house, which was adjacent to Rose's art studio, became the place I would call home for the next fifteen years, until it came time to leave for America.

When the war ended, my father was forty-five years old, and had lived through countless nights of terror. He had held our family together and kept us safe, but we were not out of the woods yet. There was a general chaos in Poland at that time. The old world order had collapsed, but we weren't yet sure what would come to take its place. Even though the Russian army had largely pulled out by the end of the year, the Russian Communists made their presence felt—Marxism was here to stay.

My father was a highly educated forester and had spent most of his life training and working in this specific field. He had such great expertise in this area that it was almost unforgivable to think that he wouldn't be working in the forests in the future. However, now that the Communists started nationalizing large tracts of what had previously been private land, he could no longer work in his chosen profession. The main reason was that he was not a member of the Communist Party, and a high-quality job like head forester for a vast property would be reserved for someone who was a loyal, card-carrying Communist. Dad did what he had to do after the war, and resigned himself to becoming a farmer.

Soon we heard from the newly formed Polish Communist government, which was acting, of course, at the direction of the Russians. The great socialist "land reform" was to begin soon, and the government parceled out all the farmland in the region to private citizens. It wasn't long before all of Rose Plehn's arable land was given away to individual farmers by the federal government. Each citizen received about fifty acres of land, which he was to use to do his own subsistence farming. Most of these parcels were taken from the large estates of German landowners who were now gone or deceased. There were also some wealthy Polish families in this region who owned land before the war, and they were allowed to keep five hundred acres of their land. If they had any land over that amount, it was nationalized.

Like most socialist propaganda, this sounded good in theory. The only problem was that farming is actually difficult to do, and few people possessed all the knowledge required to successfully sow, grow, and harvest healthy crops. Many people did not want the fifty acres and immediately gave it over to the national communes, deciding they would prefer to work there for wages. My father was one of the few who actually could manage his own farm, because he had managed Rose's forty-acre garden for more than a decade. We now had about fifty acres for our own production, and no animals to help in the field, since almost all livestock and farming machinery that had survived the war had been shipped to Russia. Each farmer was only allowed to keep a few chickens and cows—the minimum required to keep a family alive. All of the fields had to be plowed by hand, and mainly thanks to my father's great physical strength and tireless stamina, we were able to squeeze out a meager living selling our extra crops in those first few years.

A few Polish farmers had managed to hang on to an old horse and had some plows that could help the work go faster, and while they would share their horses when they could, most people plowed by hand. All able-bodied people, including children, were involved in the work of weeding and watering. My father built large wooden sleds to pull harvested grain from one end of the field to the other, and he and a few of his strong friends would help pull the sleds in.

The Russians immediately started rationing food, but there still wasn't enough for everyone to eat. The one thing which prevented mass starvation in the year immediately after the war was the fact that rye is a perennial grain, and had thus been seeded in Rose's fields in the late summer while the thousands of acres of farmland were still functioning like they were supposed to, under experienced farm managers. This grain grew in the spring so when Poland was in total disarray, at least the people had grain to make bread. While we didn't have much meat, our family did have eggs, milk, and butter, and so we weren't starving, as others were.

My father immediately started plowing the fields by hand, and set up a new orchard similar to the one he had maintained at Lady Rose's estate. He planted plum and cherry trees, tomatoes, raspberries, and red and black currants. The fruits would ripen quickly, and he would ride his bike to the market and sell them in town. Dad also decided he would start raising honeybees, even though he had never done it before. He knew it would be good business. Within a few years he had about fifty hives, and we would harvest the honey twice a year, producing several hundred liters of honey, which always sold quickly in the market. The honey harvest was one of my favorite times of the year because Dad would always save a piece of wax about two inches thick from the bottom of the hive just for me. I always looked forward to licking that wax clean, and I would have sticky, delicious honey dripping all over my fingers for the rest of the afternoon.

Also, during these early years, Henry, who lived in England, was a great help. He would send boxes of goods, for instance flint stones, that were cheap in London but impossible to obtain in Poland, and my father would be able to make a handy profit. Henry would also send bottles of newly developed penicillin, which was in big demand in Poland, and my dad would sell the pills individually for a profit. By the second year of subsistence farming and selling Henry's goods, we were able to buy a horse, which made the hard work of farming much more bearable.

Within a short few years it became obvious that this system of subsistence farming was not working for most people though, and the individual farms simply couldn't produce the amount of food needed to feed the population. Many people were on the verge of starvation, and things were particularly bad in the cities, where bread and meat lines would form at four in the morning for a shop that opened at seven. My father watched what was happening with a sense of helpless frustration. What had just a few years ago been an organized operation, producing enough to feed all the villages and sell crops for export, was now in total disarray, and people were in danger of starving even though they lived on fertile land. Many locals would come and ask my father for help, which he offered as much as he could, always giving advice about how to properly handle a harvest to maximize the yield.

What's more, local farmers had to pay large taxes to the state now. If you ran your own farm, there were large contingencies that were due to the state each year. Many of the large farms specialized in raising pork, and each year you had to give a large portion of your livestock to the state as a form of tax. The government actually was selling the pork for export, because bacon brought a fine price, while the local communities that raised the animals often didn't have enough to eat.

With the desperate situation on the farms, most young people quickly left and went to work in the cities, believing they would have better luck earning wages in a factory. This only exacerbated the problem on the farms, because now there were not enough hands to do the work. The Communist ideology did something even more insidious to the Polish people—it served to liquidate all of their private initiative. Many people just didn't have the desire to work hard in the fields all day, since they were assured they were now living in a socialist paradise where the government would take care of them. In the end, my father ended up feeding many of the local families from our yield, because people simply didn't have enough to eat, and we always did what we could to help our neighbors.

All the grains had to be harvested by hand because whatever machines we had were sent back to Russia with the Russian army in 1945. My father and Henrietta would harvest together. He would walk down the rows cutting the tall rye with a scythe, which was a long implement that required two hands and considerable skill to use. Henrietta would walk behind him and tie the rye in neat bundles to prepare it for threshing. They would stack them in bigger bundles like teepees in the field to dry. They worked long hours, from sunup to sundown, and usually cousins of ours from the nearby towns of Gdańsk and Bydgoszcz would come and help with the harvest. They were glad to help, because they would always return to the cities with suitcases full of food, which was not easy to obtain in the city.

Not only was Dad a tough guy, physically capable and full of stamina—he was also educated and highly literate. Some of the peasants who worked their farms near us had trouble with reading and writing, and they would come to see my father whenever they needed any kind of official document, like a request for a reduction in taxes, written up. He would even help send official documents written in German. I always marveled that this man who only attended a formal school up until age fourteen, and who had spent most of his adult life working the land, was known for such a wide variety of skills. Even in the early days he was already becoming a kind of village elder.

Within a few years the vast majority of the land was owned by the state—specifically, an entity known as PGR, an acronym denoting Polish cooperative farming—and their management of farmland was a complete disaster. Within a few years of the war's end there was a complete collapse of food production in Poland. Unqualified people were put in charge of the large communal farms PGR was running, and this led to an unmitigated disaster for Poland. People were given positions of power based on whom they knew, not what they knew. Many of these new bosses had not even completed a grammar school education and were barely literate. Suddenly, they would become the administrators of farms employing over one hundred people on thousands of acres, and they could barely read. Some farm managers were so clueless about how things worked that they would cut down all the grain and leave it lying in the field, assuming they could come back later to get it. Grains like rye must be rolled and dried immediately upon harvesting; otherwise, they rot quickly, and of course this is exactly what came to pass in the "workers paradise" the Communists had created in Lubocheń. The managers of the large farms simply didn't know what they were doing, and what's worse—they didn't care. They were party members and would be ensured their salary and ration of food before any of the workers, and that was all that mattered to them.

Soon enough the Communists came through with a new plan: they decided they would combine all the private farms into one large farm, and all the peasants would work together as a collective. It was 1948, and this was the time when Communism really started being force-fed to the population at a greater and greater speed. At this point my father had had enough of Communist ideas, and he refused to allow his private orchard and farm to become part of the larger collective. He received a lot of grief from the local authorities, who tried to pressure and cajole him into signing over his land to the state. My dad refused to join the mob though, and held out—much to everybody's surprise. He was as stubborn as he was hardworking, and because he was so well respected in town, there was little the Communists could do to force the will of a man who actually was succeeding at their individual subsistence-farming vision. I could sense the constant stress my parents were under, as they continued to hold on to their values in the face of so much opposition. There were high taxes my father had to pay as the price for holding on to his own private parcel of land. There was a predetermined amount of crops he had to provide to the government as taxes, but he bore that price and continued with the knowledge and confidence that at least he was farming in his own way, by his own rules. As long as he lived in Poland, he never gave in to the Communists, and never became a party member. The easier route would have been to give the land back to the government.

Over the years the pressure tactics the Communists used on my father and people like him became more intense. They started an aggressive propaganda campaign against individual farmers, calling them *kułaks*—which was a Russian term for fat, greedy old men. They would create posters and leave stacks of fliers around town with caricatures of these "kułaks," whom they depicted as keeping all of their wealth for themselves and not sharing with anybody else. Of course, my father had started with exactly the same resources as everyone else who had been granted fifty acres; he had just worked harder and smarter to succeed. But at this point in the development of Communism in Poland, there was no room for private enterprise at all.

Other industries had it worse—for instance, private shoemakers would find there were no longer any places they could buy raw material from. They wanted all craftsmen to work for collective shops and get paid wages set by the government. So it was with carpenters as well, who found that they suddenly had no suppliers available to sell them raw wood, because everything had been nationalized. The Communists were slowly trying to make sure that everybody was completely dependent on the government. My father, for instance, encountered difficulties in trying to buy fertilizer, because the government was trying to become a middleman for all types of goods. The only way around this was through connections, favors, and the goodwill of neighbors—luckily my father had enough of those to get us by. Nonetheless, the pressure tactics took their toll.

It was difficult for me to attend school, where I was conspicuously known as the "son of the private farmer," and I was not very much welcome there. At the school entrance there were always fliers posted depicting the fat kułaks, of which apparently my father was one. It burned me, because I knew my father had worked incredibly hard to achieve the small modicum of success and independence he had, and yet I was at times treated as an outcast by my schoolmates thanks to this propaganda assault. Any child who was the son of a factory worker in a big collective in town was treated well, but not me.

I always dreamed of being a fighter pilot or an artist; those were my two wishes growing up. I applied to be a cadet in the air force prep school, but there was no chance of me getting accepted, because of my father's private farm. Also, the fact that I had two siblings living in America at this time made things difficult for me as well.

The private enterprises that remained were treated like the pariahs of society. A nonstop barrage of propaganda depicted them as enemies of the system. Ironically, however, local people still respected men like my father because they knew the truth of his situation. Also, the local party members in Lubocheń didn't really believe in Communism either—they were just party members on paper. They generally respected my father and didn't give him as much trouble as the higher-ups would have liked.

One of the major pressure tactics the Communists used to get private farmers to hand over their land to PGR was through taxes. There were two kinds of tax—one was the regular cash tax on goods, and the other was a kind of quota that all farmers owed to the government. You were obligated to give so many pounds of grain, rye, or livestock to the government. On a small farm, fulfilling this quota would usually mean the farmer had nothing left to feed his family with, and so many farmers were simply unable to meet the quota. One such farmer was my uncle, who, unfortunately, liked the bottle a little too much and in 1948 was unable to meet his quota. The local authorities locked him up for six months as punishment. They kept him locked up in a basement up to his knees in water for weeks as part of his torture. Right away when they let him out, he gave his land back to PGR. This was how the Communists worked.

Meanwhile, the situation on the large collective farms continued to deteriorate. Farm managers would harvest huge bundles of grain and stack it in giant mountains in the silos, where it would just rot. It was basic knowledge for farmers that this grain should be threshed before it went bad, but on a collective farm, no one was responsible and no one cared. In a small enterprise, a farmer would *never* let such a thing happen, even if he had to hire people and share the profits—it was considered unthinkable to let so much grain go to waste. But the people in charge of the government farms had a different mentality, and crops were regularly left in the fields or the silos to rot. Farm production in our region was about 30 percent of what it had been before the war. Migrants and drifters were also brought in as many people drifted towards the cities. Many farmers continued working land that was previously theirs, but now got paid in wages for their time, and the farms usually produced a fraction of the food they had before. Imagine how this worked on the morale of the people— seeing the land that was theirs being managed by an incompetent manager who was a loyal Communist and didn't give a hoot as to whether the farm produced any food. Now the farmer would get paid pennies for his labor and work day in and day out, knowing that come winter he would probably be starving.

Luckily for me, I had parents who were by some miracle able to insulate me from the worst of these atrocities. I have many pleasant memories from these times—of playing in the fields, and doing the regular activities that kids do. The truth is that despite all the hardship, no matter what you experience, if you are surrounded by people who are even worse off than you, then you will always feel just a tiny bit prosperous. This was a powerful feeling for a growing boy, and even though we were poor and daily life was very difficult, I always had a sense that things could be worse, because I saw my suffering neighbors who didn't have fathers with farming expertise and business acumen like mine did.

There came a time not long after that when the national government was pressuring local authorities to round up all the weapons in the hands of the local citizens They were trying to disarm the populace. In the immediate aftermath of the war there were firearms littering all the fields, and people were just walking around collecting them. By 1947, representatives from Warsaw were sent into the villages and were authorized to do searches of all the houses to collect weapons, because they felt there were too many in the hands of the public. However, the law specified that such searches could only be conducted within the presence of a civilian witness. My father was not home when they came to search for his gun, and once my mother realized what was happening, she quickly walked out of the house and said she didn't want anything to do with it. The local party members who knew and respected my father also refused to act as witnesses for the search and seizure of his property, and so the government was unable to find a justification for taking my father's weapon. No doubt it was in part because he was one of the few men of influence in that town who wasn't a party member, and the local authorities didn't want to cross a line that would truly anger my father.

The punishment for having an illegal firearm was seven years in prison, and it was a huge risk to carry one—thousands of people ended up in prison in those years just for that. The only exception to this rule was for people who were members of the local hunting club, and only an elite group of people were allowed to join.

Even the local Communist lackeys had to respect my father, because he was a smart, shrewd man; he always helped his neighbors, and he was also a tough son of a gun. Messing with him wouldn't do much good. As a matter of fact, after the dust settled, my father was even able to obtain a permit for a firearm in the early 1950s—a major testament to his influence. Even though he was able to get only a shotgun used for hunting, and not a rifle, this was something unheard of, because only Communist elites were allowed to have weapons. The truth was that on a human level, the low-level Communist authorities in our area liked my father, respected his knowledge, and allowed him to join the local hunting club, where there were weekly outings for deer and ducks.

Every so often we participated in public hunts for jackrabbits. There was a specific ritual in which everyone involved would make two wings that would fan out over a large area, horns would blow, and the hunt would start. The young boys like me would chase the game so that they would run inside the ring of hunters. It was one of the best jobs, as I was getting paid to run around the woods banging on trees and making a lot of noise—a little boy's dream.

The commandant of the hunting club was not from Lubocheń, and so he took issue with my dad, a non-party member, having a gun. This commandant had been making slippers before the war, and now he had a big head because he had a little bit of power as a Communist official. This was typical of the people in power at that time—they had been lowlife rabble and hoodlums who now found themselves elevated to positions of power based simply on the fact that they were the lowest elements of society before the war. People like this were especially sensitive to and jealous of any kind of status or admiration an ordinary man like my father might have. He tried to get my dad's gun taken away, and succeeded in getting his license suspended. The manager of the club was what we called a "Communist on paper"—meaning he joined the party just to make his life easier, but he didn't really believe in any of the mumbo jumbo. He and others like him would overlook a lot of the things that would make the true Communists mad. These "paper Communists" liked my father and respected him, and some of his buddies would let him borrow a gun to hunt a few times a year even while his license was suspended. They let my father join the club because they liked and respected him. Men like my father, if they were clever and stayed out of trouble, could get by.

The local commandant during this hunt knew that the best way he could get my father was to go check his house and catch him at home with a private firearm. With his license suspended, if they caught him with a gun, he no doubt would have landed in jail for a long time, and we would have never left for America. Some of the locals—men of lower society who were jealous of my dad—were present when the commandant tried to search our house, but even they didn't want to act as witnesses to the search, because they knew my father still held influence within the region.

My dad would hunt boar, and my mom would cure and preserve it for the winter so that we would have meat even in the leanest of times. Occasionally Dad would shoot a deer, and, mixing it together with a bit of pork for flavor, this would produce quite a lot of meat. My mother would cook it in gravy and can it in jars, where it would keep in the basement most of the year and taste completely fresh when opened. My mother also did a lot of canning of fruits, and so despite many people around us starving, I had fruit compote or strawberry jam every other day—along with various fruits like apples, pears, plums, and cherries in juice. Despite all the hardship and propaganda, I was one of the luckiest kids around.

As evidence of my father's character, in the 1950s my father spent a few years working as a juror, in the local district government. This job came to him because he was nominated in the local district court to work in this capacity. In Poland the system works a little differently, and jurors have the additional job of listening to many cases all day long—poring over evidence, talking to witnesses, and so on—before they make their decisions. The district court he worked for was part of the administrative body for eight local villages, and the people who ran the court knew of my father and his reputation as a fair and honest man, and they asked him to do this job. He considered this a civic duty and spent several months working in the courthouse.

These years immediately after the war also brought new terrors for Poland. While the heroes of other Allied countries returned home to victory parades and great honors, Polish heroes were treated in an unspeakable manner. There were hundreds of thousands of Polish refugees all over the world at this point, but mostly in Britain. The question that faced them now was whether to return home or not, as they couldn't stay in refugee camps in foreign countries forever. They needed to choose where to settle. The soldiers who had found themselves in Anders' Army were particularly eager to return home, because they wanted to again see the land they had fought so hard to free from Nazi occupation. Unless you have faced it yourself, it's difficult to understand what an impossible decision it is to face returning to an uncertain homeland under a new ruler, or to say goodbye and never see the beloved country of your youth again. This was the question that many members of my family faced.

The Soviet-sponsored government made a special target out of any soldiers who had fought in the underground Polish resistance and in the Polish army abroad. The underground resistance fighters—known as the Armia Krajowa (which means "Home Army"), or "AK"—were brave heroes who had formed one of the most comprehensive, organized, and systematic anti-Nazi forces from the very first days of the war. These leaders should have been the ones to inherit a newly freed Poland, but as Poles learned too late, the Allied powers—specifically, the US and the UK—had sold out Poland to Joseph Stalin. The internal security office, Urząd Bezpieczeństwa, or "UB" as it was called, was the Communist-sponsored Polish equivalent of the KGB. They made a special target out of not only AK fighters, but also any soldiers who had fought in General Anders's Second Corps and who returned to Poland from abroad. The Soviet-sponsored government treacherously encouraged these Polish expats to return home, under the false pretense that they would be welcomed with open arms. My uncle Joseph was one of these unfortunate soldiers.

When I was six years old, I excitedly greeted my uncle Joseph, my father's brother, as he returned to Poland from England in 1947. He had been forcibly drafted into the Nazi army in 1943, but like my brother Henry, he had escaped and joined the Allies in their fight against the Nazis. He should have returned to a free Poland a decorated war hero, but instead he was immediately persecuted by the Soviet puppets who accused him of being a Western spy. He was arrested just a few days after our family reunion in Lubocheń and was taken in for questioning. The Communists working in the UB beat him to within an inch of his life, knocking out all of his teeth. They beat him with billy clubs wrapped in wet sheets to minimize the external marks left from the torture. He sustained kidney damage that would stay with him the rest of his life. They wanted him to admit that he returned to Poland as a Western spy. The UB thugs had trouble accepting the truth, which was that he had returned home to help take care of his aging mother, my grandmother. He was gone for several days during his "questioning" and returned home bruised and devastated with the realization of what Poland had become. What I remember most of all though was that he didn't become bitter, and he didn't speak of what must have been his deep frustrations. He came back to Poland without the knowledge that dishonest politicians from the West had sold out our homeland to the Communist Soviet Union, and he resigned himself to the hand that he and his countrymen had been dealt. He never complained, and led a quiet life, happy to be reunited with his family.

The Russian-controlled government in Poland kept persecuting Polish war heroes, and deporting thousands of others. Millions of Poles perished in the years after the war, when the rest of the world was enjoying a hard-earned peace. This kind of persecution was especially felt in our region, where so many had been forcibly drafted into the German army, and now found themselves targets.

In the meantime however, my parents were anxious to see their other children. In 1948 Halina had already emigrated from Germany to the USA. She had married an older Polish army officer while in the Polish refugee camps the Allies ran after the end of the war, and they had moved to start their new life in America as soon as they could. Henry, however, was with the regular Polish army in England, and he had time to deliberate his choice about where he would move when the dust settled. While at first we all wanted him to return to Poland very much, it quickly became clear what kind of welcome he would receive if he came back. I remember the anxiety my father experienced as he realized he had to write to my brother, "Do not return to Poland, despite how much we would like to see you back home." He was afraid they would do the same thing to his son that they had done to his brother. Those first years after the war saw political persecution of Poles that was in many ways worse than what the Nazis had done.

Henrietta married a man in Lubocheń in 1952 and settled down to start her own family. I was a growing boy, and Casey was in high school. Political persecution was rampant all around us, and the future seemed dark and gloomy. The bearers of culture, class, and the values of our past, like the Plehn family, had been almost completely eradicated, and a new philosophy of socialism and poverty took over. It was a very dark time for Poland. As much as we missed him, it was an enormous blessing for us that Henry had not returned home. Not only did it spare him the torture he was sure to endure, but he was able to help our family tremendously from his position in England. The supplies and goods he continued to send helped us make a living after Poland had literally been stripped bare by the Nazis and Soviets. It was our start in this dark new world, and Henry's position in England gave us a leg up. With our family now split by an ocean and no prospect of reunion on the horizon, we soldiered on into a dark, unknown future.

CHAPTER 7

Life Under Communism

ONE OF THE EARLIEST CHRISTMAS DAYS I REMEMBER was in the winter of 1946, when I was five years old. Already at this time in my life I was fascinated with Africa, no doubt thanks to the treasures of Lady Rose's manor that I had been exposed to all those years. I received a book from my parents called *Murzynek Bambo*, which meant "Bambo the Little Black Boy"; it was a children's story about life in Africa, and was illustrated with gorgeous images. I read about the adventures of Bambo, and his stories would stay with me throughout my childhood. There were pictures of all sorts of exotic animals, and to this day I remember the first word I learned while reading it: "hippopotamus." The other word I learned and fell in love with was "Limpopo River," which was where many of Bambo's adventures took place. About twenty years ago when I was fifty years old, I found myself on the banks of the actual Limpopo River, surrounded by hippos, and I felt overjoyed. At that moment I had such a strong inner need to communicate with my parents—to tell them,

"Look at where I am! Look at what I have done!" If someone had told that child that so many years later he would follow in the footsteps of Bambo, he would have never believed him.

We didn't have much for Christmas, but having this book on Africa was a great luxury. Often we would also get some cookies or fruit. It didn't matter what it was, as long as it was sweet and wrapped in a piece of paper—often just plain newsprint. Because my dad was so handy with a wide variety of tools, I always had special toys that other kids didn't. During the war, my father had made a rocking horse out of the skin of a real colt that had died just a few months after it was born. He had mounted it on a wooden frame, padded it, and placed the wooden frame, covered in a real horse skin, on a curved wooden panel. It was a real rocking horse! I inherited it after my brothers grew up, and somehow it survived through the war. When I was in grammar school and could have friends over, the rocking horse was a huge hit among my friends, especially since it looked like a real horse.

At age seven, in 1948, I went to school for the first time. I started walking the two kilometers to attend the Polish school that had just reopened after the war. Throughout my grammar school years I was always the best-dressed child there. Because my sister was already in America, and thanks to the gifts she and Henry would send, I always had wonderful American-made clothes and shoes. I was the envy of all the students, who only had one pair of shoes or one pair of pants for the winter, and one for the summer. I was a truly blessed child.

One of my greatest joys was the day summer finally arrived. This was marked by the day my mother would finally allow me to run around outside barefoot. I would wait impatiently for the day when I could be free, stomping around in frustration putting my shoes on when my mom said the ground was still too cold and wet for being barefoot. When the day I didn't have to wear shoes anymore finally arrived, I was overjoyed.

My favorite thing to do in the summers growing up was to take my fishing rod down to the river, where I spent endless hours catching pike and trout in the abundant streams. However, I also got a chance to go ice fishing in the winter. One morning while walking to school, I found an axe leaning against a tree. This was a valuable tool that some poor farmer must have left during the last days of the fall harvest, and it was now easily seen among the barren trees and snow. I did what any ten-year-old kid would have done, and grabbed the axe and set off to have an adventure. I quickly forgot that I was on my way to school, and instead made my way onto the frozen pond. I decided I would hack a hole in the ice and catch some fish to bring home to my family. This was just after the war, so food was very scarce, especially in the winter. I was so proud of myself when I hacked a sizable hole in the almost one-foot-thick ice. I sat on the edge of the hole, and put my feet on the other side of it to brace myself while I looked down at all the little mouths gasping for air. It had been a very tough winter, and the pond was frozen solid. Because there wasn't enough vegetation in the water, like cattail reeds—which could produce oxygen—the fish were slowly suffocating. There were so many and they were so slippery that I decided my best option was to lean forward and start scooping them out with my entire arm, like a rake. In just a few minutes there were fish all over the place, flopping around on the ice, and I was feeling incredibly proud of myself and had no intention of stopping. Suddenly my feet slipped and my butt fell into the water! It was terribly cold and half my body was soaked. I quickly hid the fish on the side of the pond in a pile of snow and hurried off to school before my clothes froze to my body. I was almost half an hour late for class, and of course it caused a huge disruption when I walked in soaking wet and reeking of fish. I sheepishly lied and said I had fallen into a hole while crossing the pond, and the teacher made me take off all my wet clothes and lay them against the big ceramic-tile stove we had in the classroom. I was relieved they bought my story and happy to be drying off. I was thrilled to think of all the fish waiting for me back at the pond. After school, I took all the books out of my book bag, stuffed it with fish, and carried my books in my arms to get home. My mother laughed when she saw me come into the house. I didn't tell her I fell into the water, and even though she had to wash out my backpack, she was obviously happy that I had brought home a feast for us that night.

In the years after the war, many children died from playing with unexploded artillery shells that littered the entire region. By the 1950s this was clearly still a major ongoing problem, and the Russian authorities organized a campaign to round up the unexploded ordnance. Whom better to ask where all the dangerous toys are than the local children who play in the woods? I always volunteered when they came to the school asking for boys who would show them where the shells were located. I enjoyed the expeditions, because not only would I get out of school, but after they rounded up the bombs, they would bury them in a sandpit and then set off a massive explosion that would send dirt and debris over 150 feet in the air. It was great fun for a growing boy, although today I count my lucky stars that I didn't lose a limb or worse in all those hours of playing with fire.

Life slowly settled into a new routine, and we were getting by. My father would usually go hunting on Sundays, much to the chagrin of my mother, who would have preferred that he go to church. It was his one pure pleasure, and often the game he killed was able to feed our entire family through the winter.

The old house we lived in had been part of Rose's art studio, and in the basement there was a ledge along the wall at waist height. As I grew older, I realized this ledge was there for painting. It created a kind of convenient easel on which a painter could easily lean several canvasses against the wall and get to work. It was an inspiring thing to see, and as I grew older the idea of studying art and painting was always in the back of my mind. When I look at it today, it's no wonder to me that art and Africa became two of my great lifelong passions, because I grew up in a home that celebrated both.

After Stalin died in 1953, a new regime took over and the political climate softened somewhat. Thanks to the help from Henry and Halina in America, our family was once again able to buy a strong horse. In addition to all the great clothes I had from America, I was so proud to talk about my brother Henry, and how he had fought with General Anders's army during the war. I felt I really had a special family, and so much to be proud of and thankful for.

By this time we also had sheep, and my mother would spend the entire winter spinning wool, which I, unfortunately, always had to help with. We would wash the wool, and pull out the long threads. I would have to hold up my forearms like spindles for my mom to wrap the string around as she spun it, and I would have to sit like this for hours. I hated doing it, but there was never a question of disobeying mother. At around age twelve, I had to start helping with more of the serious chores around the farm, including taking care of the livestock. In the summertime I would put the cows out to pasture. I would have to clean the stables, and spend many an afternoon up to my knees in straw and manure, shoveling the stalls and laying down new hay. I worked fast and usually had plenty of time afterwards for fishing and play.

As I got older, I also liked to play cards with my friends from school. We played blackjack, although we called it "twenty-one". Once in a while, if I saw any spare change lying around the house, I would swipe it and then my friends and I could play for money. I made friends with some of the families that had been settled in Rose Plehn's manor, which was now divided into apartments for many families—probably about fifteen families altogether, all living in her house. The types of people living in this kind of government housing were of the lower rungs of society, and even as young kids, thirteen or fourteen years old, they would smoke in front of their parents; this is where we would do our gambling. We would play in the large room that used to hold the grand piano, and there was still a beautiful painting of the beheading of

John the Baptist hanging on the wall, which Rose had painted. There were also still several large mounted Cape buffalo heads hanging high in the hallway—they had just been too far out of reach for lazy looters. One day my father found out where I was and marched over and ordered me out of there, dragging me by the ear. He was always ready to enforce a specific set of values, and he wasn't about to tolerate immoral behavior like gambling from his son. He didn't want me hanging out with these kinds of friends, and it clearly pained him to see what had become of Rose's beautiful estate.

Soon it was time for me to apply to high school, and I knew I would have a difficult time of it because of my family's situation and siblings living in America. My geography teacher was the one adult in school who I felt was sympathetic to my plight and who wrote me a letter of recommendation for continued education. He had been a Polish officer during the war but had since become a "paper Communist," even though he hated them with all his heart. When I was ten years old, he had me write a report on Florida—and I'll never forget how my mind raced at a hundred miles per hour while reading the descriptions of the sand on the beach that was so hot you could cook an egg on it. I never imagined I would one day be able to visit there myself. This teacher wrote me a letter of recommendation for the air force cadet school, but of course I was rejected. The only school that would accept me was one that trained plumbers, so this was the future I had to take. In the meantime I continued to dream of becoming a pilot. I thought it would be a way for me to escape from Poland. In the early 1950s there had been several high-level defections of Polish pilots, including one who landed on a Danish island in the Baltic Sea with a Russian MiG-15, giving the West a huge advantage in the Cold War. In my youth I imagined I would become one of these pilots who escaped to the West. I also started listening to Radio Free Europe, which opened my eyes to the larger world, even though you could be sent to jail for listening to it.

In 1956 I moved to Bydgoszcz, the nearest big city, where I lived with some of my mother's siblings and attended high school. I would live there for four years, until I left for America. One of the first things I did was join the local aeroclub, where I learned to skydive and fly gliders, but unfortunately that was as far as my piloting career went. Things got interesting in 1956, when right after the attempted Hungarian revolution against the Soviets, we had similar minirevolutions in Poland. This was completely blocked in the media, as they didn't want the general population to know about it, and so that it couldn't spark a national uprising, but the students were in the street protesting in cities like Łodz, Poznań, Gdańsk, and my own town of Bydgoszcz. We got information about the revolution in Hungary from Radio Free Europe, the only reliable source of information. One weekend when I returned from a visit to Lubocheń, there were no streetcars available upon my arrival, so I walked back to my dorm. I remember walking down a street called Ulica Długa, or "Long Street," and I saw a derailed streetcar. When I asked some people what was going on, they yelled "Revolution!" in return. There was a palpable excitement among the people on the streets, who thought this might be our chance to beat the Communists back. There was a humongous radio tower in the center of town that was jamming the radio signal, so we couldn't get Radio Free Europe at the time. When I walked up, I saw that the tower was on fire, and I joined about twenty other young people like myself in storming the building. It was mostly empty, but we took file cabinets and threw them out of windows on the third floor, and felt overjoyed at the havoc we were creating. I think many of the local officials shrank back in fear, knowing they could lose control at any moment, but for whatever reason they turned a blind eye to what we were doing and no authorities came after us. Nothing much came of it, as the Communists made sure we didn't get far, but we certainly felt like we were at least part of something larger than ourselves. Soon we learned of the vicious crackdown on the Hungarian student protestors, and our own minirevolution fizzled out. I gave blood twice for the victims of the Hungarian crackdown, as I felt a strong sense of solidarity with those students who were equally trapped behind the Iron Curtain.

Almost ten years later, when I was in my mid-twenties and working in America, I had the opportunity to meet a group of young men who were survivors of the 1956 Hungarian revolution. They told me horrible stories of how they fought the Russian soldiers, using only rifles and Molotov cocktails. With those simple armaments they had fought daunting Russian tanks. These were details I couldn't have obtained at the time it was happening, but I always considered these young men the first freedom fighters behind the Iron Curtain. These gritty fighters I met in Chicago had managed to escape to Austria when the revolution collapsed. As they told their story, they always made sure to respectfully mention their many friends who faced a very different and grim future when they were captured by the Russians.

To this day, I do not understand why the Polish Communists did not interfere while we young students were protesting and then donating blood for our Hungarian brothers. It seemed like they just turned a blind eye to this insubordination, which was very unusual. Those moments when I was a teenager in Bydgoszcz were embedded in my mind as the first hope of freedom I actually felt in Poland, and I would remember it always.

Life as a student in Bydgoszcz was bleak for most, as the student rations provided in the dining halls were barely enough to survive on. I would go to Luboheń every other week by train and bring back with me provisions my mother had prepared. This included smoked sausages, canned goods, and other nonperishables, which most students didn't have access to. By the Monday after my trips home I would usually be bare of all my goods. They should have lasted me for two weeks, but I shared them with all my hungry friends right when I returned to school. If I hadn't had all that extra food from my mother, I certainly would have been near starving the entire time I was at the trade school.

In 1958 the Communist government started to thaw a little bit under the new president Gomułka, and my father went to visit America. This would be a turning point in his life, and he spent six months there visiting my two oldest siblings. He brought a lot of clothes back with him, because the shelves in Poland were still completely barren. After his return, all he could think of was how wonderful life in America was. He talked about how free people were, the opportunities they had, and how nobody meddled in their neighbor's business or tried to stop them from doing anything. It sounded like a paradise, and it was clear my father had lost the will to continue struggling to scrape by in Poland. By the end of the 1950s, so many families had been broken up by the war that the US and Poland signed a treaty on the grounds of helping families rejoin. This was my parents' ticket to the USA, and it posed a serious crisis of conscience in our family.

After the war, it was very common for several families to live together. Henrietta with her husband and their three children lived with my parents in the same house that I grew up in, and we were all very close. My parents agonized over their decision to leave their daughter with her young children behind, but we all encouraged them to go. Henrietta was actually very sick with pneumonia at the time, and my parents didn't want to leave her—it was a very difficult decision. We faced almost certain continued hardship in Poland, as the government was inept and corrupt and showing no real signs of improvement. There was nothing holding society together. By most accounts, 50 percent of Poland's intelligentsia had been killed during the war. More than half of the doctors, lawyers, army officers, and clergy had been killed by the Nazis and Soviets. There were fewer than ten thousand people with PhD degrees left in the whole country at war's end. The people put in charge of our towns often came from the worst, most uneducated stratum of our society, promoted only because they were loyal to the party. It was clear there was no future here, and our family had a way out—and thus we urged our parents to take it.

To be honest, I think we all imagined in our hearts that we would follow them shortly after, and that this would be much easier for us to do once they were established in America and could support us. On a gloomy and misty evening in late November 1959, the time had come for my parents to leave everything behind and emigrate to the USA. My brother-in-law and I took my parents in a horse-drawn buggy to the train station three miles away. That chilly, wet night matched my mood in many ways. I was heartbroken and devastated that my home and family were falling apart. I'm sure my parents experienced the same emotions, but this was my father's choice. He wasn't the sort of man to waver, and surely his resolve came from the great promise of freedom that America held. It was almost mythic to us at the time. What a testament this moment was to the basic truth that men need freedom above all else. I was eighteen years old and had spent all of my life in this small corner of Poland, surrounded by two older siblings and a set of parents who all loved, adored, and supported me. Life had been hard, but I realized I had been insulated from the worst of it thanks to the love of my family. Now it was all going to be torn apart, and I knew I would miss them terribly. I had mixed feelings to be sure. Perhaps at the time I didn't fully realize just how much I had been insulated from the worst of the war and the Communism that followed. I had grown up, I had often had more than our neighbors, and I felt like I had had a pretty good life. I just didn't know any better, and even though I understood my parents' reasons, I loved my homeland and my life. Change is often the hardest thing to face. Maybe I didn't see it at the time, but I realized that I was learning the lesson that a man will give up almost everything for freedom, and for the chance to pursue a better future for his family. My dad, even though he was almost sixty years old, never let go of that dream and that promise.

We had certainly tried to get passports for all of us, but they would only let my parents out, and even that was an ordeal. My father's relatives in Bydgoszcz that I lived with while at school had some connections because of their high managerial positions in some factories, and over the next few years one of these relatives, a man whose name was Bolek, and who was kind of like a distant uncle to me, worked hard to get a passport for me from the Polish authorities. He was the director of a factory that produced heavy manufacturing equipment, like lathes, even though he was only about forty years old at the time. He was a staunch anti-Communist, and to this day I don't know how he had the position he did—I always believed it had something to do with the military rank and position he held before the war, and the connections that it gave him. He was always the one who was able to get US dollars to me from my parents in America after they left. He had some connections in West Germany, and they would somehow launder the US money by way of expensive and in-demand products like fabric dyes through his connections in the Polish manufacturing industry. My father would send the money to the people in West Germany, who would send the dyes to the Polish company, which would then provide us with the Polish złoty equivalent of the enormous sum—after taking their cut, I'm sure. One hundred US dollars back in those days was a huge sum—it was close to a year's salary for a low-level factory worker. This was how I managed to survive in the year after my parents left. Somehow this cousin was able to arrange for a passport for me as well (passports were a commodity for which there was a serious black market), although I'm sure my parents rewarded him well for his help.

Casey, meanwhile, was working in a shipyard in Gdańsk, and although he too wanted to leave for America, it wasn't possible for us all to go. Because I was the only one who was single, everyone figured it would be easiest to get me out first; so I plotted my escape. Although Henrietta wanted to be reunited with her parents and siblings as well, Henrietta's husband, Witold Pruszynowski, was skeptical that America could really be as great as everyone said it was, which was how many Polish people felt at the time. It was hard to see beyond all the oppressing Soviet propaganda. Witold was drafted into the Communist Polish army, and he didn't really want to leave Poland, as he had a decent job and America was full of uncertainty to him.

Over half a century later, as I am writing down these memories, I am much older than my father was then. The difference in our ages is not the only thing that separates us. I try to comprehend the strength and faith he had to undertake the decisions he did. It was certainly traumatic for my mother to leave her sick daughter with three small children, and only now, with the perspective of so much time and my own family that I love and protect, can I understand how truly awful things must have been for my parents to take the leap when they did. Like many people who live in desperate circumstances under totalitarian regimes, you do what you have to do to survive. I cannot imagine how my father handled the risks, with his strong feelings of responsibility for our family, but I am so happy that he did.

Perhaps by 1959 it was a bit easier, because the Lubocheń my father knew growing up was completely gone. Lady Rose's manor had long ago been divided up into apartments that were handed out to the peasants in the villages, most of whom were unemployed. The beautiful glass-enclosed verandas that had surrounded the house had long ago been destroyed, and the brick and granite walls surrounding the estate had been crushed and disassembled. The gorgeous trees that were hundreds of years old had been cut down. The property was a mass of wild weeds and bushes.

When I think back on the residents of the manor who were my classmates in the years after the war, I am horrified. I remember visiting their crowded apartments, which had once been the various guest rooms of Rose's home, to smoke cigarettes and play cards on her grand staircase. I still remember the faint traces of the ornate wallpaper that lined the stairwell, now peeling as we sat and played. My father couldn't stand the sight of what had become of her beautiful home—a home that he had worked for so many years to maintain. The people living there had no sense of the great and rich history of this place, and treated it like a cheap motel. It was dirty and run-down and a painful sight for my father's eyes—something that I didn't fully understand at the time.

The decaying mess had been stripped of all its riches and glory, and the inhabitants had no idea what they had done. All the magic was gone. The manor eventually became a kind of public housing system for the remnants of society, and by the time my parents were ready to leave for America, it was full of alcoholics and people who were a general nuisance in the village. They would steal from the local people in Lubocheń, and generally cause trouble. It was a terrible irony that the most beautiful place was filled with the worst people. That these people acted this way, living off something they didn't earn, was a classic perversion of the socialist system. These policies worked systematically to destroy Poland's society from the inside for the next forty years.

One of the worst parts of the Communist system is that it set neighbors and friends against each other. People started to become suspicious of you if you had more than they had. Instead of attributing it to someone's hard work or skill, they assumed that successful people must be collaborators with the oppressive regime. This was one of the most unfortunate outcomes of the socialist mentality, and it would weigh on our family increasingly. My father was the most upright man around, yet there were still those who questioned him. This was especially true for poor and illiterate folk, who were easily swayed by government propaganda. The worst of society tried to pull other people down, and as the 1950s dragged on, my father was sick and tired of petty grievances with minor officials over issues that were clearly the result of simple jealousy. In the previous world, men would have been inspired to work hard themselves so that they too could advance, but as Communism strangled Poland, the citizenry at times worked to tear itself apart from the inside.

When Poland finally cast off the Iron Curtain in 1989 and became a free capitalistic system, the country was able to revive itself relatively quickly in a short amount of time. Most of the big cities in Poland have been restored and rebuilt, showing signs of their prewar glory and becoming major tourist attractions.

Unfortunately, one of the richest parts of Polish history—the wealthy manors and estates that upheld the culture and held society together for hundreds of years—never recovered. The families that lived in Lubocheń before the war and worked for Lady Rose had moved away. Most of them went to the cities to escape the new unemployed neighbors who occupied Rose's house and had no respect for or knowledge of the profound history of this home and its former residents.

When I think about it today, I remember that Lubocheń was the home of so many illustrious characters of Europe's history. The Plehn family was full of people whom the scientific world still talks about today. They made so many contributions to humanity and science that it's hard to believe they can lie buried in the ground in northwest Poland without even a gravestone to mark their resting place. The people who live there now are little better than wards of the state, using and abusing the illustrious home of the Plehn family, where I was born, as little more than cheap public housing. The dozen or so families who live in the manor today have no sense of history about this place, and in my observation are mainly concerned about where they can get their next liter of vodka from. One hundred years before this sad state, Lubocheń was home to men and women who were doctors, artists, and scientists. They traveled the world, wrote books, and agitated to make the world a better place for all of humanity—whether through sharing beautiful pictures or music or through experiments and exploration. They worked to eradicate malaria, and keep the populations of fish in the rivers and streams of Europe healthy so that the next generation could be fed. Moreover, the

Plehns formed the locus of the entire community. They provided for the townspeople and, most importantly, set an example of a kind of honor and character that would soon vanish from the European continent. It wasn't only the Plehns that mattered, but all of the old families of Lubocheń—the skilled craftsmen and tradesmen who worked for the estate who also shared the same values of dignity and honor that are absent in the faces I see living in Lubocheń today. The older era had a sense of history and a respect for it, which is almost completely gone now amidst government handouts and decades of soul-crushing collectivism.

One year after my parents left for the US, in 1960, I finished school and decided to follow them to America. They had already learned to speak English as their third language and were adapting well to the American way of life. Europe was in shambles, and I knew it was time to start a new chapter. I said goodbye to my sister Henrietta and brother Casey, and was on my way. My brother Henry sent me money for a one-way voyage across the ocean, and I was excited for my first big adventure alone.

In many ways I see myself as one of the last living witnesses to a completely different era. I was born right on the cusp of a new world order, and the changes that socialism brought to my family almost tore us apart for good. In large part it was the freedom and abundance of America that healed and brought us together again.

Rose Plehn, self-portrait

Rose Plehn's painting of her parents,
which hung in the library

Marianna Plehn

Sława in a field of popppies in Lubocheń in 1986

The town of Gniew, near Lubocheń

My family at my aunt's wedding in the early 1930s. Left to right—my dad's youngest brother, my oldest sister Halina, born in 1924, my father, mother, uncle, and oldest brother Henry, born 1926

Ewa Swiderski, my father's mother

Jan Mackowski, my mother's father

Bernard Swiderski, my father's father, in a Prussian uniform around the turn of the century

Bruno Swiderski,
my father 1936

My mother,
Waleria Mackowska

My father's sister and her family

Father playing drums in the early 1920s

My uncle, Anastazy (Nastek) Mackowski, in Polish cavalry uniform 1937

In the forest with my father while he worked

Henrietta, me, Father, and Halina, 1942

Taking my first steps outside the manor, Henry and Mom look on

My siblings in 1940—Casey, Henrietta, Henry, Halina

Father in typical dress while working as a forester, 1942

With extended family

Lady Rose's art studio where my family lived from 1945-1959

Outside the manor with my mom

My parents' silver wedding anniversary in 1948, I'm standing next to my father

My parents' 25th wedding anniversary—Casey, my parents, Henrietta, and me

Henry in a Polish uniform after
joining Anders' Army

Halina with her future husband
in Germany after the war

Grammar school picture 1950 in Gacki; I'm in the second row, second from left

Halina and the German dentist she worked for in the German Labor camp

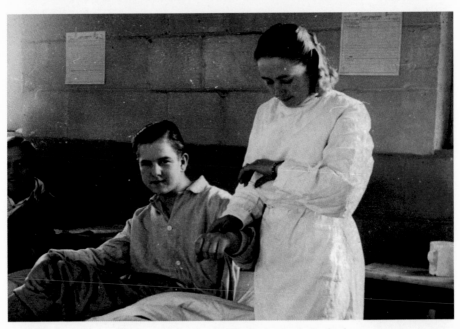

Henry recovering from appendix surgery in England

Casey with his wife and children

My sister Henia with her three daughters and Casey's wife with her daughter and son (front right)

Henrietta's Wedding 1950

Henrietta's wedding carriage

1958

1959

1964

With my airgun

At the Bydgoszcz Aeroclub

With a friend, outside my school
in Bydgoszcz 1958

With my father in Warsaw 1959

My first parachute jump from a biplane in 1957

PART II

Falling in Love with America, Falling in Love with Sława

CHAPTER 8

America at Last

THOSE MONTHS AFTER MY PARENTS LEFT FOR America were an interesting time for me. For the first time in my life I truly felt like I was on my own—no more going home to Mom's house on the weekend for pocket change and homemade meals. Without the support of my parents around, and with Henrietta and Casey busy with their own families, I increasingly thought of how I could join my family in America. It wasn't easy to get a passport in those days, but thanks to my father's connections in Bydgoszcz and the extra money we had from Henry in America, by the summer of 1960 I had a passport and a plane ticket. It was an indescribable experience of joy to think of being back with my parents living as one family, including the fact that after so many long years, I would finally to be able to meet my older sister and brother who had been forced from home so many years ago. I looked forward to my journey tremendously.

I had flown small planes in Poland after I joined the local flight club, but I had never flown in anything bigger than a two-seater. The very first commercial flight I took was from Warsaw to East Berlin in a rickety, aluminum-sided tail-wheel aircraft that rattled like an old haunted house as it barreled down the runway. The forty or so passengers looked around uncertainly at each other as we felt at any minute we would fly out the side of this shaking box-with-wings. After changing planes in East Berlin, we were quickly en route to Paris. This plane was much nicer of course, because it would be landing in the West, and the Communists always kept up appearances before an international audience. Those few hours I spent in Paris in the summer of 1960 completely blew my nineteen-year-old mind. Where I came from, everything was dilapidated and grey, and this was the first time I had ever been outside the Iron Curtain. In Warsaw, everyone almost literally wore the same jacket, because there was only one kind for sale in all the stores. It was a slick, gray trench coat that was considered fashionable because it was made out of a new material similar to polyester. In Paris everything was so colorful and vibrant. I got a good look at the city because I actually had to take a local bus between the small European airport at which I arrived and the large international terminal from which I would be departing. I got a glimpse of all the lights, fancy cars, and busy people. It was also striking to me how kind and helpful complete strangers were to me. There was an older Polish couple on the bus who had clearly been living in Paris for a long time, because their Polish was very rusty. They were thrilled to see a young man just arrived from Poland, and wanted to talk to me all about their home country. They helped me navigate the bus route and made sure I got off at the right stop. There were sensational billboards advertising Bridgette Bardot's latest movies, which I had never seen but looked absolutely mesmerizing to me from the pictures. I was wide eyed and shocked with glee at how spectacular it all was. I loved the energy, and knew I had made the right decision in leaving Poland.

At the time, Polish citizens were only allowed to leave the country with the equivalent of six US dollars, which is roughly forty-seven dollars in today's money. If you had more, they would confiscate it at the border. I wanted to buy something to prove that I had been in Paris, and so at a little kiosk at the airport, I spent three dollars on a small Eiffel Tower figurine. This was several days of wages back in Poland, and it felt exorbitant to purchase a trinket for such a vast sum, but I was glad for this new symbol of the grand adventure I was about to embark on. This trinket would continue to play a role in my life even forty years later, when I used it to inspire students with the idea that anything is possible if you just dream big enough. At the time I bought it I didn't realize how an insignificant memento from the most important journey of my life would be used as a prop for motivational speeches to school children.

That night I flew to New York City, and spent another whole day at the airport waiting for my flight to Chicago. I wanted to call my family and let them know I had arrived in America, but I didn't know how to use the pay phones, and I had no coins anyway. A kindly older man who worked at the airport and spoke Polish helped me out by taking some coins out of his own pocket and dialing for me. This simple act of generosity from a stranger had me thinking that America truly was a completely different place than where I had come from.

I knew right away that the person who answered the phone was my thirty-four-year-old brother, Henry, who had left home when I was two years old to fight in the war. This was the first time I had ever heard his voice. No one else was home, but I communicated to this stranger, my brother, that I was safe and sound in America and would be on the flight to Chicago that evening.

After that, the same man who gave me the change to call home stopped by and bought me a Coca-Cola, my very first. I found its taste mesmerizing, and I soaked in all the sweetness and good fortune I was experiencing in America. Sitting at the airport in New York, a few things jumped out at me. Right away I noticed a black man, the first I had ever seen in person, sitting on a bench and being very affectionate with a beautiful, biracial woman! This young couple was attractive, clearly in love, and while they may have been acting shamelessly by kissing and caressing in public, I thought it was great. "Holy shit, this is America!" I said to myself. I thought, if people can act like this in public, just being happy and being themselves, then it can't be that bad.

Eight months after my parents had left Poland in what I thought could be our final goodbye, I was joyfully reunited with them at 4:00 a.m. on the south side of Chicago at Midway Airport. We snapped a picture of our reunion there in front of the largely abandoned cargo terminal. Henry drove, as he was the only family member who had a car, and a new chapter of my life officially began.

My parents had a little apartment in Chicago's Humboldt Park neighborhood, the heart of the Polish community. Their home was humble, and all the furniture and accessories were secondhand, either from the Salvation Army or from friends, but it was all so much brighter and more modern than anything we had had in Poland. To me everything was shiny and new and smelled like plastic or potpourri. Even the clothing in America smelled good, and was such an improvement over the acrid, gray cleaning powder we had in Poland, which was used not only for clothes but also for floors and toilets. Every detail was better in America.

I spent the first few days getting to know Henry and his wife, Margaret. Their support from abroad had been so instrumental in our family's good fortune during the postwar period, and I was thrilled to finally spend some time with the people I had heard so much about and who had been a constant presence in my life from afar.

Margaret was only fifteen months old when the war broke out, and her father, Henry Ostrowski, was an officer in the Polish army. He sent Margaret and her mother to stay with his relatives, for their own protection. He was a captain in an artillery unit, and they battled the Germans and Russians for nearly a month after the invasion of Poland on September 1, 1939. After being surrounded by Russian forces, he and two of his soldiers were able to escape, and spent the winter hiding near Poland's southern border. Finally in March of 1940 they escaped through the Balkans and made it to France, and eventually to England after France fell. He was attached to the British army until 1942, when he volunteered to travel to the Middle East to join the Polish army in exile, forming under General Anders along with refugees from the Soviet Union. He spent over a year in Palestine and Iraq, where he served as an artillery instructor and eventually as the commander of the Ninth Field Artillery Regiment.

In what would later turn out to be an extraordinary coincidence, Henry ended up fighting in the same Allied campaign in which Margaret's father fought—Monte Cassino, in Italy. As a matter of fact, Captain Ostrowski, who later was promoted to Major Ostrowski, was awarded the Virtuti Militari for his role in the battle. The Virtuti Militari is the highest military decoration in Poland, and it is given specifically for heroism and courage— much like the US Medal of Honor.

Meanwhile Margaret and her mother had been deported to a German labor camp, and they had been separated from the rest of the family. Luckily they survived and they were able to reunite with her father through the Red Cross at the end of the war. They ended up in the Polish military bases in England, just like Henry, but they didn't meet until many years later—when they were both settled in Chicago. By the time I met my brother and sister-in-law, they had been married for several years and had two small children. Sadly, I was never able to meet Margaret's father, as he had passed away just before I arrived. My own father, however, had been able to befriend him on his first visit to America, and he spoke very highly of Major Ostrowski. He was a highly educated officer, having joined the Polish army as a cadet when it was first formed in 1920. Sadly he passed away while still quite young—he was only in his fifties, and the entire family mourned the passing of this great Polish hero.

Margaret seemed to be a good match for my brother, and I was happy for them and the peaceful life they led in America. She had attended university and had an excellent job in an administrative position with a large company. Although they were by no means rich, it was amazing to me how well they were thriving in their newly adopted homeland. They had a comfortable house and a car, and all the trappings of regular middle-class folks in the Midwest during those times. It may not seem like much looking back on it, but to a kid who just arrived from behind the Iron Curtain, their lives seemed luxurious.

After a few weeks of getting acclimated to all the new sights, sounds, and smells of the "land of opportunity," it was time to get to work. My father told me that first things first, I had to pay Henry back the $240 he had paid for my one-way ticket. That was the equivalent of about $1,880 in today's dollars, and was a significant amount of money. Henry was married with small children, and that sum certainly made a big difference to him.

The concept of saving money was kind of foreign to me, because in Poland there was nothing to save for. Any money I had in my pocket was immediately spent, even though there had been little to spend it on. My father was very stern with me that I start saving money right away, because otherwise it was unfair to Henry. To my amazement, I was able to pay Henry back in full this enormous sum within two months of starting my first job.

My father walked to work every morning, to the Saint Mary of Nazareth Hospital, which was just a few blocks away. He was a custodian and handyman: a job he was great at, because he spent most of the day fixing things. My mother also worked there as a seamstress in the nursing school. That fall, my father announced to me that we were going to attend English classes at Wells High School. We were an unlikely pair of students, he the more so at age sixty; nevertheless, three times a week in the evenings we diligently attended classes. I was annoyed that I had to go to school, but in truth that classroom was a great introduction to the melting pot that is America. I met people of every race and culture, and I saw how other immigrants were doing well for themselves after just arriving. Being a young man, I immediately started to long for a car of my own—the holy grail of status symbols back in Poland.

About a month after I arrived, my oldest sister, Halina, gave birth to a baby daughter, and I was named the godfather of the baby. It was a joyous time for all of us to be reunited. On the weekends, Henry would pick the three of us up from my parents' apartment and the whole extended family would get together at his house. A couple weeks after I arrived, Henry had a group of Polish people over at his house, along with our family, for one of these weekend visits. The discussion turned to politics as it most invariably did. The Polish expat community in Chicago was very small at the time. All of the recent immigrants were either refugees who had fled Europe during World War II, or soldiers who had fought in Anders' Army and who, like my brother, had not been to Poland in almost twenty years. They were all strong Polish patriots, and I was one of the first arrivals from a new wave of immigrants who had lived for fifteen years in a Communist Poland. At this time, there was no good way to get information from behind Stalin's Iron Curtain, so many people were naturally excited to talk to me. People in the West couldn't get information about the true state of things in letters because everything was censored. I had grown up under Communism, and so I was the closest thing to an expert on the subject that many people had ever spoken to.

To be perfectly honest, I was still a little shell-shocked by everything I saw in America—truly everything was more wonderful than even in my wildest imagination. At the same time, I was slightly confused and saddened when I saw all the people around me bashing Poland. They were of course attacking the Communist system, and Stalin's iron fist that had implemented it, but to me, who was still just an inexperienced youth, they were attacking my homeland. I saw myself as somehow different from these other Polish people, as though I came from a different place—and in a way, that was true. I came from a Communist Poland, while Henry's friends, mostly in their thirties and forties, came from a free and independent Poland. I didn't want them to think I came from some shabby place, and so my pride dictated that I had to lie about how great it was in Poland—at first. When I look back on it now, I was just making an emotional defense for my homeland, but in truth, it was mainly my immature ego making a knee-jerk reaction to defend the system I had always lived under. I wouldn't understand the full truth of the situation until much later.

Part of my defense of Communism at that time was certainly immaturity, but it also speaks to the thorough brainwashing I had received in Poland. The Communists were very clever in how they influenced young people. I arrived in America thinking that it was the moral obligation of the government to provide for all citizens, including health and education. I thought this was what a just and fair government should do, because this is what we were taught. My interpretation was that if everyone is healthy and educated, it will make for a strong nation. No one pointed out the irony that although this was the propaganda in Poland, people were hungry, and the nation was weak. We were also taught that in America, the elite few prospered at the expense of the poor, starving, exploited masses. It was pounded into our heads over and over again that in America there was a tiny group of rich elites that was squeezing and exploiting the poor.

I would often sit around talking with these extended family and friends—all immigrants, and yet all decidedly middle class and doing relatively well. They had houses, cars, and stable jobs. Somehow the Communist brainwashing was so strong I still didn't put two and two together, and I thought my family had just "gotten lucky." Yet in truth, they were not the exception, because in my experience most immigrants who arrived in America were able to find their way and be relatively successful. As long as you were willing to work, it wasn't hard in those days.

Truthfully, when I arrived in Chicago, I expected to see a lot more homeless people than I did. I fully expected there to be the "starving masses" on the streets—the millions who were oppressed by the capitalist "pigs," as we were taught back in Poland. For the first few months, I was still talking about how great it was in Poland (because I didn't know any better) at the same time that I was cautiously looking around in America and seeing everybody, even the poorest, far better off than anyone I had seen in Poland.

The longer I was in America though, the more I realized that these "huddled masses" never materialized, at least not in the way the Communists would have had us believe. I remember walking down Madison Street in the heart of the Chicago loop. This was known as "Skid Row" in the '60s, and was a sketchy neighborhood full of bums and drug dealers. Whenever I saw a homeless person begging for a dime, I would give them what spare change I had, and once in a while I stopped to talk to them. I was a young man, fresh out from behind the Iron Curtain and curious about the less privileged members of society I expected to find in America. In my occasional conversations with homeless people on Skid Row, I came to realize that most of these people were on the streets for reasons that had nothing to do with the government. Many of them had some sort of mental illness, and in my estimation close to 90 percent of them were alcoholics. It was sad to see these people fallen on hard times, but it was obvious to me that in most cases it was the result of either some sort of chemical imbalance or personal choices, not capitalist oppressors.

My experience showed me that anybody who was willing to work hard could make a living in America. Poland at the time was also suffering from a wave of rampant alcoholism, but it was because people were being oppressed by their government; their spirits were broken by the system of double-dealing, which robbed them of their human dignity. Entire Polish cities were full of men who turned to the bottle because facing the everyday reality of propaganda, corruption, and widespread scarcity was too great a hardship. Only alcohol was in cheap and abundant supply. There was a saying that was popular at the time Communism arose:

On your feet,
Or lying around,
You'll still get paid two thousand pounds.

It was representative of the general malaise and apathy that Communism instilled in people. Meanwhile in America there were programs to try to get people off the street, to give them a decent job, and to help them get back on their feet. I saw people on public assistance who were able to pick themselves up, get a job and public housing, and improve their lot. Others would make a small improvement, but then go back to drugs or alcohol and life on the streets. It was clear to me that for these people, it was a personal choice. On top of it all, there was no brainwashing in America, and for the first time in my life I was making my own judgments about the things I saw happening around me—the beauty of this experience is particularly sweet to those who have not always had it. I was allowed to roam the streets, talk to people, ask questions, and make my own decisions. The freedom felt good, and within a year of arriving I had thrown out any old ideas in my mind that Communism and socialism were good for society or humanity.

Today when I think back on it, I don't regret that I lived under the Communist regime, because I think it helped make me into a different person than I would have been otherwise. I realize I have a completely different way of relating to people thanks to what I experienced. If a person has no way to compare his life to those less fortunate, it is almost impossible to truly gain perspective on your position in the world. I was able to live in one world, and then suddenly live in one completely different. My horizons completely expanded thanks to the experience of immigration. My first few years in America were a major period of eye opening, and the progress I made both intellectually and emotionally I would not have been able to make anywhere else. It's only in hindsight that it's easy for me to see that a man who lives with a lack of freedom from birth really has no idea what he is missing. Much has to be experienced personally in order for it to be understood. America afforded me the opportunity to see the world, and make my own judgments about people, governments, and what systems worked for the good of mankind. Thankfully, I was purged of my youthful brainwashing, but those lessons would remain with me for the rest of my life. They would come in handy particularly when I later encountered unions and organized labor in Chicago.

By the end of 1960, Henry was able to get me a job at a clothing company because he was an experienced tailor and part of the local clothing workers' union. It was a huge, eight-story factory downtown called Hart Schaffner & Marx, which is still producing high-quality menswear to this day. Henry got me an apprenticeship in the cloth-cutting department. The job was relatively simple and paid well for my standards—I took home $46 that first week, which is about $362 in 2013 dollars and was more money than I had ever earned in my life. When you take into consideration that a pack of cigarettes was eighteen cents, a gallon of gas cost twenty cents, and a fancy highball cocktail might cost forty cents (my favorite was Canadian Club and ginger ale), forty-six dollars was a lot of money. I was living with my parents, but almost immediately I had enough money to buy myself a nice thirty-dollar suit, which I wore to work every day with a white shirt and tie. I felt incredibly grateful to be working for such a prosperous company. I also enjoyed working with representatives of every race and color. One time I counted and came up with thirty different nationalities just in my department. I was happy and thriving, although when I started that job, I didn't know that it would be both my first and my last place of employment in America. Before long I saw things which opened my eyes even further, and led me to think that I needed to strike out on my own.

What I was doing now in America—working in a clean, organized factory and getting paid a good wage—was so different from the last job I had held in Poland, before I left for America. Although I had applied for both the fine arts school and the flight school, my applications were denied because I was the son of a "kułak" (that derogatory term the Communists used for private farmers). The only school I was accepted to was a trade school for plumbing. I hated this school—studying sanitary installations, heating, plumbing, and gas was such drudgery for me, but it was all I was allowed to do. For the last two months of the school year, when I was eighteen, we were sent on an assignment to help install plumbing in big construction projects. In truth, the bosses who were running these state-funded housing projects just handed the blueprints to us kids and said "Go install the gas lines," without any further advice or instruction. We were a group of teenagers with no real-world experience, and we were being ordered to install the gas lines for huge apartment complexes. It was complicated work and extremely dangerous. The worst part about this whole situation was that the foundations had been poured and walls had already been built, and they had not left any opening for the gas lines to go in. We had to go in after the structure was already built, and chisel out the channels in the concrete where the gas pipes were to lie. This kind of idiocy would be unthinkable in America, but there I was, looking at a blueprint, taking a hammer and chisel to open up channels in the freshly poured floors and walls to run the pipes. I would have bloody knuckles at the end of each day because there was no such thing as work gloves. Concrete would of course be poured back over it all again when we were done. The stupidity and wastefulness of this method of operation is incomprehensible to people who have not experienced Communism. It would have taken such a minor effort and just a bit of forethought to mark out where the gas lines should go ahead of time, and leave the spaces in the foundation already prepped to receive the gas lines, but in a Communist system, nobody was responsible, and nobody cared. It was such primitive construction compared to anything in America, and yet the Communists thought it was a good idea to make every step of the process as labor intensive as possible, for the "good of the worker." Just a few proactive marks before the foundations were poured could have saved me a month of work, but that was just standard in Communist Poland. I came from a system where this was all I had known—I knew it was stupidity and madness, but I didn't know why it was that way. Only when I saw how efficiently things ran in America, and how much better off everybody was there, did I start to realize that the socialist policies were a joke.

It was clear to me that I was different from my peers, and I think it's because the experience of immigration opens your window to the world tremendously. My perspective on the world completely changed after I saw everything from both sides, and I carried around that perspective and emotional maturity with me from then on. The injustices of the Communist system didn't fully reveal themselves to me until long after I had gone. Because companies in America were private rather than state-run, and someone was always in charge and responsible for the bottom line, I saw that there was none of this kind of mindlessness that I had known before, and my eyes opened. I felt myself quickly developing a different mindset from my American counterparts, who took their efficient and capable system for granted. This would become most apparent to me when the company I worked for asked me to join a union.

At the same time, I also was growing light years apart from my friends in Poland. Within a year I was at a loss for what to write them; just after one year of being in America I felt like I had traveled ten years into the future, and I didn't know what I could talk to my old friends in Poland about. I realized that they would likely not understand all the things going on in my life. I had a desire to share my excitement with everyone, to write about high skyscrapers, colorful cars, and the life of plenty in America. Sadly, our link of exchanging letters was slowly disintegrating the longer I stayed in America.

After just one year, I was able to buy my own automobile. It was a 1959 Ford Galaxy, and buying that car was, simply put, one of the best moments of my life. For a young man who not so long ago had lived day to day in an economy so depressed that buying a pair of shoes was a big event, to be able to buy a car was a joy beyond description. As I drove it around the streets of Chicago, with the windows down, I felt as if America was everything I had expected and more. I continued to live in my parents' modest apartment, although by now I was splitting the rent with them. Of course I didn't succeed at everything I tried. Shortly after my arrival, I attempted to enlist in the US Air Force. I passed the physical tests with flying colors, but my English scores, especially on the written tests, were not good enough. Soon though, I would enroll in evening classes at the world-renowned Art Institute of Chicago, and my life would take off down another exciting path.

Amidst all my personal happiness, I couldn't help but think of all those friends I had left behind in Poland. At this time, the propaganda behind the Iron Curtain worked overtime to discredit the capitalist system. Every day, people in Poland stood in line for a loaf of bread, and very often by the time they reached the counter everything was sold out. Meanwhile, I had found a modest job, lived comfortably, and didn't just buy bread—I bought a Ford! My parents shared my excitement and joy at the quality-of-life changes. They continued to work at St. Mary of Nazareth Hospital in Chicago for very modest salaries, by American standards, but they were still able to live well, help my sister in Poland, and send money to our relatives.

After two years of being an apprentice to a cloth-cutter in the clothing factory, I was told it was time for me to join the union. I quickly realized the union meetings were not to my taste. They were agitating for things like increased pay and a more generous allowance for the cloth-cutters, but I didn't really understand why. Cloth-cutting played an important role in the factory because there were hundreds of yards of expensive fabrics that needed to be cut for men's suits, and one wrong snip could ruin an entire run. I didn't mind the work, and didn't find it too hard. You had a certain allowance of fabric from which you had to cut a suit, and the faster you did it, the more you got paid. Sure there were people who were faster and better than me, and I was glad for them that they got paid more—they worked harder! I thought I was compensated fairly for the work I did, and if I took a nap on the job, that was my business and I didn't make money during those hours. I felt in charge of my own destiny—a feeling I luxuriated in, because I had certainly never experienced that in Communist Poland.

Worst of all, the unions had a representative that worked in most factories; theoretically, he was to be on hand to mediate any disputes between workers and management that might come up. He was given a desk to sit at on our floor, and we could all see the short, fat man who mainly took naps during the day while ostensibly looking out for the rights of his fellow union members. Stewards like this one were technically supposed to be workers as well, but in truth they were paid as much as the top-earning cloth-cutter, regardless of how much work he produced. The idea of a "special representative" who produced nothing, got paid more, and mooched off the backs of his hardworking peers was exactly the situation that existed in Communist Poland. I saw absolutely no difference.

By this time I had been in the USA for almost two years, and the union meetings brought me a strong feeling of déjà vu; they were like Communist Party meetings back in Poland. It seems that in any society there will be political agitators who want to bash the old system and bring about change. Sometimes it is for good reason, and sometimes it's just political posturing. I thought my job at Hart Schaffner & Marx was relatively easy, the factory was neat and tidy, and I had more money than I ever dreamed of. Best of all, there was no foreman standing over me all day long, and I enjoyed my freedom. I attended the meetings, where the leaders bashed the company and preached about how the workers were being exploited. I had heard this language before, and I knew I wasn't being exploited, so I quickly lost my stomach for any sort of union involvement. I started arguing with some of the union guys, that I didn't agree with them, but it didn't go over well. I said that I wouldn't strike when they called for a strike, because to me it was degrading to think that I would refuse to work in such a decent job.

Around that time, Henry became the president of the local chapter—a move which I never completely understood. It was clear to me we had developed completely different mentalities, despite being family, and I chalked it up to the fact that he had never lived under Communism. I saw his forays into this misguided organization as an aberration from his normal, levelheaded nature, but there was nothing I could do. The one positive thing to come out of this situation was that I was able to speak my mind a bit more because my brother had clout in the organization. I was able to get away with being his punk younger brother, and I caused some trouble by saying things that most people wouldn't be allowed to say. They quickly started calling me the "young rebel," but because I was Henry's brother, I was given a pass.

It's hard to remember sometimes that in 1962, people still didn't know the full truth about what was happening behind the Iron Curtain and how horrible life there was. There were large numbers of people in the West who still believed that the great socialist experiment in Russia was going well. For the next sixteen years, I worked my way up in the clothing company, earning a good living and observing the union's activities with a mix of misgiving and revulsion. I was glad for the freedom this job afforded me; I had money and time—all the resources a young man needs to live the life of his dreams. Everything was falling into place to set me up for the bigger things that lay ahead.

CHAPTER 9

Becoming an Artist

ART AND AVIATION HAD ALWAYS BEEN THE TWO great passions of my life. By 1961, after the US Air Force denied me entrance, I found myself instead enrolled at one of the most prestigious art schools in the country—The Art Institute of Chicago. I had never before studied art formally, but for as long as I could remember, I had kept a sketchbook of drawings that I made with pencil and charcoal. Even when I was an apprentice working on the plumbing in those horrible Communist housing projects, I was always painting graffiti pictures on the walls when no one was looking. Many who saw my work thought I had talent, but because of the way the Communist system excelled at squashing individual talent, I was never able to cultivate it. The first time I was able to have access to paints and canvas was when I was living with my parents in Chicago and I could afford to buy some at the local art supply shop. I was very excited at the idea of being able to afford real art supplies, such as oil paints, brushes, and canvas, and I would spend many free afternoons painting landscapes and cityscapes of America in my parents' humble living room.

At this same time, there was a man named Karol Kowalski (he signed his paintings "Charlee") who was a fellow Polish-American and worked with my father at the hospital. His mother had been French, and he had studied art at Europe's finest art universities in Poland and Switzerland before the war. He was in America's *Who's Who* book of artists, and had exhibits of his work displayed at many prestigious institutions—including the Smithsonian Galleries in Washington—in the 1950s. He had been a professor of fine arts before the war, and was now working as a custodian alongside my father at the hospital.

My father mentioned to him that he had a son who was pretending to be an artist, madly painting in the living room despite having no training. Kowalski came over one day to look at my work. We immediately hit it off, and he decided to take me under his wing. He was an eccentric personality, but a very high-quality artist. He would rarely sell a painting, no matter what the offer, but he would give you one of his priceless treasures as a gift if he thought you deserved it. For the next three years I would go over to his house at least twice a week after work to study painting under his careful tutelage. Receiving years of private art tutoring from a master painter was a rare opportunity that very few artists receive. I was in love with painting—it opened my eyes to the world of art and all its amazing possibilities. I knew then that art and creating beautiful things would always have a role in my life.

My life was blossoming, and I made new friends and grew more acclimated to my new home. I joined several local Polish immigrant organizations—for instance, one that brought together Poles from the Pomeranian region of Poland, and it was here that I would forge one of the most important friendships of my life. Frank Bergman was more than ten years my senior, and worked as an industrial art designer. His friendship was formative in my life because he was a source of motivation and confidence for me. Not only did he help me get over the doubts that plagued me about my English skills, but he was a prime living example of the success and good life you could have by working hard in America. He encouraged me to enroll in evening courses at the Art Institute, and he even went with me to help me fill out the application forms, convinced my artistic talent would speak for itself. He was right, and I will never forget that it was my friend Frank who encouraged me to formally study art after he saw the works I had done under Kowalski's tutelage. This encouragement fundamentally changed the course that the rest of my life would take. It was such a wondrous idea for me; that I could work and pay for college at the same time was a dream come true, not to mention a completely unheard of idea back in Poland. I soon began taking classes in all forms and styles of art, including pastels, charcoal, and sculpting, as well as some art history courses. Mainly, however, I focused on painting. I would often attend exhibits and competitions with my work, and on several occasions I won national art awards for the quality of my pieces. I would end up going to school there in the evenings for five years, receiving a thorough art education in the process.

At that time there were many Polish organizations in Chicago. After the Second World War, with the demobilization of the Polish Second Corps army in Italy, many of the veterans decided not to return to Communist Poland. They dispersed around the world, but a majority settled in the United States. My work at the Chicago Art Institute had served me well, and a group of Polish officers approached me with a proposition to recreate some very large versions of their military insignias. They would be displayed at the ballroom of the Chicago Sherman House hotel for an annual formal ball given in honor of Polish Second World War aviators. This first big art commission had me every bit as excited as I had been by that first car. This was the first job in which I was able to use my creativity and artistic skills. I was quite intimidated at the start, because I was a twenty-one-year-old negotiating and sitting at a table with war veterans who were all senior majors and colonels in the military. I wanted so deeply to make them proud, to please them with my skills. I worked in the basement of my sister's house for many months to carve, shape, and weld those insignias out of various materials. I worked day and night on the project, restarting certain portions from scratch again and again until they were right. When it was finished, I was indeed proud. It was a big project, but I was more enthralled in that one endeavor than in anything I had ever done in my life. The experience had given me tremendous confidence and joy, not to mention my first earnings as an artist. Clearly my life's calling had found me.

Once I started at the Chicago Art Institute, I would leave the house at seven in the morning and not return home until eleven at night. Every free evening was spent studying, but this was the USA—the country of endless horizons and possibilities, and I knew it would all be worth it in the end. I was tired during those years, but I was also invigorated. By working and studying, I knew a bright future was ahead of me. I knew this was the country where I wanted to start my family and live for the rest of my life.

After two years of working and studying at such a pace, my thoughts turned to another practical matter vital to any young, single man. In the course of my work, I befriended a gentleman who had just arrived from Poland, and his wife was a highly educated and energetic woman who made a great impression on me. Her name was Ada, and as soon as she met me, she said, "I have a girl for you!" I was skeptical, but in truth, American girls didn't understand me the way I knew a Polish girl would. Ada told me this girl's name was Sława, that she was seventeen and a student in Wrocław, a town in western Poland. Given Ada's enthusiastic encouragement, and despite being on the other side of the world, I thought, what the heck, and I sent off a postcard to this anonymous girl with greetings from Chicago, signed just "George." You have to remember that in those days receiving anything from the West was a big deal, and I knew that the postcard would make an impression. I knew her mind would be racing when she received this card from a mysterious stranger, and I chuckled at the thought—and then forgot about her.

It wasn't until I had another quiet evening about a month later that I followed up with a proper letter introducing myself, including a return address and—most importantly—a picture of me with the new 1961 white Ford Thunderbird I'd just bought when I traded in my Galaxy. To this day we still have that letter, dated November 11, 1962.

Within almost no time I heard back from her and saw her sweet, smiling face and blonde hair in the small black-and-white portrait she enclosed. I was entranced from the moment I laid eyes on her—she looked like the most glamorous of movie stars, and I loved the way she wrote to me. We started off formally, addressing each other—as people did in those days, even when they were courting—as Miss Partum and Mr. Swiderski, but it quickly turned into elaborate terms of endearment. At one point the correspondence became so frequent that I was receiving two letters a week from her, and sending just as many. I would drive home from work during my lunch break just to check the mail!

I knew there was something special about this girl I had never met. It's no overstatement to say we were falling in love. Our relationship was maturing as the weeks and months passed, like good wine. You read about great love in literature, and how platonic love can be such a powerful experience—intimate and affectionate even though there was no physical dimension to it. It's hard to explain unless one has experienced it himself. My feelings became so powerful that this love affair with Sława began to consume all my thoughts. She was smart and witty, with a great sense of humor—no woman had ever kept me so enthralled just with reading! And of course she was strikingly beautiful as well. It's amazing how even when you don't physically know a person, you can build her up in your mind—and as any young man knows, a mind can work wonders, and an imagination can run away with itself. My imagination was completely consumed with this university student in Wrocław. I don't know how she did it, but to me those letters were so erotic—even though I'm sure they were completely tame by today's standards.

I'm not sure how she took it, but for me, this correspondence became increasingly personal and emotional. I was living my life, and doing the things I had always done (work, school, etc.), and yet these letters became the most important thing to me. Everything that was happening outside of my relationship with Sława seemed superficial and unimportant. Those letters had a magnetic power! It's not as though there weren't plenty of girls in Chicago—there were. But I had a hard time thinking about them. In fact, I would often be out with different girls, but all the while I was with them I would be thinking of Sława, fantasizing of her being close to me, smelling her blonde hair, and looking into her beautiful, large blue eyes. I looked often at the photographs she sent me, and I admired her graceful figure. Her letters were so eloquently written and at the same time very feminine. Despite her young age she was very intelligent and mature. These other girls had a hard time competing with this dream of a Polish girl in my mind's eye. Sława and I talked about intellectual life and school, and she would send me books from Poland that I couldn't get in America. It was exciting for me to share with someone my age what my thoughts, feelings, and emotions were about living in this incredible country, and how happy I was to have the opportunity to help my friends and relatives I left behind in Poland. Half a year after our correspondence began, in the summer of 1963, I had wanted to go to Poland, but because my father fell ill and required surgery, I wasn't able to leave. I was incredibly anxious to meet her, and I was ready to travel around the world to do so. Nonetheless, it wasn't yet to be.

I wished I was with Sława, but instead I spent that summer with my two new friends Frank Bergman and Stanley Muszynski. They would both become my mentors and role models in Chicago, taking me under their wing and introducing me to the social scene in America when I was still only nineteen. I knew early on that they were good guys, and I felt lucky that I had forged such solid friendships with people I could rely on. Shortly after my arrival in the States, I went out for the weekend to Wisconsin with a group of people to play volleyball. During the game I stepped on a piece of glass from a broken bottle and cut my foot very badly. Because it was the weekend, no medical help was readily available. It was only my new friend Stanley who showed concern for me and my situation—I had no money or health insurance, and so he took me in his car to drive around the rural back roads of Wisconsin until we found a nurse's station that could close up the wound, which stretched all the way across my foot from one side to the other. I'll never forget that it was Stanley who visited me while I was homebound and recovering for the next three weeks at the height of the summer. I was new to this version of American generosity, but I knew then that Stanley and I would be close friends. We were inseparable until his untimely death twelve years later, and I still miss him.

By the summer of 1963, I was very well adapted to the ways of life in America. I was amazed that I already felt so at home here, and I loved spending the weekends with my friends in some of our favorite spots, including Wisconsin, Michigan, the Indiana dunes, Lenard's Casino, and of course the beautiful beaches of Lake Michigan. When we stayed in the city, we frequently went out to parties and went dancing, meeting new people and many Polish-Americans along the way. It was by far the best life I could have ever imagined for myself as a young boy in Poland.

In the meantime, I was busy with work, classes at the Art Institute, Polish Boy Scouts meetings, and the Chopin Choir. I participated a lot in charity organizations that supported Polish causes, as they were very active in Chicago at the time. I particularly enjoyed and became very active in the choir, which consisted mostly of much older Polish-American gentlemen. They treated the younger guys like me, who just arrived from Communist Poland, with a special compassion and tolerance. I realize now that these men knew, better than non-Poles, that we came from a place where a dictatorial regime ruled everyone with intimidation tactics. I felt a special compassion from them because they knew we had overcome the attempts to brainwash us through endless barrages of Communist propaganda. By then I had fully embraced my identity as an American, and I was grateful for the camaraderie.

One of my favorite things about those early years in America was developing a close relationship with my sister Halina. Although she was sixteen years older, she was able to level with me. She knew how to read her twenty-one-year-old brother and quickly became my confidante. She was talented in arts and crafts and would prove herself by creating different beautiful objects she would present as gifts to her friends and family. Unfortunately, tragedy struck suddenly in her home. Her husband, Zbyszek, fell ill with cancer, and after suffering for many months, he passed away. Halina was left as a single mother to three small children, and I tried to substitute for their father as much as I could. I never felt like I could do enough. Being with Halina during this trying time for her family, I began to think more and more about that long-delayed trip to Poland. Another year had passed by, and by the end of June 1964, I began to make travel plans. I was allowed two weeks of vacation, and I took an additional three months leave of absence from work.

I was incredibly eager to meet Sława, and felt a wave of relief and excitement when I finally booked passage on the Polish MS *Batory*, which would leave out of Montreal, Canada. I of course wanted to bring my gorgeous white Thunderbird with red leather interior with me! My friend Paul Kowaluk had an uncle who lived in Montreal, and so he decided to come with me and visit his uncle and later return to Chicago by bus. I was glad for the company on the long drive. The day before we left, I loaded my car with my personal belongings and dozens of presents for my family, my friends, and—of course—Sława. At the last moment, I decided to take my water skis with me, waterskiing being a sport I greatly enjoyed at the time. I wasn't certain if I would have the opportunity to water ski in Poland, but I decided to take a chance. Either way, it was going to be a grand adventure.

The morning I said goodbye to my parents was a happy one, but at the same time, they were full of worries that I was going back to Communist Poland—a place we had managed to escape only with great difficulties. They were now sending their youngest son there for over three months, and to be honest there were all sorts of concerns that the Communists wouldn't let me come back. Technically I was still only a US resident, not yet a full citizen, so I didn't have the comfort of an American passport. Looking back on it now, it was a great risk I took, but in my mind it was for love and it was all worth it. Besides, I missed my sister Henrietta and brother Casey, and it seemed like a good time to visit. As my parents walked me to the car, I realized my mother was crying as we hugged, and for the first time in my life I witnessed tears rolling down my dad's cheeks. Today I understand his emotions; his youngest son was going back to a land where he lived for almost sixty years, a land he himself would probably never see again. There were so many emotions happening because those were the worst years of the Cold War, and my dad knew his son would have to navigate the tensions of those politically fraught times. There was also the additional possibility that his youngest son might come back as a married man. Dad's tears were those of joy and concern. As I was leaving, I didn't think I would come back married, but perhaps they knew something I didn't, because they saw how passionately I wrote letters to the girl I loved. Five decades later, I realize they knew me better than I knew myself, and yet saying goodbye to them still feels like yesterday. I can still see in my mind that moment when Paul and I took off for Detroit and from there to Montreal.

In one day we covered over one thousand miles. Our progress would perhaps not be possible today. But at that time the speed limit was not strictly observed. On some stretches of road that were as straight as the eye could see we were pushing a hundred miles an hour. Cruising along at this high speed, all of a sudden we saw a car approaching from the other direction, coming just as fast as we were. It all happened in the blink of an eye, but with only a couple of seconds before our paths crossed, I realized the car was coming towards us in our lane. For a split second the thought flashed through my mind to jump over into the left lane. Fortunately, I stayed in my own lane and the other driver jumped back into his lane at the last second and passed us by on the left side like a bullet. It took a few minutes before Paul managed to squeeze any word out of his mouth, and we were both in shock at how close we had come to a head-on collision. When we finally did emerge from our mutual shock, we decided to drive much slower for the remainder of the trip. We arrived at night to Paul's uncle's place in Montreal.

We hung out together there for almost a week before my ship was ready to leave. One evening we wandered around downtown Montreal, and I noticed from the gangway between two buildings a lot of young people coming out of what looked like a hidden nightclub. The staircase leaned against the side of the wall, and people were walking down from a room on the second story. The folks were young and looked like they were having a good time, so we decided to check it out. When we got upstairs, we were greeted by a few burlesque girls and some bartenders in a very narrow, long room with a row of tables. We sat at the first table and ordered a couple of drinks. A few girls brought them over and at the same time started to charm us and kept asking if we would like to have "some fun." We declined the offer, and the girls went on to the next table, but we noticed they all kept staring at us.

As soon as Paul finished his drink he started to complain that his head was spinning, and at the same time my vision was getting blurry. I said, "Let's get outta this 'bleepin' place," and we managed to exit onto the busy street to catch some fresh air before whatever they had laced our drinks with kicked in. We quickly headed back to his uncle's place and realized how close we came to being robbed, or worse. In my wallet I had well over $3,000. In those days, this was a substantial amount of money. In Communist Poland, a good craftsman would earn only about twenty dollars a month. I had been close to losing the entire fortune that I'd saved for my journey to Poland.

Finally the day arrived to drive to the harbor and load my Thunderbird aboard. In those days you did not have to go through customs—all you needed was a passport (I had my Polish one with me) and a ticket and you were ready to cruise. Quickly enough, I made friends with the Polish crew on the ship. I had access to my car, and whenever I needed to get some personal items I was free to do so. The officer who was in charge of the gym with the swimming pool even allowed me to use the facilities whenever I wanted. I made friends with the other passengers, too. There was a hockey team from Canada traveling to Sweden for some games and a bunch of girls from Denmark and Holland returning home from their postcollege graduation trip to the US. Also, there was a young doctor going to Leningrad and a guy from Texas in his midthirties who worked for Interpol who was going to Poland to visit his friend. I started talking specifically to a girl from Canada of Polish descent. It turned out that her parents financed her trip to Poland as a college graduation present. She was going to Warsaw to meet her relatives. We developed a great group of friends on that trip and stayed up late most nights partying and having a great time. We were a young international group of people having fun and enjoying our voyage—each of us heading towards an important destination. I was glad for the company because it made the time pass quickly, and before I knew it, the day would arrive when I would once again touch the shore of my homeland.

CHAPTER 10

A Visit Behind the
Iron Curtain

O N THE NINTH DAY OF OUR VOYAGE, THE MS *BATORY*
pulled into the port in Gdynia, Poland—the very town
where I knew Sława was staying with her aunt at that exact moment. We had never before been closer—she was somewhere in
this town, and she consumed my thoughts as we docked, but I
wouldn't be able to see her until the next day. Luckily for me,
the voyage had passed quickly, but as the last twenty-four hours
before our meeting stretched before me, the hours dragged on
in excruciating slowness. All the excitement and anxious nerves
were upon me at once as I said goodbye to the friends I had made
on the ship, and every thought I had was about meeting the woman of my dreams.

I also felt great anticipation about returning to the place I
had spent most of my life. Admittedly it was quite strange for a
young man to return to the land behind the Iron Curtain just four
years after he left—and at the height of the Cold War. The Cuban
missile crisis and Bay of Pigs had both happened in the four short

years since I had been gone, and US-Soviet tensions were at an all-time high. President Kennedy had just been assassinated the year before, and the world was still reeling from that shock. I had changed since the last time I had been in this place. I was more mature, was able to speak another language, and had gained familiarity with many of the different cultures that made up the "melting pot" of America.

There were crowds of people waiting near the dock for their relatives arriving from the US and Canada. Many of my fellow passengers had left Poland before the war or during it, and for them it was the first time since that hasty departure that they would see their families and friends. I was certainly one of the only ones who had grown up here, and was now back for a visit. My brother Casey, his family, and some of my cousins were waiting for me on the dock, and I was overjoyed to see them. After I left Poland, the only way to communicate with my family was by writing letters. Most people in Poland were not lucky enough to have phones—that was a privilege reserved for top Communist Party members. My brother Casey worked in the Gdańsk shipyard, as did many of my cousins, and they certainly were in no position to have phones. I had not heard the voice of my brother for four years, and our reunion was one of the highlights of that trip. I loved seeing his growing family and visiting with them.

That night I could barely sleep in the crowded apartment. I could hardly keep still I was so excited. I told Casey that by noon the next day I had to be in the nearby town of Sopot, in front of the Grand Hotel to meet a girl. He was a little curious that I was meeting someone I had corresponded with for almost two years and clearly had strong feelings for, even though we had never met. The next morning my brother said he would come with me to show me some shortcuts to ensure I wouldn't be late. That was the first day I traveled on the Polish streets with my own car, and heads were turning everywhere I went. My brother couldn't stop admiring this beautiful vehicle and all the high-end trimmings like air conditioning and power windows. It was a huge vehicle, weighing in at almost five thousand pounds, and I felt a thrill knowing I was very likely the only person in Poland driving a Ford Thunderbird.

I parked right in front of the hotel to make sure everyone noticed me, and Casey took the streetcar back home. I knew I was about to meet my destiny, and could hardly think of anything else. The Grand Hotel was an old, beautiful structure surrounded by ancient trees and gorgeously landscaped grounds. Before the war, the hotel had been the meeting ground for rich and famous personalities of Europe who wanted to vacation on the shore of the Baltic Sea. Now it was midday, and there were hardly any people around. I walked along a U-shaped walkway towards the hotel. In the distance, I saw the slender figure of a girl walking towards me. I began to feel a million butterflies in my stomach as I saw for the first time, in real life, the blonde girl from the black-and-white photographs. We approached each other from years and miles away, and the thought crossed my mind that my imagination had gotten carried away with me all these months and that this whole meeting might be a total disaster. As she walked closer, I could make out her well-defined features, which emphasized her striking beauty and gave her an aristocratic look. She had a long neck and graceful figure, an alabaster complexion, and large blue eyes that for a moment locked with mine as we were within a few steps of each other. She was dressed in modest clothes, and I was overwhelmed with her beauty as we both broke into large smiles and embraced in a lingering hug and a gentle kiss.

"Happy birthday, Sława," were the first words I said to her, and it was in fact August 5, 1964, her twenty-first birthday. "Have you been waiting here long?"

"Not at all," she answered. "I just arrived."

We both wondered what to say next, and for a tense few minutes as we walked to my car the atmosphere between us was full of nerves. She was even more gorgeous than I could have imagined, but when imagination meets reality, especially in the mind of a young man, things can be a little uncertain. I was excited to show her my car, but little did I know she had already seen it! She laughed and launched into the story of how she had in fact spied on me the day before.

Sława's university in Wrocław was about a six-hour drive from the port in Gdynia, but the truth is that no one in those days drove, because no one had cars. The main means of transport was by old, rickety, and dangerously overcrowded trains that would make the trip in about eight hours. The trains were the equivalent of what you might see today in developing countries—dirty toilets, no amenities, and people climbing through the windows to try to get aboard. Sława made the long journey to Gdynia, where one of her mother's friends had an apartment she could stay at in anticipation of my arrival. It turned out that the day my ship pulled in, she had tucked herself among the crowds waiting on shore as the ship docked, with the intention of giving this American boy a once-over from a distance. She was overcome with curiosity and anticipation, and couldn't bear to stay away from the place where she knew I would be. She had seen the crane lift my enormous white car off the ship and place it onto the dock, and had stared along with everyone else as I drove the Thunderbird away. She had observed from a safe distance, and saw that in fact I was what I said I was—a young man, dressed in a sports coat and tight pants (as was the fashion at that time) as I greeted my brother and his family. The truth is, it wasn't that unusual for Sława to come and watch the ship from America pull in; the whole event was a bit of a local attraction, and people would come from all over just to get a glimpse of anything arriving from America—even just a ship full of passengers. As was the case with my Thunderbird, you never quite knew what you were going to see, and that ship from America made only three trips a year to Gdynia, so watching it arrive was a big deal for the locals. Just the cost of the ticket alone was something an average Pole couldn't fathom—I had paid $475 for my ticket, which included my car, and was several times as much as a Polish family made in a year.

With that we quickly settled into a comfortable conversation. We had written so many letters to each other about almost every subject under the sun that we felt so close already. We had spent nearly two years building this incredible platonic love, and there was plenty to discuss now that we were finally together! First things first, we went to the apartment where she was staying so we could spend a few minutes alone in each other's presence for the first time. We already had an inkling that we might not make it back that night, so she packed some sweaters and a few things she would need, and we got back in my car to go cruising. It all started happening so fast—acting like we were a couple—and everything fell into place so naturally that in almost no time we felt like we had been doing this for years.

We finally headed out for an expedition in my car. First we wanted to stop and buy some food to enjoy a picnic. I had beach towels in my car and we just needed some supplies. As we drove around town with the windows down on a beautiful summer day, I almost felt like I was in America—it was one of the best moments I had ever experienced in Poland. The stores in Communist Poland were poorly stocked, and all we could find was some bread rolls, cheese, strawberry nectar, and cookies. We had no place in particular to go, so I chose the road towards Bydgoszcz, where I had been attending school and which was the last place I lived before I moved to America. It was about a two-hour drive on a largely deserted and barely paved two-lane road. Driving through the beautiful forests of northern Poland, we pulled over into a clearing in the woods to enjoy our picnic on the side of the road. She was supposed to go back to her mother's friend's apartment and I was supposed to go to my brother's, but it was clear within a few hours that we were headed in the opposite direction, and wouldn't be back that night. We didn't tell anybody where we were going, and I don't think we knew ourselves. We were just cruising in the grand American tradition, one of my favorite pastimes back home and something I was happy I could share with Sława.

It was almost midnight by the time we got to Bydgoszcz, and I came up with the grand idea to knock on my cousin Klara's door. Everybody was asleep, so we threw pebbles at her window to get her attention. Klara and her husband were young and levelheaded. We knew that they were more liberal than my siblings, that we could count on more privacy at their house, and, most importantly, that they only had one spare bed, which Sława and I would have to share, which was of course the whole point, in my mind at least. Klara and her husband, Chester, didn't mind being woken up in the middle of the night, and they could hardly believe their eyes when they saw me. I had lived with them for two years before I left Poland, and seeing them now was a joyful reunion with two of my favorite family members. There was a lot of commotion as they ran down the stairs to greet us, and plenty of hugging and kissing. I introduced Sława as my girlfriend and they immediately brought out snacks and vodka flavored with sour cherry syrup to celebrate our reunion. We stayed up until nearly morning talking, and I was answering all of their questions about life in America. During the war, my cousin Chester had been in the same Polish army unit as Henry, and had fought bravely in the Italian campaign. When the war was over, unlike Henry, Chester had decided to return from England back to Poland. He later very much regretted that decision, not knowing that he was entering what he now quietly called the "trap of the Communist paradise." They were incredibly curious and intrigued to hear that all the propaganda the Communists spread about America wasn't true. They listened to my stories as if I were telling a fairy tale about a magical, made-up place. Finally it came time for Sława and me to lie down on the futon that Klara had prepared for us in the living room. That first night that Sława slept beside me was one of the best nights of my life. We had been together for less than twenty-four hours and already I felt I had met the woman I was going to marry, and I had an inkling she felt the same way.

To be perfectly honest, it didn't even occur to me that the rest of my family might be worried about my whereabouts. My older brother and sister surely thought something had happened to me, as I was a young kid with a flashy car and a lot of money. In reality, the only danger I faced was brought on by the radiator in my overheating Thunderbird. I couldn't believe that my first day driving Sława around in Poland, my car started to act up. It serves me right I suppose, because I had traveled the thousand miles from Chicago to Montreal without once checking the cooling fluid, and by now I was dangerously low. I'd already had to stop the day before to find some water to add to the radiator, and we were lucky to make it to my cousin's house without any major breakdowns. The only real problem was that a bearing from the air-conditioner compressor had seized, and I had to spend my first day in Bydgoszcz looking for someone who could repair a vehicle they had never seen before. I drove through town looking for a repair shop, and a man approached me while I was stopped at a light. He had noticed my highly unusual Illinois license plates, and it turned out he was also just visiting from Chicago—so he recognized I must be a tourist just like him. As we talked, he admired my car and I explained my problem. He mentioned that the girlfriend he was visiting was actually the daughter of the fire department chief in town. The mechanics who managed their large fleet of cars and trucks were surely the best equipped in town to fix my unique problem, and he offered to put Sława and me up in their apartment while we waited for the repairs. They presumed she was my wife also visiting from America, and in order not to make things too complicated, we didn't offer any explanations. I marveled at my good fortune, that I managed to find probably the only other American in the entire city. Thanks to this fellow Chicagoan's kindness, my car was ready to drive the next day.

After this small hiccup, we resumed our visit with my cousins in Bydgoszcz, catching up on everything that had happened in the intervening years. Chester was one of my closest relatives, and it was obvious he found me much changed. I had matured significantly, and my horizons had broadened far beyond the place I had been in when I left Poland in 1960. We often turned our discussion to his time in the war, and how much he regretted leaving England in 1946. He dreaded the prospect of living in Poland for the rest of his life, being persecuted by the Communists. Like many returning veterans, he had been interrogated and abused by Communist officials upon his return to his homeland. He was viewed suspiciously, as a suspected enemy of the state, solely because he fought for Poland's independence during the war. A few years after he returned, the Communist Party dangled a carrot in front of him and offered him a better position as a general manager of the printing company where he worked, which would include a much higher wage, but it came under the condition that he join the Communist Party. It was against Chester's values and principles to join this organization he despised, so he turned down the job and spent the rest of his life working in a factory at a meager wage. I always knew he had made this decision, and to me he was a beacon of upright character, and I admired him tremendously. It was a great joy to visit with him during these few days in Bydgoszcz. I couldn't imagine it then, but this summer would be the last time I would see him. It was with a sad heart that just a couple years after that visit I received one last letter from him, telling me that he was ill and giving me an update on his bleak life. By the time I received his letter, he had passed away. My cousin Klara later told me that this was the last letter he wrote in bed the day before he died. It was such a great shame that the Communist system held down a man of such integrity and character as Chester, but the truth was that there were demoralized men like him—that could have been something truly great—all over Poland.

After two more days in Bydgoszcz visiting all the relatives, Sława and I left for my brother's house back in Gdańsk. Everything was happening in such a short period of time that it made me feel almost euphoric. It was so exciting to meet my relatives again from my new station in life—an accomplished young American with a newly broadened worldview. Seeing my other relatives, I realized just how truly far I had come. Most amazing of all, sitting beside me all day long was this beautiful girl to whom I'd written letters for over two years. I was twenty-three years old and I had everything I ever wanted. I had three months of vacation in Poland to look forward to, with a pocket full of money, a nice car, and the girl of my dreams beside me. Sława stayed with me one more night in Gdańsk at my brother's house, and the next day she returned home by train to Wrocław, while I continued to visit my siblings for two weeks in Lubocheń, where I had grown up.

There was a big celebration when I arrived in Lubocheń. My extended family of course knew I had arrived almost a week earlier, and they gave me grief for appearing after what they viewed as an unacceptably long delay. Someone had seen a fancy car passing by through the nearby city of Świecie several days ago and news had traveled fast! As a matter of fact, it seemed that the entire village knew that that car belonged to the young boy who had grown up here, and who had left for America just a few years before. The news had spread like wildfire, and my sister had been expecting me since her neighbors had delivered the reports.

After ribbing me about driving around the whole country before coming to visit, we settled in for a long and wonderful visit. We caught up about the members of our family who weren't there—Halina, Henry, Mom, Dad—and I was pleased to report how everybody was flourishing in the land of opportunity. For my nieces, it was Christmas in the summertime when they opened all the gifts I had brought with me. I was so filled with joy and satisfaction that it was like Christmas for me, too. We stayed up late into the night, and Henrietta told me stories about our parents and about our oldest siblings, whom by then she hadn't seen for twenty years.

I was excited to catch up with my friends as well, even though we had mostly stopped corresponding. I was lucky to run into Gerhardt, who had been my friend since childhood and was home on leave from the army. We had not seen each other since I left for high school in Bydgoszcz almost nine years ago. It was a bittersweet moment. I was thrilled to see him, and yet it seemed to me as if he had not advanced in his life at all. He was a caricature of a soldier. The uniform he was wearing was about three sizes too large, he was clearly malnourished, and he had none of the high spirit I remembered from a decade ago. The worst part for me was that he spent much of our time together openly worrying that his superiors might find out that he was associating with somebody from America, for which he could suffer some serious consequences. The paranoid Communist authorities were suspicious of any visitor from the West, for this was, after all, the height of the Cold War. In their eyes, even a native Polish kid could be a spy or an agent spreading capitalist propaganda.

Largely thanks to the charm of my Thunderbird, I managed to talk Gerhardt into worrying a bit less, and took him for a drive. He couldn't get over the performance of my car, and we cruised smoothly down the two-lane paved road lined with massive linden trees. The trees reached up over us as we drove, forming a leafy dome above with trees looking like Greek columns lining our way. Once in a while, a diffused stream of sunlight lit the road, and the effect was magical, as if we were driving through a tunnel. On this August afternoon, the wheat fields colored both sides of the road a brilliant shade of gold. The rays of sunshine filtered through the canopies and made the trees look even more majestic. On one straight stretch of road, I showed Gerhardt how the trunks of linden trees could create the illusion of a solid picket fence as I pushed the pedal all the way down. The poor guy stretched his legs out straight on the floor and clenched his teeth, bracing his body in vague contortions as we raced along in probably the fastest ride of his life—well over one hundred miles per hour. I could see he was enjoying it, and I was thrilled to share this little piece of American freedom with my childhood friend.

All of a sudden, from between the trees a peacock stepped out in front of my car. Unfortunately for the bird, it was too late for me to brake, and in the rearview mirror I could see a cloud of peacock feathers scattering all over the road. We were already racing away when suddenly Gerhardt got shaken out of his stupor.

"Stop, let's get some peacock feathers!" he shouted.

I could see from a distance a farmhouse up on the hill; obviously the bird was somebody's pet. Peacocks do not live in the wild in Poland. I felt very bad about that incident, but at the same time I did not want to get in trouble; so I kept going, to Gerhardt's great disappointment. My friend had been completely petrified by the ride up until that point, but the prospect of gathering some rare peacock feathers had stirred him awake. Usually, the only place you could see peacocks in Poland was in a zoo, and their feathers were prestigious symbols and highly valuable. I was sure someone else would gather them and put them to good use.

Lubocheń was only about an hour away from Klara and Chester's house in Bydgoszcz, so I decided to take Gerhardt to visit them. We organized a group of my cousins and their friends and decided to go to a restaurant and have a party. Years before, when I lived in Bydgoszcz, I had often passed by a particular five-star restaurant, but had previously never been able to afford going inside. This time I decided to make up for all those past years and took all eight of us out for dinner. When the maître d' greeted us in the lobby, he informed me regretfully that we would not be admitted because Gerhardt and I did not have proper evening attire. Gerhardt was wearing a private's army uniform and I had my standard American outfit of checkered shirt and jeans. My always resourceful cousin Chester pulled the maître d' to the side for a short conversation. I'm not sure what he said, but in a few minutes the manager of the restaurant emerged with a navy blue blazer for me to put on. Apparently Chester had convinced him that I was an important guest from America, and the manager decided to make an exception and let me and the soldier in. I was happy it all turned out well in the end, but I was disgusted that these Communists had their priorities so completely turned upside down. The uniform this poor soldier was wearing was what the government had given him, and he should have been treated with great respect for serving his country. After all, they had drafted him. In the Communist regime, everybody paid lip service to all citizens being "equal," and yet the soldier tasked with defending this "equal" society wasn't worthy of admission to their fancy restaurant. By the time we were seated, several waiters were hovering about—I think word had spread about this special American guest. There was a live band for entertainment and we ate and drank well past closing hours, until almost four o'clock in the morning. The three waiters designated to our table stood by the entire night, and I felt incredibly satisfied when I tipped them generously at the end of the night—probably like they had never been tipped before. It was amazing to see what a difference I could make in Poland even with just a basic American factory worker's wage. No doubt none of those people had any idea I was just an average American twenty-three-year-old.

The next day, Gerhardt returned to his army unit, and I returned to my sister's house in Lubocheń. I enjoyed being back in the village where I spent the early years of my life. This turned out to be a special time to reminisce more with my sister. At the time, about fifteen families lived in the village of Lubocheń, and there were by then only faint glimmers of the charming country estate that had existed when Lady Rose Plehn ran the manor. I was lucky I could be here to enjoy Lubocheń at the height of summer, when the lush rolling hills and fragrant meadows were at their full bloom. America certainly had its advantages, but the delight I felt at being surrounded by those vast ancient forests I grew up in was unparalleled. All of these thousands of acres had been my playground growing up—a fact that I appreciated much more now that I had been gone for several years. I strolled again through the forest with Henrietta and my nieces, and watched them climb those hardwoods just as I had done as a child. Luckily for them the forest was no longer littered with the artillery shells and unspent grenades that had killed or maimed so many children in my youth. The place seemed peaceful and beautiful, even if the people were terribly poor.

During those two weeks that Sława was with her family in Wrocław, I traveled frequently between my sister Henrietta's in Lubocheń and my cousin Klara's house. One afternoon when I arrived in Bydgoszcz, I parked my car in the courtyard behind her building, where tenants kept their trash cans and where clothes-lines were stretched out for laundry to dry. There also was a horizontal beam, about five feet off the ground, to hang carpets to be dusted. This was the only spot where I could park my car close to Klara's apartment. Her building was three stories high and seemed like it must have been built three hundred years ago. The streets around it were narrow and paved with cobblestones, and it was always a bit perilous getting in and out of those tight spots.

As I was parking my car, I saw a pack of teenage boys from the neighborhood loitering around my usual parking spot and acting as though they were looking for trouble. Before I opened the door, they surrounded my Thunderbird, peering in and running their hands along the chrome trim. I managed to open the

193

door and get out, making my way through this bunch while they were making wisecracks about how it might not be safe to leave my car there. One of the oldest, probably about seventeen, said, "Ain't you worried that something might happen to your fancy, shiny toy?" I paused, and without a word turned back and passed through them again. I unlocked my car and retrieved from under the backseat an air gun I had been carrying with me. To them it looked like a semiautomatic German Luger pistol—one of the most common handguns carried by the Nazis during World War II. I tucked it into my belt, turned to them, and said, "Do you see that window up on the third floor? I'll be there, watching," and I walked away. They had no idea that what I carried was little more powerful than a BB gun, but it certainly looked real, and that was what mattered.

To this day I'm amazed that the paranoid Communist authorities allowed me to bring this weapon into their country. Before departing from Chicago, I had to get a permit from the Polish consulate to bring it with me. I had justified it on the grounds that I was a member of a marksmanship club and that I might possibly participate in competitions in Poland. I also look back in wonder at how my youthful bravado walked the line of foolishness. Just having that air gun was asking for trouble, and now I had threatened a group of young kids with it. At that time I was not a US citizen, and it would not have taken much for the Polish authorities to revoke my passport and prevent me from leaving the country.

When I got upstairs, I told my cousin and Chester about my encounter. We looked through the window and, sure enough, the neighborhood troublemakers were all gone. At that time, Poland was a police state, and anyone who possessed firearms represented the ultimate authority. Although I had succeeded with my bravado that time, I realize now that I was probably a little overconfident, even for my own good. I got away with a lot by being an American guest visiting Poland, but I certainly didn't realize the kind of consequences that could have befallen me if a member of the Communist security apparatus went on an anti-Western rampage and wanted to give me a hard time. Clearly there was a lot of good luck on my side, and while I strayed a little too close to the edge at times, fate and fortune were still on my side for the time being.

I had been an oddity in America by being one of the first immigrants from behind the Iron Curtain, and now I was an oddity in my hometown as a kind of local celebrity, thanks to the simple fact that I had made something of myself in America. People I knew from my previous life couldn't comprehend how the young punk they had known in 1960 could return with such obvious prosperity and success to his name. I was a living, breathing testament to the power of American capitalism and democracy as I drove around behind the Iron Curtain in that summer of 1964. I was taking everyone out on the town, and paying what to them were extravagant prices. I had more money in my pocket than most families made in a year. There were even rumors that I was an American agent driving a car that belonged to the US embassy in Warsaw and that I was being paid to spread Western propaganda. People literally couldn't believe their eyes when they saw me. Of course, the saddest irony of it all is that I had just done what millions of other immigrants in America had done before me—I had worked hard at a simple job. People in Poland had the same impulse, but whereas their hard work got them exactly nowhere, keeping them enslaved in a vicious cycle of near-poverty, hard work in America actually moved a man to the next level. I kept telling people over and over again this simple truth, but I know that quite a few of them had trouble believing it could actually be so.

The time with my family flew, but Sława was constantly in my thoughts. For the past two years we had corresponded nonstop, so it was strange during those two weeks to not be in touch with her. We were so close, yet I missed her more than ever. Our meeting had confirmed we were in love with each other, and during those brief first few days we were together, I had promised her I would write her a postcard to let her know I loved her and I was thinking about her. Clearly this was a period of high excitement for me, and, well, I forgot to send that postcard. I had told Sława I would arrive in Wrocław in two weeks to visit with her family, but before I realized it, three weeks had passed and I had not been in touch. No one except high Communist officials had phones in those days, and even with my savings and American ingenuity, I did not have a way of getting in touch with her. So, after three weeks had passed—and not realizing what state I had put her in—I showed up at her doorstep in Wrocław. As soon as she answered the door, I quickly realized that she was not expecting me at all. I had made a terrible mistake in being out of touch, and arriving so late. Almost before we had begun I had my first big challenge in patching up the rift I had unwittingly created between us.

CHAPTER 11

Blossoming Love

S ŁAWA WAS NOT EXPECTING ME AT ALL WHEN I
showed up on her doorstep on an early September afternoon,
one week late. When she saw me, she was less than pleased, and
I immediately realized I had to move quickly to make amends.
She told me that as she waited for my arrival, with each day that
I didn't come, she began thinking that I was some kind of playboy from Chicago who took advantage of her. By now, she fully
expected that I had gone through a few other girls as well, and
that she would have to forget about me. Poor Sława was simply
devastated by these thoughts that had been swirling around in her
mind for the last week, and to express her disappointment in me
she had written me a letter full of sorrow to say goodbye.

I begged for her forgiveness and explained how difficult it
was for me to leave my family after such a short stay. I should
have written her a postcard to let her know she was constantly in
my thoughts; for this there was no excuse. After some time and
convincing she accepted my apology, and we kissed and made up.

However, I still wanted to read the letter, because I was curious to see what the true feelings in her heart were. At first she refused to let me read it, but after a little tender wrestling, she finally let it go. This letter was filled with all the tormented thoughts that had been plaguing her mind because of what I had put her through during the last week.

"What about the hundreds of pages of letters you wrote to me?" she wrote. "This is unbelievable. How can you be so cruel?" I realized how much she truly cared for me, and as much as I was sad I had hurt her, I was secretly thrilled to see how deep her feelings for me were. She said she had not planned to mail the letter, but that she needed to spill her feelings onto the page so she could move on when she thought I had abandoned her. Today, fifty years later, I still have that letter as one of my most precious possessions.

For the rest of the day we talked, kissed, and caressed. Sława's parents were divorced, and she lived with her mother, who was at work, and sister, who was currently at a summer camp. We enjoyed our day alone, and I was in heaven at being reunited with my love. That evening we decided to go out, and as we were getting ready, she remarked, "George, look at my face. It hurts!" Her delicate, alabaster skin was all red as if it were covered in some kind of rash. I looked closer and realized it was from my unshaved face. I felt a little guilty, but she laughed at me and said, "It was all well worth it."

We changed and went to the students' club, where she used to hang out with friends from the university. On that day, the sky was brighter, the sun stayed up longer, the birds sang louder, the grass was greener. I felt more handsome than I had a right to feel, and she was the most beautiful girl I had ever seen. To this day, she remains so.

Sława's parents had divorced when she was very young, and her father lived across town. He was the manager of a big factory, and the Communists had tried many times to get him to join the Party, but he had refused. His was an interesting case because he had been very active in the underground resistance during the war, and had fought in the Warsaw Uprising of 1944. Like many freedom fighters in Poland at the time, he had lived in the sewers for several weeks while fighting the Nazi occupation. During this time, he had seen his first wife die during the bombing of Warsaw as she was running across the street holding their daughter. As the war ended, he was left with a son, and soon after that he met and married Sława's mother.

Before the war he had been the director of a big telephone factory, and he was an expert in managing and running these kinds of large enterprises. After the war there were very few people with this kind of expertise left, and so even though he would have been a prime target for the Communists' brutal tactics, they knew they needed him. They put him in charge of one of the largest railcar factories in the country. It was very unusual for someone to have such a high position and not be a member of the Communist Party. He truly had specialized skills that filled a niche they weren't capable of handling without him. Still, just to put things in perspective, even though he was the equivalent of the president of the factory, he didn't have a private phone at home, because only Communist Party members had phones.

Sława's half brother, Andrzej Partum, was several years older and had already moved out, and was living on his own in Warsaw. Andrzej would in many ways take after the father he shared with Sława, and become a prominent critic of the Communist Party in the 1970s and '80s. He was an artist, and through his paintings and writings, he became quite famous in Poland for his anti-Communist activism. Nonetheless, that day I arrived in Wrocław, there were no family members of hers available for me to meet just yet. When her mother finally came home later that night, I could tell she was happy to see me. She was very friendly and obviously pleased that I was not in fact a playboy who had been toying with her daughter. I think like any mother in those times, she had it somewhere in the back of her mind that her daughter might have the prospect of moving to America, if Sława and I chose to marry. Needless to say, I was on my best behavior and was well received. We had her full blessing as we undertook the adventures before us in the coming months.

After one week in Sława's hometown, we again went to visit my cousins Klara and Chester in Bydgoszcz. Sława's classes had resumed at this point, so she kept up with her studies in between our family visits. While she had been studying literature at Wrocław University, she had also occasionally worked for a movie studio, playing small roles in feature films. In Bydgoszcz we attended the one movie theater in town, which was playing a movie in which she had a small part. It was a Second World War movie, titled *Giuseppe in Warsaw*. She played the part of a messenger for the Warsaw underground. I was so proud of her that I almost felt like telling the person sitting next to me that the actress on the screen is sitting right here and she happens to be my girlfriend. Sława glowed at my praise over her performance, and I felt lucky to have such a beautiful and talented girl on my arm.

Later that week, we decided to take a drive out into the countryside with Klara and Chester to a small cottage that belonged to the company he worked for, and that high-level employees were allowed to use for vacation from time to time. On the way there, we decided to take a shortcut on a dirt road through some farm fields. Since my Thunderbird was built for American highways, we did not get very far. While trying to bypass a big puddle of water in the middle of the road, we got stuck in the mud. We found ourselves in a hopeless situation. After trying everyone's ideas to get us unstuck, I walked to the nearby farmer's house to ask for help. It did not take much for me to convince him to participate in our little adventure. He gladly brought his horse to pull this five-thousand-pound American car out of the mud, and still the poor animal needed help from us. As it pulled, we were pushing the car from the rear. Together, but mostly through the strength of that big steed, we dragged the vehicle out. I paid the farmer well for his time, and he was clearly very happy for the extra cash. He needed it far more than I did, because private farmers in Poland made a very meager living. The Communist authorities were trying to destroy independent farming, and they oppressed farmers with high taxes and penalties. Most had to give up their endeavors and join collective farms, which killed all incentive to work hard because all profits were taken away by the government anyway.

For our rescuer and his horse, I imagine that pulling a fancy car from Chicago out of the mud was one of the biggest events since the Second World War. Sometimes I think back on that farmer and hope he managed to hold out in his private enterprise, just like my father had for the fifteen years after the war. Maybe my little gift to him helped in some way, and I hope he enjoyed telling the story for years to come of how he had to help the big, rich American and his fancy car.

We arrived at the humble cottage situated in a beautiful forest and got settled in for the few days we would be here. By then Sława and I felt like we had known each other for years. To me, it felt like we had been together since we started to write those letters to each other years ago. I knew she was very pro-Western, as most Poles secretly were at the time, but occasionally the Communist indoctrination she had been subjected to would surface. The propaganda in the media at her university was relentless, and of course she had very few outside sources of information.

Surprisingly, we got in a little argument over the principles of US involvement in the Vietnam War. By 1964, the war was escalating rapidly and President Lyndon Johnson had been sending more and more troops into combat. As a young man, I was rather conservative in my political beliefs, but I still believed that the president, a Democrat, had the best intentions for American interests. Sława, on the other hand, believed that it was wrong for Americans to get involved in the conflict. Like many conservatives of the time, I believed that if we could win that war, we would take one more step in the direction of defeating Communism for good. She thought that it wasn't worth it.

Today, almost fifty years later, I must agree with Sława. The Vietnam War cost us over fifty thousand lives and far too much precious US treasure. In the end we gained little and lost credibility as a world power. Now I realize Sława was right, but in the heat of that Polish summer, I firmly disagreed with her and I told her so. I didn't like arguing with her, but luckily it didn't last. After our brief squabble, we put politics aside and made love. All was well between us.

We didn't discuss politics often, because usually the most interesting topic of conversation for everyone I encountered in Poland was the quality of life in America. Those nights at the cottage we would stay up late into the evening talking with my cousins around a bonfire, and their questions were endless. Most Polish people were intensely curious about the true nature of the American system, and speaking personally to someone who had been there was the only way information could pass through all the levels of Communist censorship. I told them everything I could, but by now I had fully realized that the two worlds were so completely different that it was often very hard for me to explain fully the wonder and opportunity that America provided. Everything I experienced was the exact opposite of what the Communist propaganda tried to teach.

After a few relaxing days at the cottage, Sława and I drove to my sister's house in Lubochen, which was only a few hundred meters from the now run-down manor that had once belonged to Lady Rose Plehn. My sister's home was adjacent to the beautiful orchard my father had planted after the war, and its roughly two hundred trees were in full bloom this time of year. We enjoyed a feast of many varieties of apples, plums, pears, and cherries when we arrived. Throughout the garden, walking paths were laid out, and along each of them grew gooseberries, four different varieties of currants, and red, black, and yellow raspberries, as well as boysenberries. The orchard had been my father's labor of love, but he had never had an opportunity to see his efforts grow to maturity. The constant harassment by the Communist government drove my father to abandon all of his hard work. Only later in my life, when I was dreaming of having my own family and property, did I understand how agonizing it must have been for him to leave everything behind and travel to a distant land to start a new life. It hit me for the first time as I strolled through the glorious orchard that day what a profound loss it must have been for him to just walk away from everything he had worked for.

One of the rare plum trees my father had planted was a sight unlike anything I had ever seen before. It was so loaded with plums that the branches were almost breaking under their weight. They were a golden color with a little reddish blush on one side, and absolutely beautiful. As I popped one perfectly round plum after another into my mouth, I felt like they were saturated with honey as they went down my throat. Sława was a city girl and had only occasionally visited the countryside for summer vacations. To roam these orchards that belonged to my family was a rare treat for her, and we spent many afternoons eating plums directly from the tree. For the two weeks we spent there, we indulged ourselves continuously, and basked in the beautiful scenery of the place in which I had grown up.

By now I had seen all the family I needed to see, and I could focus more on spending time with Sława. She was, after all, the main reason I returned to Poland just a few short years after I had left. I was falling more deeply in love with her with each passing day. It was just over a month since we had first met, and already I could barely imagine my life without her. We decided to take a trip to the northeast region of Poland known as Mazury, which is full of interconnected lakes and is a popular summer vacationing area.

I can still recall that late summer morning when we set off through the Tuchola forests where my father had worked as the administrator before the war. The traffic was very light and we seldom saw other cars. On the rare occasions that we did, the other driver would slow down almost to a stop, staring at this beautiful, strange white car passing by, looking back and wondering if by any chance he had fallen asleep and was dreaming. We traveled on a narrow, two-lane road that was lined with rows of huge oak trees that obscured the view at the curves. At times we worried that we would cause an accident as those drivers looked backwards. Fortunately, we never did. Every few kilometers, as we passed through another charming little village, we were forced to slow down to avoid running over geese, chickens, dogs, and other small farm animals. We weren't exactly sure where we would go or what we would do, but we just wanted to be together and be alone. We had money and time on our hands—what else could two young people in love want? We passed through a few small cities such as Grudziadz, Gniew, and Kwidzyn, and eventually we stopped in a small town called Piławki, which was just on the outside of the city of Ostróda. We had no particular reason for stopping there other than that it looked charming and peaceful.

We hoped to find a place on the outskirts of town. Driving on this beautiful road through the trees, we noticed an old white frame house surrounded by a veranda. It was set back about one hundred yards from the road and had tall flowers growing halfway up all the windows. It was a beautiful setting in the woods, with glimpses of a lake in the background. Intrigued, I pulled down the lane in front of the house, and a lady immediately came out. Sława and I introduced ourselves and asked if the woman knew where we could find a room to rent for a couple of weeks. She knew of a small hotel in town and assured us they would probably have rooms available since the tourist season was over.

The thought of staying in a cramped hotel room in town didn't seem very appealing to us. There were few opportunities for leisure and tourism in the countryside, so we knew our options would be limited. Seeing our disappointment, she asked if we would settle for simpler accommodations. "Maybe," we responded. She then proposed to rent us a part of the veranda with a private entrance facing the woods. It had a view of the lake and a bathroom nearby.

At her proposal, our eyes lit up. I thought this was a perfect place for us to spend some time. It turned out that the lady's husband was a forester just like my father. She wanted to check with her husband when he got home from work, to see if he would agree, as they had never had guests stay on their veranda before. She asked us to return in a couple of hours, so we drove to town and stopped for ice cream. We did a little sightseeing and drove back to the forester's house, hopeful that it would all work out. When we arrived back in front of their house, they were both waiting outside, and they received us warmly. I noticed, however, that the forester was focused more on my Thunderbird than on what I was saying. It turned out both of them were very lovely people. They showed us around and we moved in.

While the accommodations were not the most luxurious, it was a beautiful location surrounded by gorgeous forests and many lakes with small islands. Thousands of years ago glaciers sculpted the surface of this terrain with rolling hills and ravines. We had found a perfect country house in which to enjoy ourselves for as long as we liked, and the nearby town of Ostróda provided some entertainment if we wanted more options. Within walking distance of the house there was a roadside kiosk, and we went to buy some basic supplies for our stay. We spotted a large can of Polish ham called Krakus in the back on a high shelf, and told the lady we wanted to buy it. She took it down and dusted off the top, for it had probably been there for a very long time. We could see reluctance on her face. She said, "I cannot open it and only sell you a part of it. I won't be able to sell the rest. You have to buy the whole five-pound can." We looked at each other and said, "That's exactly what we want, the whole thing and a case of strawberry nectar juice and some freshly baked rolls."

We went back and had a feast on our veranda. The rolls we bought at the kiosk were freshly baked and tasted just like those my mother used to make in Lubocheń. The ham was a special treat for Sława, as the constant shortages of food in big cities were especially problematic when it came to meat supplies. Even though it was a Polish brand, Krakus ham was actually a rarity in Poland. The Communists were selling Krakus brands, and whatever else they could, to Western countries so that they could obtain the hard currency they needed to keep their Communist "paradise" afloat. Polish agricultural products of any real value were mostly sold on international markets. Polish people had trouble buying much of anything that they really wanted. Nonetheless, the Communists kept up their arrogant propaganda, and insisted year after year that they were on the road to surpass the Western economies. Most Polish people, after years of seeing just how false and shallow those promises were, knew enough to laugh at this nonsense. The only pockets of plenty in Poland were in the countryside, where individual private farmers produced their own goods in their backyards. If you were lucky enough to live near one of them, then you might have access to fresh dairy products, meat, and eggs. The majority of the country, however, faced bread lines and had meat only on special occasions.

For two days we lived on ham, rolls, and strawberry nectar, and we felt content and happy just to be together. On the third day, we decided to head into Ostróda, and found a restaurant where they served good food, and where we enjoyed a nice dinner out on the town. Later we came across a nightclub with a live band, and decided to stop in. The year 1964 was the year "Beatlemania" took the world by storm, and the Beatles were at the peak of their popularity. In Poland their records were considered contraband and were selling for astronomical prices. When I realized this, I regretted not having the foresight to bring any of the records with me to sell. If I had, I would have been able to stay in Poland for an additional six months!

It was ironic that the demand for anything related to the Beatles persisted despite everything the Communist government did to try to prevent it. Their censorship policy was aimed at preventing any Western cultural influence. Of course, the more effort they put into preventing Western influences, the more the demand grew. Very few Western movies were shown in theaters, and if by chance that movie depicted a version of the "good life" in America, the government would make sure to let everyone know this was simply a depiction of how the "super wealthy" lived, oppressing and taking advantage of the poor. There were times during my visit when I had a hard time biting my lip while speaking to someone who had swallowed this propaganda. In America, I had seen many examples among my immigrant friends of how the capitalist system works for people who are intelligent enough and who are willing to work hard. The car I drove around Poland for those few months was perhaps the clearest refutation of that Communist propaganda. After just four years of living in America, I was able to take a three-month vacation, and take my car with me to travel in Europe. I had done this on my own, working at a simple job in a factory! Such success was unheard of for people in Poland. Under their Communist system, even most of the high-ranking cronies could not afford what a working student in America could.

The nightclub in Ostróda was actually the only place in town that had any kind of nightlife, but everyone said it was the place to be for evening entertainment. We ordered a few cocktails and enjoyed the American music blaring in the background. Despite the government's best efforts, young people still listened to Elvis Presley, and any other American music they could get their hands on. Sława and I were sitting at a table listening to Elvis's "Hound Dog" when two young Polish officers walked up. The captain asked Sława to dance, and while I didn't object, I certainly didn't like it very much. I figured he should have asked first whether it was okay with me, and I stewed silently in my seat while they danced. He brought Sława back to the table after the dance, and just as I was about to give him the cold shoulder, he asked if he and his friend could come sit with us. They were very inquisitive about America, and they couldn't help themselves from expressing their eagerness to speak to an American. The tension between us softened and we started chatting. Somehow we got on the topic of waterskiing and I asked them if there would be a possibility to rent a boat in this area. After I had loaded my car up for the trip in Chicago, it turned out I had plenty of space in my vehicle, so I had brought my water skis with me. It was my favorite summer sport in America. To my surprise, the captain told me it was not a problem to rent a boat. He could get one from his unit, and he said he also liked to water-ski, but unfortunately he did not own the equipment. It was all going to work out perfectly it seemed—he had a boat, and I had the skis!

I was very excited for our rendezvous the next afternoon on the shore of the lake. The captain met us there, along with a soldier who was driving the military speedboat. I insisted that the captain should ski first, since he had provided the boat. He obliged, but it turned out his methods were a bit more complicated than I anticipated. For some reason, the captain needed a kayak to get started, which confused me. Fortunately, they were available to rent at the beach, and a puzzling scene unfolded in front of us. The captain got in the kayak, and to my surprise the soldier, in his well-fitted uniform, stood knee deep in the water to assist him. He held the kayak so the captain could sit on it while holding on to the rope, with his feet in the skis on either side. The private then climbed into the boat and took off, pulling the captain off the kayak. Because he started off sitting in the kayak, he at first cruised in a seated position. Then he got some speed and was able to stand up, leaving the kayak bobbing in the water behind him. Once he got up, he looked like an experienced skier, but I was genuinely amused by the whole procedure. I explained as I chuckled to Sława that this guy had a pretty expensive hobby if he needs two vessels and an assistant in order to water-ski.

After a couple of minutes the captain fell down, and the soldier turned around to pull him back into the boat. I then tried to gently explain to the captain how it was in fact possible to come to a full upright position on skis while starting low in the water. I demonstrated several times how just keeping your tips up and facing the right direction would allow you to get up in a more simple and efficient manner. Luckily for me, the captain took kindly to my instruction, and within a few tries he also got the hang of it, and we ditched the kayak. It turned into a great day of fun for us. It was the only time I water-skied during my visit to Poland, but it was well worth it to bring my skis for just that one memorable day.

Those few weeks we spent at the forester's house in Piławki were some of the best days of my entire visit, and probably some of the best days of my life. The weather was beautiful and warm and we spent a lot of time on the beach, enjoying the lake. I found fishing rods in our veranda, and we even caught some fresh fish for dinner. A few times we went back to the same nightclub at which we had met our water-skiing captain. On one evening we befriended a nice couple a few years older than us, from Krakow, the second-largest city in Poland and home to some of the most beautiful architecture in Poland. It turned out the woman was a custodian in the royal castle there, known as Wawel. We spent the next few nights with them, enjoying dinners and good conversation, and by the time they were preparing to head back to Krakow, they invited us to come stay with them at their home. Krakow was on our itinerary of places to visit before I left Poland, so we gladly accepted and looked forward to visiting them in a few weeks.

Meanwhile, with every passing day that we spent together, Sława and I grew more and more in love. We spent the last full day of our countryside-paradise vacation on the beach. It was late September and the shore was practically empty. We had the place to ourselves as we lay on our towels in the sand; the reality began to sink in that my stay in Poland was slowly coming to the end. Lying on the warm sand so close to each other, I had plenty of thoughts spinning around in my mind.

I began to think back on the two years we had been writing letters to each other and how anxiously we had waited for the moment when we would meet for the first time. Now it felt like we had just met, and it was already time to go back to America.

The time was passing so fast, and I just wanted it to slow down so I could enjoy being with Sława. I realized that a lot of my visit to Poland had to do with luck, and that there was no guarantee I would be able to come back any time soon. I also worried about my own state of mind—would these intense feelings last? Would I meet another girl back home that might interfere with my feelings for Sława? The world was a changing and unpredictable place at that time, and I realized that there was a chance I might never see Sława again.

I realized that the Polish Communist government would never let Sława out of the country to visit me—it was hard enough for those of us who had family, money, and connections in the West to get out. The thought that they could keep us apart made me furious. She was such a beautiful girl, and I worried that it might be asking too much of her to continue this romance at a distance for what could potentially be a very long time. Would she be able to keep up her determination to keep our love going through letters? Would I? These questions were tormenting me, and there was silence between us as she knew my mind was wandering all over the universe trying to find the best resolution to the dilemma we faced.

After lying on the beach side by side in silence for some time, I finally got my thoughts together. I sat up, took a deep breath, and said, "Sława, I would like to ask you something," and I looked into her beautiful blue eyes. "Would you marry me if I asked you to?" I do not remember her exact words, but I do remember the big smile on her face, and that whatever she said, I understood that her answer was an emphatic *"Yes!"*

From that moment on, our relationship took on a different meaning. I now looked at her as my future wife. It seemed like making that decision took a heavy weight off my shoulders, and we were both thrilled. I was twenty-three and she was twenty-one, and we realized we had both just made the biggest decision of our lives. I had always been something of a free spirit, and had always liked to do things exactly my way. Both my brothers were in their early thirties when they got married, and I wondered what my parents would think of me getting married at such a young age, especially considering my lively character. That night we didn't think of much else though, as we enjoyed the last fading evening of the summer on our veranda. We were incredibly excited. We were just like two kids who had gotten the biggest present of their dreams.

CHAPTER 12

A Wedding and a
Honeymoon

T HE NEXT MORNING, WE SET OFF FROM PIŁAWKI AS A
newly engaged couple, and headed back towards the port
city of Gdańsk. On the way there we stopped in Malbork, home to
one of the largest brick castles in all of Europe. Neither of us had
previously seen this magnificent medieval structure, which had
been built over eight hundred years ago by the Teutonic Knights.
The architecture and craftsmanship were second to none. It had
survived through numerous tumultuous times, and parts of it
had been rebuilt after the Russians bombed it during the Second
World War. I marveled at my good fortune—at how I finally
had the time and resources to tour all the famous and beautiful
spots of Poland while on this vacation, things I had never had the
chance to do when I lived there. I felt proud to be Polish.

Just after Malbork we stopped in a small town called Elbląg,
where my mother's brother lived. After a short visit with my uncle,
we had to cross the river Nogat by ferry to continue our journey
to Gdańsk. While driving onto the platform that was connected

to the ferry, the entire exhaust system of my Thunderbird got torn off. I had to drive all the way to Gdańsk without the mufflers. Ironically, the best stretch of road in Poland lay ahead of us. It had been built by the Prussians before the war, and had stood the test of time. There was hardly any traffic, and since we didn't have to worry about approaching cars, I drove my Thunderbird with the pedal pressed down all the way to the floor for the very first time. The speedometer moved all the way to the right and stayed there. The car was going at full speed and so was my level of excitement. I'd always wanted to be a fighter pilot, and soaring down the road like this was a dream come true—I felt as if I were flying. It sounded like I was flying, too. Without the exhaust and the mufflers, and while going about 140 miles per hour, the huge V8 engine sounded like a Russian MiG-15 fighter jet taking off.

Not everyone found it so pleasing. We came over a slight hill and saw an old farmer plowing a field with the horses on the side of the road. As we flew past him, he stopped walking and let go of his plow while his horses kept going. He must have been wondering what was happening. Since we were driving so fast, we quickly arrived in Gdańsk to visit my brother Casey. I knew he would be at work at the shipyard, along with my cousin Casimir, who was a manager in one of the shipyard's departments where they built hulls for large ships. They were happy to see me after a few weeks of absence, and I told them the good news that I was engaged, which didn't surprise them, because they had already met Sława and knew what an amazing girl she was. After I explained the situation with my car, they pulled some strings and told me they had arranged to have it repaired right there at the shipyard. The following morning I arrived at the main gate with my car, and two guards armed with Kalashnikovs waved me through. The shipyard was massive, almost like a city by itself. Inside, I was met by another set of armed guards, one of whom made a phone call and then told me to head down a street on one side. In a few hundred meters, I came upon a group of middle-aged workers dressed in greasy jumpsuits. One of them got behind the steering wheel of my car and drove it into the huge factory hall. Inside, it was so noisy from the banging of steel that there was no way one person could hear another speak. Sparks were flying all over the place, and there were slabs of steel moving over my head that were as large as a wall in a garage. I realized I was in the heart of the Communist workers' "paradise"—and it was a filthy, noisy mess.

That same Gdańsk shipyard was the place where the Solidarity movement was born fifteen years later. At the time I went to get my car repaired, Lech Wałęsa was probably working there as an apprentice electrician. In 1980 he would lead the workers as they walked out onto the streets to protest against the Communist regime. These demonstrations, of course, were the famous shipyard strikes that caught headlines around the world, and launched the Polish Solidarity movement, which would bring about the peaceful downfall of Communism within a decade. Wałęsa would go on to win the Nobel Peace Prize in 1983, and then become the first president of a newly democratic Poland in 1990.

Only many years later did I realize what a big chance my cousin took by letting an American car onto the terrain of the shipyard he managed. At the time I was still just a kid and did not comprehend the seriousness of the situation. While my cousin had power in that setting, it certainly wasn't without its limits, and one of the main things you didn't want to get caught doing during those days was lending a helping hand to a capitalist.

My cousin Casimir had somewhat of a reputation for being a rebel though. A few years earlier he had played a central role in a major act of protest against the Russians. The workers in the shipyard were paid abysmally low wages, but on one particular occasion, they were told that they had an order for one of the Western countries. Everyone was very enthusiastic and jubilant, because they assumed they would be paid better and that their conditions might improve if they were doing business with the West. Up until that point they had been producing ships for Russians, and Poland was essentially being robbed in the process. It was the same kind of oppression the Soviets imposed on farmers—forcing them to "sell" a certain quota to the Russians every year. In truth it was robbery, and the prices farmers and producers received in Poland for their goods didn't even cover the costs of materials in Poland. Poland, for example, was also a producer of cement, and of course it was all exported to Russia. The prices Polish manufacturers received for their cement barely covered the expense of the paper bags the cement was shipped in. Such was life behind the Iron Curtain.

When this particular ship was finished, everyone waited for the foreign crew to arrive and hoped they would finally see their fortunes turn for the better. Instead, they arrived to work one morning and saw Russian flags flying on the masts of the ship they had just built "for one of the Western countries." Casimir was already the shipyard manager at the time, and he climbed the mast of the ship and tore down the Soviet flag.

They could have easily thrown him in jail, where no one would have ever heard from him again, but the Communists knew they needed him for his expertise in the shipyard. He was demoted from his position as general manager, but he never apologized for the anger he felt on behalf of all his men. Despite having this kind of controversial history at the shipyard, he still stuck his neck out to help me. Although his job could have been in jeopardy for helping an American, he nonetheless showed fearlessness in the face of the Communist regime and gave the order to repair his cousin's car. In those days, no one was permitted to enter an important industrial area like a shipyard without the proper documentation and permits. Signs were even posted all around prohibiting the most innocent of photographs. My youthful bravado and audacity in entering the shipyard in a fancy American car could have caused some very serious problems. The whole visit could have been easily twisted into an international affair by a paranoid Communist official who was in a bad mood. If they had searched the car and found my gun, I would probably have been accused of being a Western spy and thrown in jail with my passport revoked. Those kinds of episodes happened to many people in those years, and I was still traveling on my Polish passport since I only had an American green card. For my cousin, who was already on the "blacklist" for taking down a Russian flag, it could have been even worse.

Nonetheless, the men in charge of repairing my car worked fast. I was lucky I hadn't lost that many pieces from my exhaust system when it came apart. In just about one hour they welded whatever was broken. They improvised new parts for whatever I was missing, and soon I was ready to go. I gave my cousin and brother some money to take care of the guys who helped me, and drove out. At the gates, the guards just waved goodbye. I waved back with a smile as the Thunderbird rolled quietly past them on the way out. Sadly, Casimir did not live to see the Solidarity movement. If he had, I'm sure he would have been a brave leader of that group. I never saw him again after I drove off the shipyard that day. He passed away before I returned to Poland twenty-two years later. Luckily, however, I did see my brother Casey again, and soon. Approximately seven months later we finally managed to get the paperwork in order for him, and Casey joined the rest of our family in Chicago.

For the next week we stayed in Gdańsk visiting other relatives of mine, cousins from my mother's side of the family. All of these people were relatively poor, even though they worked for the biggest enterprise in town. Still, it was the custom among Polish people to receive any guest with a special feast, and so many feasts were had. The simple working-class food they provided was undoubtedly one of their biggest expenses, and I appreciated their sincere generosity and delicious food with all my heart. In return, I was often required to stay up late consuming alcohol with them for many hours. Alcohol had taken on a new meaning in Communist Poland, and vodka, the traditional drink of the Russians, became commonplace among Poles. It certainly provided an escape from the dreary reality of their sparse living conditions, and everywhere I went in Poland during those years I noticed the drinking being worse than I remembered from even a few years before. Having an out-of-town guest was a truly special occasion to celebrate, and glass after glass was filled to the brim, with everyone required to drink to the bottom. A refusal would have been considered rude behavior, and if you fell behind, your tablemates would quickly prompt you to drink up. The vodka consumption was at such a level of excess that even I had to protest. I was thrilled to be with my family as well, but I warned them that I wanted to be able to remember my stay with them, and the only way for me to accomplish that was to drink a little less. I got some grumbles of protest in return, but obviously the way alcohol was consumed in Poland during those years was not something my American blood could, or wanted to, keep up with. Besides, I had my new fiancée with me and I needed to maintain some civility! After I laid down the law about the drinking behavior, I realized that I might be changing and maturing after all. I had never enjoyed getting drunk, and now that I was soon to have a wife, that was even more the case.

The rest of our visit passed without incident except for one small accident. One evening, Sława and I were visiting my cousins, who lived on a fourth-floor walk-up. While we were walking up, she missed a step, fell on her hand, and broke a nail. Actually, the nail separated from the finger and was rather nasty looking. She got lightheaded and almost fainted because of how horrible it looked. Being the gentleman my father brought me up to be, I carried her up the remaining flights of stairs like a princess. I loved treating Sława like a lady, but in truth she was such a brave and accomplished woman. She had even been the swimming champion in the three-hundred-meter butterfly, an extremely difficult and grueling sports event, at the University of Wrocław—a major accomplishment. Everyone knew what a talented athlete she was, so the running joke for the rest of our stay became "George carrying the champion up the stairs because she broke a nail!" It was quite funny, and we didn't mind the poking. Luckily she recovered just fine from her "injury," and a week later traveled back to Wrocław by train. She had been gone from her studies for almost a month, and had some catching up to do. Meanwhile I went to Lubocheń to spend more time with my sister Henrietta's family. Sława and I agreed to meet in Wrocław in a week, and this time I hoped to spend more time with her family.

During my second visit to Wrocław I was able to get to know Sława's mother. I was impressed with how well she had done for herself considering she had divorced her husband when Sława was only sixteen. She was certainly in an unusual position for the time, being a single mother supporting two girls on her own. Nevertheless, she had managed to successfully navigate the harsh economy and had always provided for her family. Unfortunately, when I arrived, Sława's younger sister, Urszula, had contracted meningitis and was in a special quarantine unit in the hospital. Once again, I would not be able to meet with her. We could only wave to her third-story window from outside the hospital.

I truly enjoyed my stay at Sława's apartment. We already had decided in Piławki that we would get married that week, and we were eager to get on with our honeymoon. It just felt like the right thing to do; we had been together for two months now and we knew we wanted this to last the rest of our lives, so why wait. Unlike the elaborate weddings of today, we had a simple ceremony, and dinner at her mother's apartment as our entertainment. Sława's family and some of her friends were our only guests. It was too far to travel and too much of a financial burden to ask my family to come all the way from the other side of the country to attend. Sława's closest friend, Cyla, an artist from the Wrocław Pantomime Theater, spent much of that week crying about the fact that Sława would soon be leaving for America, which was of course what everyone expected. While they were happy for her, it was certainly bittersweet on some levels. Sława realized that getting married meant a life in America awaited her, and who knew if she would ever return to Poland.

We had a small but special ceremony in the Wrocław City Hall to make it official. The building was actually a twelfth-century Gothic building, which made it feel a little bit like a church. We arrived in front of the city hall in my white Thunderbird, and Sława stepped out wearing a simple and elegant white cream dress a seamstress had sewn for her just that week. I had prudently packed my tuxedo from America, and together I thought we made quite the handsome couple. My chest was bursting with pride and happiness as I escorted my beautiful bride up the front steps. Scenes like that did not occur in Wrocław very often, and within minutes a crowd of spectators gathered to see what the fuss was all about. I laughed inside, and I thought to myself, *Too bad this crowd doesn't know that this guy in a tux with a fancy car is almost broke!* I had already spent most of the $3,000 I had brought with me, and realized at this point that the crowd should have felt sorry for me instead of admiring me. We tied the knot then and there, in what seemed like the perfect crescendo to the magical two months that had passed since we first met. After we had gotten engaged, I had written a letter to my parents informing them of the news. In return, my father wrote a warm letter to Sława welcoming her to our family, and I gave it to her to read now. Sława's mother hosted a small party for us that went on well into the wee hours of the morning, and we woke up the next morning as overjoyed newlyweds.

We decided to head to the famous Polish mountain town of Zakopane for our honeymoon. I had never visited the scenic Tatry Mountains, which formed Poland's southern border, so this was the perfect opportunity. We set off towards southern Poland, and I was tremendously excited, as I had never been in these regions before. Even though we had been traveling around Poland together for many weeks, this trip through the rolling hills in the south of Poland felt different. We were now married! It gave new meaning and excitement to everything. We passed through small villages and charming towns, and before we arrived in the mountains, we stopped in the famous Polish city of Krakow, which was along the way. Krakow had been the capital of Poland before the fifteenth century, and it was home to an old royal palace known as the Wawel. I remembered that I had written down the address of the couple we met during our countryside visit in Piławki, and we paid them a visit. They were tremendously happy to see us, and they offered to put us up for the few days of our visit. What was even better was that the following day, our friend arranged for a special treat and instructed us to meet her at the foot of the hill the castle was built on. To this day I'm not sure how she arranged it, but she managed to have the large iron gates that stood across the entrance to the royal courtyard opened up for us. There was a long, inclined road, paved with bricks, that for about one hundred meters led up to the archway entrance and the gates. She told me I was to drive my car through the gates, up this dramatic, iconic path, and park my Thunderbird in the courtyard right in front of the palace. It was a tremendous honor and something normally reserved for the motorcades of foreign dignitaries. We had already become close friends with them, and I think through a combination of the fact that she truly liked us and that I was driving a Thunderbird, we received a once-in-a-lifetime experience. Because she was the head custodian for the entire palace grounds, she then took us on a tour of many of the hidden rooms of the castle that were not even open to the public.

I was truly amazed with this special gift our friend gave us just as we were starting on our honeymoon. They were probably about ten years older than us, and I had a feeling they had been charmed by what they saw as "two young lovebirds" when they first met us, and wanted to treat us well. They clearly had some sort of status, because they also lived in a beautiful villa on the outskirts of town, but I don't think they were members of the Communist Party. Perhaps because of their highly specialized artistic knowledge they were given these special privileges. They never spoke about it, as they were incredibly humble. Even if they were involved with the Party, they were what we called in Poland at the time "radishes"—red on the outside, but white on the inside. We learned a tremendous amount of Polish history from them, and I couldn't help getting the feeling that all of their kindness was rooted in the hope that I would return to America with news of the many Polish patriots who were proud of their heritage and holding out against Soviet Communist propaganda. These two souls were a beacon of intelligence and civility, immune to the glorification of the Communist system. They were bastions of Polish culture. I was proud to know them, and although we never saw them again after our few days together in Krakow, I always remembered the example they set for us as Polish patriots quietly keeping their culture alive.

Our honeymoon continued on to Zakopane, and once again we ended up renting a room from some local people, known in Poland as "Górale," which means "people of the mountains." Although it was October, the weather was warm and beautiful and the snowcapped mountains were breathtaking. On one of our first days, we decided to hike to the top of Mount Kasprowy, which was one of the highest peaks, instead of taking the cable car. Coming down those steep slopes was precarious, and the next day our legs were terribly sore and we decided to spend a day in bed recuperating. We were newlyweds and enjoying our time together was one of the main things we wanted to do.

Over the following few days we made friends with some locals, and enjoyed some of the food delicacies of the region. The Górale people are generally very skilled woodworkers and creative carvers. Their homes are usually traditional log cabins, surrounded by ornate embellishments. Like the mountain folk of many parts of the world, they have a special reputation for their rich history of folklore and are somewhat suspicious of outsiders. They have a very specific dialect, which at times was hard even for us to understand; it would be the equivalent of a proper New Englander from Boston trying to speak to someone from the Deep South in America—some things might get lost in translation.

One day I took some pictures of Sława, including a series of her posing on the hood of my Thunderbird, and I dropped the negatives off at a local photo studio for printing. The next day when I came to pick them up, the photographer had a strange expression on his face.

Sarcastically, he asked, "Where did you pick up this starlet? She is hot!"

I replied angrily, "Listen, buddy, this 'starlet' is my wife!"

Needless to say, he was quite embarrassed, and he handed me the pictures and complimented me on my photography.

Today Zakopane is a very popular tourist destination in Europe, but at the time of our honeymoon it was still quaint, charming, and not crowded. It was the ideal place to spend our honeymoon. Sadly, after just another week it was time to start heading back north. We still had to cross the entire length of Poland to make it back to port in Gdynia in time for me to catch my ship. Of course a few more adventures awaited us before we made it safely back. Just a little bit outside of Zakopane, my car completely came to a halt in the middle of nowhere. Apparently the alternator had gone bad. After a short while a passing car stopped, and the driver offered us help. Of course, there were no tow trucks in the area and we didn't even know how close the nearest town was. The kindly driver told us he had an idea and asked us to wait. Before long he returned dragging an armful of heavy wires. He had cut them from the fence that was running along the side road. This entrepreneurial guy tied the wires to my car and then to the bumper of his car and slowly pulled us a few miles to the closest town!

It turned out this Good Samaritan ran a small repair shop from his garage, and he promised to fix the car by the next day. In addition, he had mercy on these stranded tourists from America, and since we were in the middle of a small town in the dark of night, he offered us a room in his house. He and his wife kindly prepared a supper for us with a touch of customary vodka, and we were glad to be the recipients of Polish southerners' famous hospitality. In the morning we found out that we'd actually slept in their bedroom, and that our hosts had slept on the couch. After breakfast the next morning he got to work on my car, and to my amazement, it was fixed by early afternoon. It's beyond my comprehension how he managed this feat. His garage looked more like a blacksmith's shop than a mechanic's repair establishment. He explained that, for him, it was a matter of pride and a priority to fix my car, knowing that I had to arrive on time in Gdynia to make it back home to America. We parted like good friends. When I think back on this last encounter with a complete stranger in Poland, I often wish there were more people like that in today's world. Good, simple, hardworking men like this Good Samaritan restored my faith in Poland.

CHAPTER 13

One Last Adventure

THERE WAS ONE MORE IMPORTANT STOP WE HAD TO make as we passed through central Poland, and that was to visit Sława's mother's side of the family in the city of Radom, which was also Sława's childhood home. Her grandfather was the president of the famous "Radom Factory," which produced firearms. However, under the Communist system the mission of the factory was a heavily guarded secret. Officially, they were making sewing machines, but most people knew the truth.

Sława's grandmother came from a wealthy and prominent family in what is today the Czech Republic. As a matter of fact, her great-grandfather was one of the wealthiest men in the Czech Republic. He was a powerful industrialist in the railroad business, and had made a fortune building the Trans-Siberian railroad around the turn of the last century. The family was living in the city of Dniepropetrovsk, in what is today Ukraine, while Sława's great-grandfather ran his business building the railroad. His daughter, meaning Sława's maternal grandmother, was sent to posh Russian finishing schools in the pre–World War I days, when Poland was still partitioned.

Sława's grandfather, meanwhile, was a Pole living in the area of Poland that fell under the Russian partitions. He had been drafted into the tsar's army, and had fought in the Russo-Japanese War in Siberia from 1904 to 1905. Sława's grandfather attended a military school under the tsar, and this school was near the town of Dniepropetrovsk; he was also then stationed for work there in the town, and this was where Sława's grandparents ended up meeting. They actually spoke French to each other, as was the custom for educated society at the time. Sława's mother was born under these privileged conditions, to a wealthy, military family, in the years before Poland existed on a map.

When the Bolshevik revolution broke out in 1917, Sława's grandparents had to flee, along with her mother (who was just a little girl) and her mother's younger brother (Sława's uncle Henry, who was only five years old at the time). They made their way to the Black Sea and started heading towards their old homeland in Poland. The family recognized that the little boy had an uncanny prophetic ability. One morning, before the revolution, he woke up very distressed and told his father that his factory was on fire and that he had to go there quickly. Sława's mother was three years older than he, and remembered this day well—the boy was right, and there was in fact a fire in their father's factory that morning. The factory ended up burning down, and it was a great setback for their father. Of course, they were slightly unnerved by the boy's ability to know things he couldn't possibly have known. In fear that people might think their family somehow planned the fire ahead of time, they kept the boy's prophecy quiet. While the family made their escape, the boy made some other interesting prophecies as well—for instance, repeatedly stating that he wouldn't survive the journey. Sława's grandmother was explaining to her children that they were now going to Poland, where they really belonged, but her five-year-old son told her he would never see that land, and he was right. He passed away on the boat.

Sława's mother had stacks of prerevolution Russian rubles, which we still have in our possession today. Back then you could buy a whole village with one banknote, but, of course, immediately after the Bolsheviks killed Tsar Nicholas II, the rubles became worthless. Sława's grandparents ended up settling in the Polish town of Radom, in a newly constituted Poland, after World War I. Her grandfather became the director of the Radom Firearms Factory. Eventually, her grandmother gave birth to two more sisters, and a brother, all of whom would become very active in the Polish underground army during WWII.

While in Radom, I also met Sława's uncle Sławomir Szafranowski, who was a decorated officer in the Polish army. He had fought the Germans during the war, and was lucky not to have been executed in Katyń, where Russians executed over twenty thousand Polish officers. He instead had been captured by the Germans and sent to Buchenwald, a concentration camp, where he had somehow miraculously managed to survive the remaining years of the war. After the war, he was awarded a medal for heroism and bravery in battle.

After just a short drive from Radom, we finally made it to Warsaw, Poland's capital, where I finally met Sława's mother's sister, Aunt Lusia, and her husband. Both of them fought in the AK—the Polish resistance movement—throughout the war. Aunt Lusia had been captured and sent by the Germans to the Ravensbrück concentration camp, which was infamous for the horrible medical experiments they carried out on female prisoners. Aunt Lusia was even awarded a medal for her service in the AK. It was here at Lusia's house that I finally learned more of the history of Sława's family, including information about Sława's father. Her father's family hailed from Lithuania, where they had been wealthy aristocracy before the Bolshevik revolution in 1917. The Bolsheviks hanged her paternal grandfather in front of his wife and son, Sława's father, who was named Henry Partum. With the help of their servants, they dressed in rags and managed to escape to western Poland; having had their previous land holding seized by the Bolsheviks, they now faced a bleak life in this new country. I also learned that Sława's father grew up to be a brilliant mathematician, responsible for developing some key mathematical theorems in the field of electrical engineering. Before the war he had been the president of a Polish branch of the Swedish telephone company Ericsson, which still exists today. During World War II he was active in the underground resistance, and had barely escaped with his life from the sewers of Warsaw. After the war, the Communist government hired him to rebuild the famous Polish company Pafawag, which built train wagons in Wrocław and was one of the largest and most well-known companies in Poland.

For various reasons, in 1949, Sława's parents divorced, and part of it had to do with the way her father's experience in World War II had left him a somewhat troubled man, dependent on alcohol. Sława's mother would explain to me years later that she loved Henry, and that he was a brilliant man and that they tried to make it work. They actually even remarried, and were together for a few more years, until they finally split for good when Sława was sixteen years old. He left Wrocław, where they were living at the time, and moved to Warsaw, and Sława never saw him again.

Since that time, he loosely kept in touch with some of his extended family members, like his former sister-in-law, but by the time I arrived in Poland, nobody had heard from him in several months. Also perhaps because tensions were still high between Sława's mother and father, Sława lost touch with her half brother from her father's first marriage, Andrzej Partum. At that time, he was well on his way to becoming a living legend, for he was an outspoken critic of the Communist system, and wasn't afraid to make strong political statements in his painting and writing, which earned him a kind of notoriety. Sława never connected with him during that time, but her younger sister, Urszula, would befriend him and become close with him in the years to come. Urszula also reconnected with their father, and stayed in touch with him until he died on March 1, 2002.

When it was time for us to say goodbye, Sława's cousin Janusz escorted us to the outskirts of Warsaw, where we would pick up the road heading north. If we knew then that it would be the last time we'd see him, we might have spent more time there. Tragically, Janusz, who graduated from the Polish Naval Academy, badly injured his back in the line of duty as a naval officer during a voyage to Asia. He underwent surgery and, unfortunately, died from complications. We never saw him again.

The last leg of our journey was before us, and we headed towards Lubocheń with somewhat heavy hearts. On a rainy night just before we arrived at my sister's house, we took a wrong turn. We had been driving on a nicely paved road, but suddenly it turned to sand and we realized it was under construction. I attempted to get out of this trap, but it was too late and we were dug in, with our wheels spinning in the air. I found an ice scraper in my trunk, but my attempts to dig us out were futile. We had no choice but to sleep in the car. It seemed we were in the middle of nowhere, with no lights to be seen in any direction.

As we sat in the car, I looked out across the fields and finally saw a small light far off in the distance. I decided to see if I could get some help and told Sława to lock herself in the car. The light turned out to be much farther away than I anticipated, and just as I thought I was getting closer, I suddenly heard a pack of dogs heading in my direction. As soon as I realized they were approaching me, I sprinted off back towards the car, and got back inside just in time to avoid the barking mob. The dogs gave up, and we slept the rest of the night in the car with one window open for some fresh air.

Just as dawn was about to break, I heard a strange sound next to my ear that woke me up. At first I thought I was having some sort of bizarre nightmare, but as I looked out the window, I realized this was no dream. I looked up and found myself face to face with a cow! A farmer was leading his herd to pasture. One of the cows was very inquisitive and stuck her head through the window, greeting us with a loud "Moo." Soon the farmer joined the cow, with a puzzled expression on his face, and tried to figure out what these two people were doing sleeping in the car in the middle of nowhere and stuck in the sand. After I explained the situation, like all those other good Polish Samaritans before him, he jumped at the chance to help us. He set off towards his farmhouse and in a short while came back with his son and two horses to pull us out. It worked! We were finally on solid ground; all we had to do was turn around and be on our way. I put my car in reverse and nothing happened—the car wouldn't move. Apparently the previous night when I was trying to extract us from the sand, shifting gears back and forth with the wheels spinning, I had ruined the reverse gear. We had no choice but to continue on, only from now on I could only go forward. For the rest of the week I had to be very mindful of how I parked, because if I didn't park appropriately, I would never be able to get back out.

Finally, after more than a month away, Sława and I arrived at my sister's farm in Lubocheń. When I told them about all of the adventures and misadventures we lived through, they couldn't stop laughing.

"And on top of all of that, you got married!" they exclaimed. We were happy to be reunited with them. Sadly, this truly was the last stop of my grand summer tour behind the Iron Curtain. When I arrived in Poland, I had four brand-new tires on my car and a spare in the trunk. I realized that after driving these past three months on the subpar Polish roads, there was no way I would make it back to Chicago once I arrived in Montreal. I would have to get new tires, but I was all out of cash. Hat in hand, I asked my older sister for money, and promised her I would pay her back as soon as I got home.

The day finally came for my departure in the port city of Gdańsk, where the MS *Batory* waited to take me home. Sława and I were very sad. The good days were over, and we had to part not knowing when we would see each other again. There was no telling what kind of bureaucratic obstacles the Communist government would put in our path, and for all we knew it could be years before Sława was allowed to come to America as my wife. The regime at the time was not inclined to give passports to many people, not even the wife of a foreign resident. My brother Casey and his family took us to port on that gloomy morning. I said my goodbyes to my brother and then held Sława in my arms. I told her I loved her and that we would manage to get through this time and would see each other again soon. We both were brokenhearted, and tried to reassure each other as best we could. I stood on the deck for a long time waving to Sława, and I watched her waving back to me with tears rolling down her cheeks.

For me, this was the second time I had to say goodbye to my family and my country. But now I also said goodbye to my wife. Finally, the ramp was lifted up onto the MS *Batory*, and with a deafening sound the loudspeaker announced that we were departing. The trawlers started to pull the ship from the shore and out into the open Baltic Sea. I stood and stared at my wife, waving to me in the distance, for as long as I could make out her tiny spot on the deck. During the night I wrote a long letter to Sława expressing all of my joy and all of my love for her, as well as my gratitude for the past three months. I mailed it from Copenhagen, where the ship stopped the next day to pick up more passengers before heading to Canada. It seemed appropriate that the journey home was miserable. The MS *Batory* hit some severe storms, and the rough seas bounced the ship around like a toy boat. It was impossible to walk on deck, and I spent most of the ten-day journey seasick in my room. My physical body, which normally did not get seasick, was an accurate reflection of the heartsickness I felt on the inside, not knowing when I would see the love of my life again.

Soon enough the storm passed by and we grew closer to the Atlantic Ocean. We had a long trip ahead of us, but sadly the social life was not quite the same as on my voyage to Poland. Most of the passengers were older people. The weather was chilly, and I spent most of the time indoors. We formed a small group of young people, and we tried to make the best of it.

One evening we were having a good time by the bar. One of the guys in our group was a Danish fellow who was an ex–merchant marine sailor. He claimed that he traveled all over the world, and after having a few too many drinks he began to entertain us with the stories from his voyages. As proof of his adventures, he took off his shirt and showed the scars he got when he was attacked by robbers in Bombay, India. In our group there was a very attractive young Polish girl. He announced that never in his life had he met such a beautiful woman, and declared his love for her. The party was coming to an end and someone jokingly suggested that the two lovebirds should get married. Before the sentence ended, the sailor took out his passport and put it on the bar, but no one from the group was willing to perform the wedding cere-mony. Finally, after having a couple more drinks, I volunteered to act as justice of the peace and marry them. The girl did not have a passport with her, so I wrote the marriage certificate in the sailor's passport. It was the last night of our voyage, and the next day I did not see either one of them. We did not even have a chance to say goodbye to each other.

During the wedding ceremony, a young lady traveling to Chicago to visit her relatives came up with a proposition for me; she asked whether instead of her flying from Montreal to Chicago, she could hitch a ride with me. This way I would have a compan-ion and she would have the opportunity to see North America. I never took advantage of this offer.

I missed Sława terribly on the trip back, but I felt we had a lot to look forward to, so I kept my spirits up. I was looking forward to seeing my family in Chicago again, and telling them all about my adventures. In a way I felt like a changed person from the young, single bachelor who had made the voyage to Europe three months ago. I now had a new purpose in life—figuring out a way to rescue my wife from behind the Iron Curtain.

CHAPTER 14

Married in America

I ARRIVED IN MONTREAL A DIFFERENT PERSON FROM THE one who had left. My car was a little rough around the edges, and so was the one suitcase with all the clothes I had been wearing for the last three months—not to mention the fact that I was penniless, and that I had overstayed my leave of absence from work by at least two weeks. I had no idea whether I would have a job waiting for me when I returned to Chicago. I found a mechanic that would fix the transmission in my car, and replace the tires, but I had no way to pay him. I checked into a nice room in the humble Victoria Hotel near the harbor, and put in a phone call to my parents. Hat in hand, I asked them to send me $300 via Western Union. I must have done something right in a previous life to have such wonderful parents, but luck was indeed on my side as well, because in just two days I had paid my bills and was on my way speeding towards Chicago.

I drove the one thousand miles from Montreal to Chicago only stopping to fill up the gas tank. My parents were anxiously awaiting my arrival, and wanted to know everything about my trip, especially about Sława. We stayed up all night talking when I got home, and while I may have left out some of the juiciest details about some of the more wild adventures, they got a full report on our families, our friends, and—most importantly—their beautiful and intelligent daughter-in-law. It took me a couple of days to decompress from this life-altering journey overseas, but I had to get back to work as soon as possible. I had a family to support now! I was nervous going in to work knowing they had expected me back two weeks previously, for I knew they had fired people for missing just one day on the job. As luck would have it, they took me back without much of a fuss, and I threw myself into my work with new gusto.

Then I had to take care of some personal matters. First, I filed all the documents with the immigration office for Sława to obtain a visa and permanent residency in the USA as my wife. All the procedures went smoothly and the paperwork was sent off to Poland for their approval. I wrote a letter to an American girl I had been casually seeing before I left, and told her that I had gotten married in Poland and that we would not be able to see each other anymore. Other girls were the furthest thing from my mind, and I just wanted to be with Sława. It was difficult to adjust to reality again—I had just completed possibly the most astonishing life adventure that I could have dreamed of at that time, and now I was back at work in the factory and living with my parents. I had to concentrate on earning money and saving for the arrival of my bride. I also went back to the Art Institute in the evenings and started selling my oil paintings for additional income. In sum, I had very little free time. I wrote letters to Sława, and since it was winter, most of the time I stayed home.

A few months passed, and Sława was still unable to obtain a passport from the Polish government. At the time, citizens had to apply for a passport; they weren't allowed to just have one with them at all times. Moreover, it had to be returned to the government when you got back from your preapproved trip. It should have been a simple matter, but she kept getting the runaround at her local immigration office, and so I decided to take matters into my own hands.

When I arrived in Poland the previous August, I was required to visit the regional police department in Gdańsk to register the air gun I had brought with me. The assistant to the chief of the police department and I had gotten friendly and had killed time talking about our hobbies as he filed the paperwork for my air gun. In this Communist system, the police force was called the Milicja—also known as the "Citizens' Militia"—because the Communists didn't want to call their law enforcement "police," as it was considered too bourgeois. This man told me his passion was collecting stamps, and when I told him that I worked with people from almost forty different countries, I could see his eyes open wide at the prospect of being able to obtain so many precious foreign stamps. At the time, I told the guy that I would send him some stamps from my foreign friends when I returned, and I had done so when I got back to Chicago in early December. I'm sure he was thrilled to see the stamps from all the exotic places that I collected for him—Venezuela, Panama, Italy, Colombia, and Lebanon, just to name a few; I wonder if he even knew where all of those countries were. I had seen many high officials in high Communist positions who didn't necessarily have an education. This man seemed to be a good, if simple, person. He was polite and had a highly polished uniform. He opened up to me a bit during that conversation, and I could see that even in his position, his horizons were narrow because he never had any real opportunities in his life; yet he was curious about the outside world.

I thought the stamps would be a nice Christmas present for him. He was one character I remembered in particular because as I was filling out the paperwork for the air gun, he had commented on what a nice pen I had. To me it was just a basic ballpoint pen you could buy at any corner convenience store in America, but to him it was a luxurious Western good. Without a second thought, I gave him the pen. I had plenty more of those. He was so thankful for my gift, and shook my hand and patted me on the back as I walked out. I remembered thinking, this poor man is the assistant to the chief of police in one of the largest cities in Communist Poland, and yet a simple pen from America is a status symbol in this country that tries so hard to spread propaganda about life in a worker's paradise. Moments like this revealed to me what a sham it all was.

In early 1965, I sent this gentleman another collection of foreign stamps, and this time I included in my letter to him an explanation of how unfortunate it was that my wife was having trouble obtaining a passport, and how much I hoped to see her soon. Within two weeks of my sending that package, Sława received a phone call from the chief of police in Wrocław, where she was back at university, informing her that her passport was ready and waiting for her. This time she was treated with utmost respect and kindness, and none of the dismissive attitude they had treated her with in the past. It was sad but true that the only way to accomplish anything in Communist Poland was through exactly this kind of corruption and bribery. It was a foreign concept to my American friends.

Finally the letter I was waiting for arrived; Sława had purchased her first plane ticket and would be arriving in Chicago on May 5, 1965. It would be six months since we parted, and I was elated and quickly jumped into action. I rented a nice two-bedroom apartment for $125 per month in an upscale Polish neighborhood on the north side of the city, and started to prepare it for her arrival. My parents helped me greatly—especially my mother, who did an excellent job of organizing a functional kitchen and preparing a home with all of the feminine touches my young wife would appreciate.

When the day finally arrived, I just couldn't wait to be with my Sława again. I could hardly focus on anything. I left work early and rushed home to take a shower, change, and drive to the airport. It turned out her flight from Europe had arrived early, and she had been waiting at the airport for over two hours! I rushed around what was by now a nearly empty terminal looking for her graceful, blonde figure. I finally spotted her at the end of the long row of baggage claim areas, and she spotted me at the same time. As we walked towards each other, things moved in slow motion, and I was overjoyed when I was finally able to hug and kiss her again. We were together as husband and wife in America, starting a new chapter of our lives side by side, just as we had been imagining for years now. It was a dream come true. Poor Sława said that those two hours she waited at the airport seemed like forever, and of course I could understand her eagerness to commence her journey in America.

Henry and Margaret also met us at the airport, and then all four of us drove to our parents' apartment. I was incredibly proud to present Sława to my parents, and I knew she would make a strong impression. My family welcomed her warmly, and we spent several hours talking over dinner, with everyone getting to know the newest member of the Swiderski family.

The time finally came for me to drive Sława to our new apartment. It was part of a two-story apartment building, and our home consisted of two bedrooms, a dining room, and a study. I was eager to see what Sława would think of her new home—after all, she had just left behind everything she had ever known and moved to a new country. As we walked in, Sława stood in the doorway, and I could tell immediately that she was overwhelmed. She could hardly believe that the fully furnished apartment before her eyes was her new home. Everything was decorated down to the smallest details, including modern chairs and side tables that were all the rage in the 1960s. We had contemporary Danish furniture I had purchased from a local European furniture importer. Everything was in hip olive tones, complete with velour armchairs and modern area rugs in abstract asymmetrical patterns. I also had a couch, end tables, and all-brand-new top-of- the-line appliances, like a refrigerator and a stove. In truth, I had taken out a loan for almost $2,000 to obtain all the furniture, but it was well worth it to see Sława's reaction. My mother even filled the refrigerator and pantry with all the basic provisions we would need. It was a wonderful beginning for newlyweds. We could hardly believe that the seeds of all our wildest dreams, which were planted in that first letter three years ago, had come true.

I had planned to take the next few days off of work, and Sława and I enjoyed our second honeymoon. I introduced her to the rest of my family and took her sightseeing in Chicago. She was amazed by the beautiful streets and tall buildings, just as I had been. Of course, one of the first big stops we had to make was to take Sława shopping. She had arrived from Poland with all of her earthly belongings in one suitcase, and I knew it would be an incredibly special treat to take her to an American department store. There was so little available for purchase in Poland, and in all her twenty-one years she had only ever purchased one pair of high-heeled shoes. She had saved and saved for those shoes for a long time, and on her eighteenth birthday she made an appointment at the special, private, high-end store where they were sold. Even so, there were usually only one or two colors and styles to choose from, but she still felt it was a glimpse into the lap of luxury. She had told me how one day she left those precious shoes under her bed, and unfortunately, her dog had chewed them up. She cried for three days, and took them, in tears, to the shoe repairman to see if they could be salvaged.

Now I was by no means rich, but I knew I could take her to the store and even on my humble salary it would far exceed all of her wildest shopping fantasies. At the time, I was making about

$120 a week, which is about $880 a week in 2013 dollars—and it was a solid middle-class income. For Sława, this amount of money blew her mind, and overnight she felt like she was incredibly wealthy—which of course, compared to where she came from, she was. I remember that on the first shopping trip I took her on we spent about $240, and I knew I had far surpassed any of her wildest dreams. Not only did she have a new wardrobe with multiple pairs of high-heeled shoes and elegant dresses, but she also had a beautiful brown boucle winter coat with a mink fur collar—unheard of in Poland.

For Sława everything felt like a kind of paradise. In the stores, all the sales ladies were incredibly nice and accommodating, not like the rude store attendants in Communist countries, who acted as though they were doing you a favor by helping with an object you wanted to buy. The abundance of tropical fruit also enchanted her, and for the first time in her life she ate a banana. She also ate oranges by the dozen, because while they were available, at most, once a year in Poland and only at an exorbitant price, you could buy them for pennies at any grocery store in Chicago. During this time, Sława also tried to cook for us, but she was not yet familiar with English, and so she had some difficulty preparing meals with all the new products and labels. We ended up eating a lot of sandwiches, but food was not important—we just lived on love.

After about two months of getting acclimated to life in America, she was finally ready to start looking for a job. All my friends liked her very much—she was intelligent, funny, beautiful, and had no problem communicating with people. I knew she wouldn't have trouble finding work; I just hoped she would find something she liked. Her education in literature didn't lend itself to many fields of work in Chicago, and she had only just begun taking evening classes in English. Our landlord arranged for Sława to work as a quality-control inspector at the wire factory where he worked. This was her first full-time job in her life, and while it was not a very glamorous one, she was earning American dollars, and that was something to be proud of.

We settled into a stable life enjoying our two incomes, and had plenty to cover everything we needed. I finally traded in the trusty old Thunderbird that had driven us all around Poland, and got a new one. This one was sky blue with a black vinyl roof and black interior. It was certainly nice, but we missed the old one, which carried with it so many good memories of the time in Poland. Meanwhile, I continued to study at the Art Institute in the evenings, and was painting more and more in all of my free time. Sława's arrival sparked a new kind of artistic passion in me. She was my critic and my inspiration, and I wanted to show her what I was truly capable of. I felt myself reaching new levels of expression with my artistic abilities. I maintained a vigorous exhibition schedule, and each season we would be booked at four or five major exhibits, where I often won awards and my works sold for very respectable amounts of money. Today I would gladly buy some of those works back, but at the time, I was just proud to also be earning an income as a painter. Sława loved coming to these exhibits, and meeting all the fascinating personalities that came through and held intellectual conversations on the merits of various art pieces. I enjoyed always having her at my side, and

I loved how she lived emotionally through my success. We were becoming such a team, true partners in life.

For the next ten years or so, I would focus intensively on my paintings. I joined the Polish Arts Club in Chicago and participated in many art exhibits with my fellow Polish countrymen. My confidence increased and I consistently started winning first- and second-place prizes, even in big regional competitions. My work was getting so much attention that I started to believe I really must have a talent, and I decided to expand even further. I became seriously interested in creative photography. Gradually, I was able to buy a good camera and an enlarger, and I set up a darkroom in our apartment. Sława adopted my hobby too, and we spent many evenings developing our black-and-white negatives and doing our own printing in our pantry.

As a matter of fact, Sława enjoyed photography so much that she decided to look for a job in that field. She had been at the wire factory for about a year, and was feeling much more confident now in her English and her other abilities. One day she picked out a downtown photo studio from the yellow pages, and she took the train downtown. She knocked on their door and applied for a job, as simple as that. She may have fudged a little bit about her experience to get the job, but what she lacked in knowledge she made up for in eagerness and ambition. To her and my amazement, she was hired by that very first studio she applied to. It was very convenient because our offices were close to each other and we could now drive together to work and back home.

After about a year, she was offered a job in another photo studio for higher wages and a better position. This job put her at the cutting edge of photography work in that day, and she quickly developed the high-tech skills she needed to get the job done. She worked on creating various stills and slides that would be used in television presentations and by big advertising agencies. Before the digital era, everything had to be prepared in a special format for TV, and this is where Sława found her niche. There was even an article written up about her in the local newspaper, which discussed how this charming young woman had become an expert in this particular field of photography. She worked there for several years and enjoyed the creative aspects of her job. In the meantime, we further developed our photography hobby. We had access to her work studio on the weekends, and we would oftentimes go there while no one else was around and work on producing our own materials. We split our free time between our small home studio and her work studio on the weekends. This was a great period of artistic exploration and expression for us. I made endless photographs of my beautiful wife; she was my muse and model. We did all the developing and printing ourselves, and soon our house was covered wall to wall in pictures and paintings of our own creation.

In 1968, three years into living this wonderful life, we invited Sława's mother to visit us, and Sława had a joyful reunion with her after not seeing her for so many years. During the six months she stayed with us, she was also able to find a part-time job in a local factory, and earned enough money to live like a queen when she returned to Poland. That same year, Sława got pregnant, and we knew everything in our lives was about to change. I decided not to reenlist in my courses at the Art Institute, because I wanted to come home earlier on most nights to be with Sława, whereas school kept me away usually until 11:00 p.m. I was only a few credits short of attaining an advanced art degree, but I knew I did not want to be a professor or academic, and since I felt I had learned everything I wanted to learn from that institution, I had no problem ceasing my classes. We were very excited about the prospect of having a child, and at the same time, our outlook and perspective on life changed. We realized that raising a child is a big responsibility and not something to be taken lightly. Not a day would go by that we were not talking and planning extensively for our future. We wanted the best for our child, as any parent would, and we thought of that unborn baby every single day as we eagerly awaited her arrival. Sława was voraciously reading all of Dr. Spock's books on childrearing, as was all the rage in those days, and we nested and prepared a small nursery.

As the time for the arrival of our baby was getting close, and not having much experience in these matters, we had a few false alarms—hurrying to the hospital only to realize it was not yet time. Finally, on August 14, 1969, it was clear the moment had arrived, and I drove Sława to the hospital. The nurses checked us into the maternity ward and a couple of hours passed, but our daughter was taking her time. Sława was worried it was another false alarm. Feeling sorry for me, she suggested that I go to the waiting room to take a nap, and assured me that if anything happened, she would send the nurses to come wake me up. Well, what happened instead is that she came and woke me up early in the morning where I slept (on a couch in the waiting room) with the news that I was the father of a beautiful, healthy girl. We named her Krystyna Dorothy Swiderski, the Polish equivalent of Christina, but we called her Krysia, the sweet, diminutive form of Krystyna in Polish.

The next few years passed with much the same rhythm as before, but now we had a toddler in the mix! We continued working on our art and photography, and I continued with my primary job in the clothing factory. Family life suited me, and Sława was the perfect partner for me. Nonetheless, I started to grow a bit restless. By 1972 my father was seventy-two years old, and I had to start thinking a little more clearly about how I would be able to support my parents in their old age. I realized it might be time to move out of the city and establish ourselves somewhere more substantial in the newly developing suburbs of Chicago. By this time Henry and Halina had already moved to the suburbs on the northwest side of the city, Henry in Skokie and Halina in Franklin Park, and so we decided to expand our search in that direction as well. I had some money saved up, and we started looking for the right property. In truth, I was concerned about my parents' well-being. They were getting older and didn't drive, and it didn't feel right to leave them alone in Chicago while all of their kids moved out to the suburbs. Our plan was to find a place that would accommodate two families, yet we did not want to live in one house, under the same roof. It was quite a challenge to find something that would fill these requirements, and we engaged one of my real estate broker friends to find something that would meet our needs.

Within a few short weeks my friend called with the news that he had found just the place for us. From what my friend described over the phone, it was perfect for us, and I drove the seventeen miles from downtown to Palatine as quickly as I could. The property was about one acre, and the house was a small three-bedroom Cape Cod with only one bathroom. However, there was also a large shed, about twenty feet by fifty feet, and a substantial garage that the previous owner had converted into a small office for his electrical business. I instantly saw the perfect opportunity to add another section to the office for a bedroom and convert the whole structure to a small carriage house where my parents could live. There, they would still have their privacy, but at the same time, they'd be close enough to us for me to help them if they needed it. The next day I told my parents about my plans and brought them to see the property. They liked it very much, and from the beginning they also liked my idea. Sława and I loved the serene setting amongst the fields and trees of the suburbs; we thought it would be a wonderful place for Krysia to grow up. We made a decision to buy it.

Sława and I had enough money for a down payment, and my parents financed the construction of the addition that would become part of their carriage house, which I would build with some hired help. The owner accepted our offer, and within a month we were the proud owners of our first house in America. We had been here less than ten years and we felt a major milestone was now behind us. For the time being, though, we still lived in Chicago. Every day after work I drove to Palatine to work on the addition. After two months everything was finished and all five of us moved in. The area was still mostly cornfields and farmland at the time, and it reminded me of the Lubocheń of my childhood.

Our house was only nine hundred square feet, but it was big enough for us, and we loved it. It was a great joy for me to see my family and my parents as happy as I could ever remember seeing them. I often took a moment to just look around at everything I had accomplished, and I felt so grateful that I was able to provide for my wife and daughter as well as my parents. Every week Sława took my mother shopping for groceries and various household things, and my father never failed to keep himself busy. Within no time he had mastered the local bus schedule, and with his senior citizen discount card he got around the suburbs to take care of his errands just as well as he had in the city. Krysia was starting kindergarten, and we loved watching her grow and learn. We were all flourishing. Sława's mother came to visit us again, and we were truly happy living together as one big family on what we saw as our own little slice of American paradise.

When the first springtime came around, we all set about improving the landscaping of our mostly bare lot. We planted dozens of trees and bushes, and slowly the empty field around our home began to look like a beautiful park. For the first time since World War II, my father could truly invest all of his considerable gardening knowledge into a plot of land that he felt solely responsible for. My mother too was thrilled at the chance to let her considerable gardening skills flourish—and her "green thumb" had rows of flowers growing in no time. Every morning she would wake up and talk to the flowers, encouraging them to bloom, and their lovely scents filled our homes all summer long.

During this time I started developing a more serious interest in an activity I had only dabbled in a few times before: hunting. I also was able to take my father hunting as much as his health would allow, and he truly enjoyed it. It was the first time since before the war that he was able to hunt freely and for fun. It was a true bonding experience for us. As I developed this new passion, I increasingly enjoyed my time in the suburbs.

Despite this, I began to grow restless with my job at the clothing factory. I had been there for nearly sixteen years, I had been married for over a decade to the woman of my dreams, and I had a beautiful home and a healthy, growing family. The success I had achieved was beyond any of the wildest dreams I had as a teenager. Yet I knew there was something greater still on the horizon for me, although at the time, I didn't know what it would be. America had already made so many impossible fantasies come true, and yet I knew there was something more I could achieve. Soon enough, an opportunity presented itself in which I would leave behind my livelihood as I knew it, and make the decision to never work for another person again as long as I lived.

CHAPTER 15

A Revival of Old Traditions

B UYING THE LAND IN PALATINE OPENED UP NEW horizons for my family and specifically for my father. Hunting had been a way of life for us growing up in Poland, but obviously things had been different since World War II. During the fifteen years of Communism we lived under in Poland, many of the traditions my father enjoyed as a boy had been restricted under new oppressive regulations. Now, living in America so many years later, I thought he might be able to reclaim a small part of the lifestyle he had lived before the war, in Luboń.ień. When he worked for Lady Rose, he had always traveled through the forest with a shotgun, for his own protection and also because it was part of his job as administrator of this land to act as law enforcement. He would sometimes catch thieves trying to cut down trees, and he had to protect himself from the occasionally dangerous beasts that he might come across like wild boars or bull elk. Occasionally Lady Rose would ask my father to kill an elk or deer for food, as she had exotic taste and meat wasn't easy to come by in the store. She also enjoyed various birds and even squirrels. During the war my father was one of the few Poles who was still able to carry a weapon under the Nazi occupation, and it was only because Lady Rose insisted, that he had permission to do so. My father's old rival, Herr Niehoff, had been viciously set against it, but Lady Rose prevailed, and my father felt safe for the time being. After the war, the Communists exercised tight control over all weapons, and confiscated most firearms that were in the hands of private citizens. My father was only legally allowed to carry a weapon thanks to his friends in the hunting club, and the fact that he was generally liked. Nonetheless, it was always a risky business to carry weapons after the war, as a Communist in a bad mood could use any excuse to throw you in jail, or at the very least confiscate your property. It was nothing like the freedom my father had grown up with.

When I was about ten years old, in the early 1950s, I remember participating in group hunts that would be organized by the hunting club. Two long lines of people would fan out over a massive area of forestland and herd the game, mostly jackrabbits, towards the shooters in the middle. These two lines would eventually form a very big ring, about a mile in circumference, when the two point men would meet and then close in progressively to catch the game inside. This was a very common and enjoyable method of hunting for us at the time. There were strict rules about what distances you could shoot at, and you had to wait until the spooked game would pass outside the circle before you could take aim. I was too young to participate in any shooting, but I had a very important job as a chaser. We were given loud noisemaking toys, the kind used in New Year's Eve parties, and we got paid to stomp around, bang on trees, yell, and generally make a lot of noise—it was a little boy's dream job. I remember being so impressed with the hunters because by the end of the day there would be close to eighty massive, twenty-pound jackrabbits hung along the side of the wagon. Unfortunately, each family only got to keep one, and the rest were sold off to markets in Western Europe, which paid big bucks for game meat. Still, this was a period of incredible learning for me, and I couldn't wait for the day when I could graduate to becoming one of the hunters myself.

My chance came sooner than I expected. When I was about fifteen years old and already attending high school in the town of Bydgoszcz, I came home to visit my parents and received a major surprise from my father. It was the middle of winter break, and my father was entertaining guests at our house. A group of local men, including the priest, Jerzy Pietrek, who had often come to play piano and sing with Lady Rose, were at our house. The priest had just finished leading the local parishioners in a round of Christmas carols, and the final stop, as usual, was our house for smoking and drinks. Henry had sent a box of cigars from England, as they were a major treat; cigars were completely unobtainable in Poland. Even though these were probably cheap cigars, they were considered such a luxury in Poland, and the men savored my father's treats. As usual they were talking politics, and I sat in my room bored.

Before he went in to join the men, my father came to talk to me, and told me about some foxes he had recently seen in the haystacks in our fields. After the wheat was separated from the chaff, we would keep the chaff because it was good feed for our livestock. Large wooden planks were laid out in the fields and the straw was stacked on top of them, and it would form a little chamber inside under the straw. The foxes would stalk around the outside of the haystacks, looking for mice. To my great surprise, my father handed me his shotgun, and told me to go out into the field and kill the fox. I could hardly believe what has happening. I felt enormously important, and the confidence my father showed in me was one of the best feelings a young man can have. To be perfectly honest, what I was doing was illegal and could have easily landed my father in jail. He warned me to carry the shotgun under my coat, and to make sure that no one saw me while I was out in the fields. Our fields were in a very rural area, and it was already dark out, so the chances of anybody seeing me were slim. As my father handed me the shotgun, I think I grew about three inches in height. I had walked into the house a high school kid on break and that evening walked out of the house feeling like a seven-foot-tall man. That my father had trusted me with this illicit matter made me feel like such a grown-up. He was an upstanding person in every area of life, and for the first time in my life I saw a glimpse of how a grown man takes measured risks when he believes the laws of his country are at odds with what is natural and right for the people.

As I walked toward the haystack, I could see the telltale shape of the fox from a distance. Its long fur and bushy tail stood out as it darted around the haystack. I moved quietly, and took aim carefully. I wanted so badly to make my father proud. I killed the fox with one shot, and I was far enough away from the house that I knew that nobody heard me. When I came back, I snuck in through the kitchen and presented the fox to my mother, who gave me a big smile and took the animal out of my hands to clean it for its fur, which could be sold in town to government furriers for a high price. Foxes were considered pests because they hunted jackrabbits and small deer, which were our main source of meat in those days. I really felt I had done a very good deed in helping my family, and I couldn't wait to show my father. She told me to go change my clothes, and after I did that, I waited impatiently for the last of the guests to leave so I could show my father what I had done. He was proud of me and told me I did a good job; I fell asleep feeling like a changed person.

My father was violating the law by giving a weapon to someone who didn't have a permit, never mind the fact that I was a minor. I respected how he insisted on keeping with tradition, irrespective of the unscrupulous Communist laws we lived under. Before the war it was customary for a man to teach his son to hunt, and this practice was now outlawed. In my dad's mind, he was keeping with age-old tradition, and I had already been primed for this hunt thanks to all of my participation in the group hunts in Lubocheń.

About a week later, my father gave me a new assignment in the middle of the day. He told me to head off into the woods and look for more foxes there. I was under strict orders to hunt only fox, and not to even think about being tempted by bigger game. "Just hunt the fox," my father said sternly. Then he added, "And whatever you do, don't open your mouth to any of your friends about what you're doing."

That first day out in the woods, I tried my hardest to stalk the tracks I had seen of foxes in the snow, waiting outside their dens, and using every trick I knew to lure them out into the open. Sadly, I didn't see a fox all day, and I never even fired a shot. I went home disappointed that I didn't experience the thrill and ease that had come with my first fox the week before.

The second day I went out again, and of course by now my head was growing a little big, and I started considering myself a real grown-up, who could do whatever he wanted. Despite my father's warnings, I had to tell someone—and I went to my friend Gerhardt's house and casually asked him if he wanted to go hunting with me. He looked at me in disbelief, but when he saw what I had tucked under my coat, he quickly got dressed and joined me. I thought I was an adult and could now make all of my own decisions, despite my father's dire warnings. With two of us tramping around in the woods and making double the noise, we stood even less of a chance of ambushing a fox, and so the second day ended empty-handed again. We stayed out late, and I crawled into bed that night disappointed. I consoled myself that at least I got to show my friend that my father trusted me with a gun, and I looked forward to impressing Gerhardt on the following day.

The next morning my father woke me early while I was still in bed, before he left for the day.

"Did you see anything yesterday?" he asked.

"Not a thing," I replied in my disappointed voice.

He paused, and then asked, "What did I tell you?"

I tensed up, because I knew I had screwed up, and I didn't know what he would say next.

"What are you talking about?" I answered, feigning ignorance.

"I told you not to talk to anybody about it," he said in an even tone. "And above all, not to take anyone with you."

He was right, and I remained silent and downcast.

"That was the last time you went hunting on your own," he said, and quietly left my room. There was no physical punishment, no slap on the butt that I knew I deserved, but I was devastated and felt awful that I had betrayed his trust in me. Later that day I walked out into the bright daylight and realized that Gerhardt and I had left behind two clearly marked tracks leading into the woods, almost as if I had been asking to get caught in a lie. My father would live in Communist Poland for another four years, and he would never again allow me to touch his gun. The year after the government confiscated my father's shotgun once and for all, he emigrated to America.

What a relief it was to arrive in America in the 1960s, where people could still own guns and shoot freely. It was very much like Poland before the war. Large portions of the country were completely rural, where kids grew up on farms, rode horses to school, and kept their guns inside the classroom on a wall-mounted gun rack. Before the assassination of President Kennedy, gun laws were very liberal. I bought my first handgun within a month of arriving in America, and kept it in the glove compartment of my Thunderbird, often tucking it in the back of my jeans whenever I had some business to take care of in an unsavory part of town. It was a .25-caliber Spanish Astra, a small, black semiautomatic pistol, and I thought it was beautiful and modern. It was a thrill for me to own something for which I would have been put away in jail for a long time in Communist Poland. All variety of arms had been like a forbidden fruit to me growing up, because I was one of the first men in my family who grew up without free and easy access to them. I jumped at the chance to start my own collection in America.

Once Sława arrived in America, I started investing more heavily in my firearm collection, and by the time we moved into our apartment, I had five different long guns hanging on a wall rack. Now that my personal life was more settled, I could focus a bit more on other extracurriculars I had always wanted to pursue. About a year after Sława arrived, I went on my first hunt in Chicago. A few hours' drive south of the city there were state forests that allowed pheasant hunting. Hunters would have to wait in front of the gates that blocked the entrance to the marshes in the forest preserve, and it was on a first-come, first-served basis because only about forty people were allowed in each day. I liked this system because it was completely unbiased—whoever showed up first got to hunt first. I remember thinking that if this were Poland, it would be a corrupt system where only those who had connections or paid off the guards were allowed to hunt, but in America everybody got a fair shot. We would form into groups of two and three guys, and they would designate an area that we could cover for the day.

Just like back in Poland, we would walk in a line, spaced about 150 feet apart. It just so happened that on my first day hunting in America, I was paired with some fellow hunters who I thought were stupid and, worst of all, greedy. The unspoken rule in hunting was that if I was the guy walking the right end of the line and a pheasant flew off to my right, he was mine to shoot. My partner was ignoring the rules and going for every bird he saw, regardless of which area it was in. It was frustrating, but I still managed to bring home two birds to Sława. I had grown up cleaning and gutting ducks for my dad when I was young, so I was familiar with all of the work even though I hadn't done it in years. When you grow up on a farm, these things never leave you.

I enjoyed the opportunity to explore other parts of America that were in my own backyard. During most of the next ten years, we would spend most of our family vacations taking road trips to sites that interested us, including many travels to the western states. We would pack up our car and our daughter, Krystyna, and set off in a direction, usually without much of a plan in mind. Most of the time we camped, and occasionally we would stay in a rented cabin. We truly enjoyed the beautiful scenery, history, and breathtaking vistas of the American West. We would often drive until we saw a beautiful place we wanted to stop, and there we would put up our tent and make camp with just some simple camping gear and a little gas stove. There weren't many tourists in those days, and we felt like we had the world to ourselves. America's highways were brand new and wide open, and all the beautiful scenery was open for anyone to explore. We watched many a golden and red sunset on a deserted road surrounded by high desert or dense forest, the likes of which I hadn't seen anywhere else in the world.

At a certain point, I realized my father had not been hunting in years, and I got excited at the prospect of taking him hunting somewhere in America. Henry was also a fellow hunting enthusiast, and he had some friends who owned a ranch in Wyoming. We decided the three of us would make the drive in November of 1975, to take Dad on a big-game hunt, the likes of which he hadn't done since before the war in Poland. Sadly, Casey couldn't come because he had two small children at home, and his job wouldn't allow him the time off. We stayed on our friends' gorgeous property in the foothills of the Rocky Mountains, and we could see the magnificent and iconic Devils Tower landmark in the distance. The view was spectacular.

In the early morning the three of us would walk across the property spread out in a line with several hundred yards between us as we stalked our game. In 1975 tourism in the American West was not as developed as it is today, and there were still many amazing artifacts of the frontier days to be found. As I was walking, I saw something strange that didn't fit into the environment, and I bent down and realized it was an Indian arrowhead made of flint. A few minutes later I found something even more peculiar—a perfectly shaped metal ring of some sort, jutting out from the hard, cracked earth. It looked like a pipe, and as I dug it out of the dirt a bit, I realized it was a rifle. This was not just any gun; this was a Winchester 1873 lever-action rifle—the gun that won the West! This rifle had been the most prominent weapon among American frontier settlers at the turn of the century, and here I found a perfectly preserved one in the middle of an empty field. What was more striking was that there was still live ammo in it—as if the person that it belonged to had died right there on the spot and this was all that remained of him. None of the parts moved, as it was about one hundred years old, but I polished and restored it and still have it in my collection to this day. It is one of my most prized mementos from that trip with my father.

At that time, Dad already had a bad heart, and the altitude was significant in the areas in which we were hunting. At one point we had to climb up a steep embankment as we were stalking the deer, and our father became alarmingly short of breath. He started turning blue in the face and had to sit down. It took a long time for him to recover. At that point, Henry's friend came with his pickup truck, and we put Dad in the truck because it was too strenuous for him to keep walking. He could still ride along with us, even though he couldn't stalk the deer on foot and could only shoot from a greater distance. We realized the end of his hunting days was near. Nonetheless, the hunt was very successful; all three of us bagged big whitetail bucks. For my father it was a great experience hunting for the first time in America. For years afterward he would often reminisce about this adventure.

This would be my first and last big hunting trip with my father as adults. If we had grown up in a normal, free Poland, we would have been participating in these kinds of activities together for years. I'm just glad that after so many years had interrupted this traditional father-son activity, I was able to take him on one last, memorable trip. The trip took about two weeks overall, with the drive from Chicago and back, and to this day is one of the favorite memories I have of my father.

After we came back, we knew our dad's hunting days were over. He wasn't able to do any local pheasant hunting with us, either, because it required walking long distances through swampy and difficult terrain. However, our house in Palatine proved to be a kind of rural paradise. I even persuaded my brother Casey to buy the property that was for sale right next door, and it was great that I could have one of my brothers in the neighborhood. Even though today Palatine is a busy, bustling suburb with over seventy thousand people, back then there were a few hundred at most. On the weekends, everybody was out shooting game birds, so much so that it almost sounded like a battlefield around our house, with the distant sounds of gunfire constantly going off. From our house, Dad could sit on the porch and shoot doves, and they would fall either on my property or on Casey's right next door. We had purchased a hunting dog for him a few years back, a half-beagle mutt named Dolly. Dad named her after Lady Rose's spotted Dalmatian hunting dog, Dolly Do. Our dad's Dolly was a smart and kind dog, and she was his faithful companion as he sat on the porch. She would run to retrieve any bird he shot, and bring it back right to his hands so my mom could prepare it for dinner.

In the wintertime my father would prune the branches on the trees and bushes he planted throughout our four-acre property. He would leave the branches on the ground around the base of the trees through the winter, specifically because they would attract animals like rabbits (because it was a favorite food of theirs). One day we even saw a bobcat on the other side of our fence, stalking the small game in our yard. When it was too cold, Dad would sit inside the house and shoot the rabbits from the kitchen window.

Dolly would fetch the rabbit Dad shot, and Mom would prepare some of the most delicious hunter's stews we ever had. One of my favorites was rabbit meat stuffed with apples and marinated pumpkin that turned golden after stewing for many hours. The food was amazing, and my father got such a sense of satisfaction from providing dinner for us.

One day I came home from work and could smell another delicious hunter's stew on the stove. My mother had a smirk on her face as I walked in, and she told me my father shot a rabbit that day. Then she walked me over to the window where he had been sitting, and showed me the perfectly round bullet hole that he had blasted through the window! Our house was equipped with double-paned windows to keep out the frigid Midwest winters, and while Dad had opened the main window, he had apparently forgotten to open the second storm-window pane as well. He shot the rabbit straight through the glass, and got it anyway. That bullet hole has been in the window for over thirty-five years, and is a precious reminder of how much he enjoyed the fun and adventure of hunting even during his twilight years.

Surprisingly, it was thanks to my father's habit of shooting game birds from the porch that I got my start in what would become one of the greatest passions of my life: taxidermy. One day I came home from my job at the clothing factory in Chicago, and my father came to me right away and said he had something to show me. He approached me with the sun at his back, holding something in his hands. I thought it was a dove, because I could only see the silhouette, but as he placed it in my hands, I realized it was a sparrow hawk—the smallest predator bird in North

America. It was a gorgeous, delicate bird—blue, brown, and reddish in coloring—and since it was not a game bird, we knew we weren't allowed to shoot it. It had been an innocent mistake by a senior citizen, and he felt bad about killing this lovely creature. We weren't sure what to do with it, but it was so beautiful we knew we wanted to preserve it somehow. For the time being, we put it in a plastic bag and put it in the freezer.

At the time, I had been dabbling in woodworking and wood sculptures on the side for extra money, and one of my clients was a local taxidermist. I had all the relevant tools because we were working on remodeling our house, and so this kind of work came naturally to me. I was making large ornate wooden panels for him to use in his mounts for his clients. I also became interested in jewelry and silversmith work at this time; I enjoyed working with my hands, and sculpting small objects out of precious metals was fun and rewarding work. Many of the wooden panels I made for the taxidermist would have silver inlays or accents on them. Occasionally a hunter would want a bear claw made into a pendant, and this was work I excelled at.

I watched with interest as the taxidermist went about his work, seeing how much skill and precision it took to bring the animals he worked with back to life. I knew, however, that I couldn't take this sparrow hawk to him for mounting, because it was an unauthorized kill. I resolved that I would try to mount it myself. My dad had brought with him from Poland a small pocket guidebook that was something like a hunter's almanac. It had a few pages with simple instructions on how to dress and mount a bird, along with recipes and other tips of interest to hunters. It was the kind of guidebook boy scouts might carry with them in the woods, and this was all the instruction I had to begin with. First, I practiced on a dove and a common starling, which there were dozens of in our area. Finally, I felt I was ready to try the sparrow hawk. In those days, taxidermists were a secretive bunch anyway. They protected their trade secrets for fear of competition, and even covered up their works in progress when they had visitors to their shops. Nonetheless, I had visited enough taxidermists' shops and absorbed the basics just from seeing the tools, supplies, and methods they employed.

With my hunter's almanac, artistic skills, and a bit of guess-work, I was able to mount the beautiful bird my father shot by mistake. It was challenging work. First I had to follow the diagrams to make the wire body to support the bird. After creating the basic structural part of the bird, it became quite a delicate balance to position it just right.

It was difficult working with such a small specimen. I was always good with my hands, but this was painstakingly precise work, and one of the biggest challenges I had ever undertaken. Once the bird skin has been prepared and persevered, it lies flat and dull, as if a car ran over it. It seemed it would be quite an accomplishment to make that little body look alive. I positioned the wires in the wings, head, tail, and feet, and each feather had to be placed just so to make it look as if he was still full of life. Another thing to be careful of was that after the bird fully dried over a period of a few weeks, the skin would shrink. You would have to be careful not to overfill it; otherwise, it would look very strange. Back in those days we used something called wood wool to stuff the animals (the technical term for it was "excelsior"). It was basically fine wood shavings. You would wrap the shavings with a bit of cotton twine and keep wrapping and adding the wood wool as you created the shape you needed. Essentially, it was like sculpting but with a dry material. You keep wrapping and squeezing and molding until you have the perfect shape you are looking for. It was a laborious process, but the end result was superb—light and firm, with just enough give in the wings and head to allow final positioning. Nowadays, people use prefabricated fiberglass or Styrofoam molds, and while it has simplified the process greatly, it has taken out a great amount of the artistry that was required in those early days.

I couldn't display our sparrow hawk for anyone, because it was a protected species, but that beautiful bird sparked in me a whole new passion. Taxidermy work was demanding—it required both great technical and artistic skill, as well as in-depth knowledge of anatomy, and I found myself enthralled in the process. I was just over thirty years old and I realized I had found my calling in life. The whole legacy of who I am today and what I have accomplished begins with the story of that little bird. After my father passed away, I donated it to a local high school, where it has been on display for the last thirty years.

CHAPTER 16

Becoming an Entrepreneur

I WAS STILL WORKING AT THE FACTORY DOWNTOWN, but nonetheless I hung a shingle out in front of my house that said "Taxidermist." Within a few days I had my first clients. The first one who stopped in brought me a fish! I had no idea how to mount the slick, gray carcass he brought in, but I took the job. I had never even used an airbrush, but I spent the next week taking a crash course in preserving and painting fish scales. I wasn't thrilled with the way it turned out, but luckily the customer thought it looked great and went away satisfied. A few days after that, a lady brought in five quails her husband had bagged and said that she wanted them mounted in a group—taking off. This was a big job for me, and I didn't let on that I had never done anything like it before. I had to recreate parts of their natural habitat and capture them in midflight. Luckily it was my years of art training and painting that helped me assemble a realistic scene for this woman. She was so thrilled with the job that she took my first masterpiece to a local magazine, and they took pictures of it and did a whole article on my studio. Of course, my name was mentioned in the article as a young local taxidermist doing great work, and this boosted my confidence and served as encouragement for me to continue in this line of work. After that, the clients started trickling in at a steady rate.

It was now late 1976 and I wanted to go on another hunting trip to Tennessee to hunt boar. I asked for a two-week leave of absence, without pay, and to my surprise my supervisors refused my request. I could not understand their logic, because we certainly weren't busy at work. Jimmy Carter had just been elected president, the country was experiencing a recession, and people were waiting in line to buy gasoline. I grumbled about it and thought I would have to skip the hunt. Imagine my surprise when just two weeks later they announced they would have to lay off 30 percent of the workforce! My first thought was, "Great! Now I can go on my boar hunt," but it turned out I was a little hasty. Because of my seniority, I was not one of the people who were laid off. I was annoyed because, in truth, I wanted the time off more than I wanted the job. I wasn't worried about making ends meet, because I always knew I would figure something out. One of my Italian coworkers, Nino, who was notified he would be laid off, was devastated by the news. He had just bought a house and had a wife and three small children to support. He wailed about his "bambinos" when he got his notice, and I felt bad for the guy. I went to my union representative and asked if they would lay me off instead of my friend, who truly needed the work. It was a win-win situation in my opinion; I got the time off and my friend kept his job.

What surprised me most, however, was that I was still getting paid, even while I was on layoff! This seemed to make no sense to me, and I could see that the others around me were trying to take advantage of this situation, mainly because they were lazy. In those days, unlike today, being on unemployment was rather uncommon and was considered a shameful situation. Back then, everything still had the flavor of the true America, where everyone had a chance, and if you worked hard you would find a job and advance your position in life. In those days, if you went on unemployment, you knew you weren't going to get anywhere; so, few people wanted to do that. In today's world many things have changed, and some people try to game the system instead of making something of themselves. I was not one of those people.

The very next day, I left with my brother Casey, our mutual friend Greg, and his brother. The four of us drove all night and arrived in the Smoky Mountains in the morning. It was my first time in this part of America, and it was truly beautiful. The rolling hills were filled with fall colors and everything shimmered with a touch of frost. There were magnificent oak trees full of acorns the size of small walnuts. The hunting lodge we were staying at was in a remote area, and we were planning on hunting wild boars, which could be a dangerous business, especially if you encountered a sow with young ones by her side. Those tusks could gore and kill a man easily. I was paired with Greg, who wasn't very experienced, and oddly enough spent most of his time up in a tree to protect himself from the boars. I didn't think he was going to have much luck stalking a boar from his position, and so I wandered around the areas rich with acorns, one of their favorite foods, hoping to spot one. That first day we didn't see anything, but it was nonetheless an invigorating day spent in the woods. We returned to the lodge happy and hungry, hoping for better luck the next day.

I was thrilled to set out again the next morning, despite the fact that the terrain was very dangerous. There were large caves covered with overgrown vines, and one could easily fall into them. The rolling hills also contained some steep canyons with similarly overgrown edges that gave the illusion of solid ground but on which it would be easy to lose your footing and have a nasty fall. This was also a habitat for poisonous coral and rattlesnakes, and in general, you had to really be careful where you stepped in those Smoky Mountains. When I think back on it, I realize most people might not enjoy tramping around for hours in this environment, but to me it was heaven, and I loved the thrill of the chase. Over the next few days my brother and I bagged our first wild boars, and it was a thrilling experience because of the challenging terrain, and the difficulty in stalking this animal. I felt each hunt left me more ecstatic than the last, and as soon as I got home, I wanted to start planning the next big hunting trip immediately.

At the time, I also had a burning ambition to start mounting my own trophies. I was doing more and more work for hunters who were bringing me increasingly complex and exotic animals, and I also wanted to be a part of their hunting tradition. By now I felt confident doing birds and small game, and with some help from my friends, I mounted the boar I brought back from Tennessee. Next I set my sights on something bigger, and in January 1977, a few months after the boar hunt, I went to South

Dakota to hunt bison. I gathered a small group of hunting friends, and together we drove an old van the several hundred miles from Chicago in the middle of a very harsh winter. The heating system in our van was broken, and a few hours into our trip we had icicles hanging over our head inside the van! Nonetheless, it was worth it. One of the friends who joined our group on this trip was my taxidermist colleague that I had been making wooden panels for. We kept seeing snowshoe rabbits dead on the side of the road, and my friend, who was something of a scavenger, couldn't help but try to use some of them in his profession. I hopped behind the wheel while he ran out and collected one from the side of the road. He was mounting a coyote for a customer and decided he could use a rabbit as a prey for the mount. He jumped back in and proceeded to skin the animal on his lap while I was driving.

After almost twelve hours we finally arrived in Pierre, South Dakota, in what felt like the middle of nowhere. We were visiting the huge property of one of my friend's clients, who happened to be a former lieutenant governor of South Dakota, Roy Houck. His property was so vast that he had to fly an airplane around when he wanted to inspect his nearly forty thousand acres. Mr. Houck was breeding American bison on his property, animals which in the previous few decades had come dangerously close to extinction. To a large degree, his efforts brought that species back from the brink, and they were now thriving in sufficient enough numbers to be taken off the endangered species list. On his property, he allowed a certain number of bison to be hunted each year, and the profits allowed him to fund and continue his conservation project.

Each of the three members of our little group got a bison during that visit. We drove back home with the icicles hanging over our heads, but I was proud to bring home some buffalo meat, the entire skin, the skull, and the horns. Best of all were the memories from what was the first truly big-game hunt in my life. I was hooked. Later I mounted the buffalo in his full size, the first I had ever done in such a manner. To this day it stands proudly in my trophy room where visitors can admire it, and kids can touch it and learn about this animal's rich history and how it sustained entire tribes of American Indians, who hunted and used every part of the animal for sustenance. Hunting always engendered a great amount of education both for the hunter, and also for the people who would share in the experience later on. I was proud to be a part of this tradition.

I was only sad that my father's health prevented him from coming with us, but he loved hearing all the details of our stories when we returned. Back at home my father was fascinated by the details of my hunt. I'm sure in his heart he wished he could have the opportunity to experience such an adventure. I was very happy that I got to spend more time at home with my parents, thanks to the layoff. I had plenty of side jobs to keep me busy, and it was good I was home because I frequently had to take my father to the doctor's office.

In truth, I had already long forgotten my job at the factory while I was on layoff. I had time to hunt, I was making many wooden panels and silver jewelry, and I was making increasingly more mounts for hunters in the area. I was surprised when in April of 1977 the factory called and told me I had my job back.

I was so busy during my months off that I hadn't given the job a second thought. We had started the first big addition to our house, adding two floors and a basement. I had salvaged an old spiral staircase with a gorgeous railing from a pump house downtown, and was busy polishing and installing it in our living room. A friend of mine ran the demolition company that was in charge of tearing down this massive building, which took up a full city block and had been used to pump water throughout the city since the 1800s. I asked if I could take a look around the building before they tore it down, to see if there was anything I could use in the addition to my house. This historic building was full of gorgeous marble and hand-carved details, but most of it would be too difficult to bring back to Palatine. However, I noticed a solid cast-iron staircase with ornate brass railings that was about three stories high. To me it was a beautiful piece of art, and I knew if I didn't save it, it would likely end up in the junkyard. I had to disassemble the staircase, which weighed about four tons altogether, and I carefully brought it piece by piece back to my house in Palatine. It was a huge project to install it—I had to adjust the placement of the floors I was adding, and I added a third story just so I could include the entire staircase in my home. Just as I was starting the addition, a customer came in to have a fish mounted and saw my staircase. He was an architect, and on the spot he offered me a huge sum for it—more than the whole addition itself would cost me. It was a tempting offer, but I declined. As with most things, this was a labor of love, and the money didn't matter.

I had my workshop out back and was happy that I got to do what I wanted to, and when I wanted to do it. The last thing I desired was to go back to work in the factory. Nonetheless, out of a sense of obligation, I went back to work the following Monday, and the place was no longer as I remembered it. Most of my friends were gone, except of course for Nino. I worked that first full day, but I didn't like it. Mainly, I didn't like the lack of privacy, and the way the union and the bosses were constantly keeping tabs on you. Things had changed from when I started sixteen years ago. I had just experienced six months of being self-employed, and I was making a pretty good living, so I wasn't sure what I was doing here. The next day, Tuesday, Nino and I took our lunch break together, and we went to get gyros and martinis at a local joint on the corner of Franklin and Wells Streets. We caught up over lunch about how much things had changed, and how bad the economy was. I felt underpaid compared to what I was making working for myself, and I was just fed up with the unions. I was still a little bitter about how the union had handled my request for a leave of absence, especially in light of the layoffs they must have known were coming at that point. I realized the union would always only do what was convenient for itself, and not necessarily for its members. They didn't care about me, and I didn't care about them; that much was clear.

"You know what, Nino," I said to my friend. "I'm not going back there."

"You're outta your freaking mind!" he told me. He looked at me like I was crazy, but I assured him that I was dead serious. I finished my martini, and instead of walking with him back to the

GEORGE R. SWIDERSKI

factory, I walked the three blocks to the train station and caught the next train back to Palatine. I had just quit the first and last job I would ever have in America, and it was a liberating experience. After six months of working one on one with hunters and getting paid for my services, I felt such a thrill and sense of self-determination that I knew there was no going back for me. I knew I would never be happy working for someone else again.

I decided to quit then and there. I officially opened my business, giving it the name Old World Taxidermy, and began to advertise and hope for the best. The economy was not doing so well, but of course it was a little easier knowing that Sława had a good job in the photography studio and could support us while I expanded my own business. She was completely supportive of my decision and saw that I was passionate about what I was doing.

Starting to hunt more frequently, and becoming a serious hunter, marked a major turning point in my life. All of a sudden my horizons opened tremendously, and the whole sport of hunting and mounting animals drastically changed my life for the better. All of a sudden I was meeting various types of people, from all walks of life. Many of them were very well-to-do, and from old, established American families. I relished in the experience of working one on one with clients. When you work for someone else, you are looked at differently compared to how people look at you when you are in business for yourself, and they are dealing with you as an equal. I was also in a different line of work than someone who was making cabinets, for instance. This wasn't a simple service business—it was very personal work, and I was developing real relationships with my clients. I was working with some of their most prized possessions, and capturing their most treasured moments. I would see them again and again, for many years—and this, of course, turned out to be one of the most rewarding parts of my career.

The best decision I ever made was to quit my job while my father was still alive. He only lived for another year and a half after that, passing away in August of 1978. Spending every one of his last days with him is one of the best things I have ever done in my life. He and my mother had been married almost sixty years, and it hurt me to see my mother suffering in the wake of his passing. I was, however, consoled a little bit knowing that she wasn't completely alone, and lived right next door to us and had her many grandchildren and her garden to keep her busy. I wish my father had been alive just a little bit longer to see the success of my business. In the next few years after his passing, I would build a successful business out of what had always been one of our greatest shared lifelong passions.

CHAPTER 17

Flourishing

B ECAUSE MY BROTHER CASEY BOUGHT THE PROPERTY next to mine, we now owned half the block. That year Sława's mother also came to live with us, and our daughter, Krystyna, was flourishing. She was now ten years old and attending a local grade school. She was a lovely, healthy girl, and I loved sharing my passion for the outdoors with her. Thanks to my mother, our garden was overflowing with flowers during the summertime, and we often entertained our friends and family in our beautiful outdoor setting.

I continued working on the addition to our house, mostly working by myself and occasionally hiring help for the bigger jobs. It took me a long time to complete it, most of 1978 in fact. Once it was finished though, we truly felt like we had a place to settle down, and we concentrated on decorating our nest. It was the first time we had ever owned a large home of our own, and we were now well on our way to living the American dream.

The summer after my father passed away, Sława's younger sister, Urszula, came to visit with her family for an extended stay. Sława and Urszula, only three years apart in age, were very close. Luckily, Urszula had been able to visit us twice already since we got married. Each time she visited America, she came away with a new business idea. During the six months she spent with us in 1974, she worked as a draftsman for an architecture firm (she was an architect by training), and had saved up a sum of money that would allow her to live like a rich woman back in Poland. With her savings, she bought an ice cream machine from Sweden, and set up a small shop at the zoo in Wrocław. In those days it was the only one of its kind—and she was a huge hit with the locals, who would form a line down the block for a taste of her ice cream. Urszula had an architecture degree from Wrocław Polytechnic, but of course, as was usually the case in the Communist system, she could only be successful in her job if she kowtowed to the Communist officials. Luckily, she was resourceful and found other ways to make a living for herself.

The second American-inspired business she opened, around 1975, was Wrocław's first pizzeria, which, like anything imported from the West, became a tremendous success. Urszula had also been taken with the American notion of breakfast cereals, which were very popular in America but had not yet made their way to Europe. She took it upon herself to start mixing bags of things like oats, seeds, and fruits and selling them at the local market as her own version of American breakfast cereal. Now she came to America for the first time with her husband, Wojtek, with the aim of vacationing with us, rather than working and making money. Sława's mother went to Poland for the summer, so she was available to watch their children, and it was a rare opportunity for Urszula and Wojtek to have a little honeymoon vacation. We decided to take them on one of our favorite pastimes—the great American road trip. Over the course of three weeks, at the height of summer in 1979, we drove them all the way to Wyoming to see the dramatic landscapes of Yellowstone National Park, one of our favorite places in the American West.

We were so thrilled to be able to spend an extended vacation with Urszula and Wojtek, especially because we would finally have a chance to show them how beautiful America really was. Our first stop out of Chicago was to visit the Badlands—an area filled fantastic natural phenomenon, such as sharply eroded pinnacles and canyons amidst large untouched grassland, the likes of which can only be found in America. The landscape there stretches for endless miles, and it was quite a sight to behold for our visitors.

After a few days of driving through South Dakota and Montana, we finally arrived in Wyoming, and rented a cabin inside Yellowstone National Park—one of the greatest natural wonders on earth. Our guests were mesmerized and overwhelmed by the beauty of the majestic Grand Teton Mountains, which frame the southern edge of the park. It reminded us of the Tatry Mountains, which run along Poland's southern border and are the second highest mountains in Europe after the Alps.

Interestingly enough, however, one of the things that fascinated them most on this trip was all the massive semitrucks parked at rest stops and behind motels. No such trucks existed in Poland, and Wojtek in particular was mesmerized by all the chrome and shining lights on these massive cabins. Throughout that three-week trip, whenever we stopped at a roadside motel or rest area, Wojtek would always walk up close to the trucks to get a better view. The trucks were gigantic, trimmed out with glittering lights and painted in bright colors. They were fascinating objects for Wojtek, who marveled at their luxury and comfort—as most of them even had sleeping cabins. We befriended a few drivers who let us see the inside of their cabins. Wojtek had an advanced degree in mechanical engineering from Wrocław Polytechnic, and seeing these giants of American industry, he was like a little kid again. I could completely relate to how he reacted, because I felt the same way the first time I came to America—everything was grand, colorful, and overwhelming, in contrast to the gray reality of Communist Poland.

After several days of hiking, exploring, taking pictures, and building campfires, we decided it was time to head out of the park and take some side roads to explore more of the American West. We were enjoying the sights on what were mostly deserted roads at that time, and we found ourselves on a dirt road, driving in some mountainous terrain somewhere in central Wyoming just as the sun was setting. We had been on this road for several hours, bumping and jostling along, and it was clear it was now getting much worse—it was barely discernible among the brush and boulders we were driving among. The road narrowed to such a point that it looked like little more than a walking trail with boulders lying across it every couple of yards. We were very frustrated by our situation, and were tired and lost. Wojtek, who was a big man, volunteered to walk in front of the headlights to roll the boulders to the side to make enough room for the car to pass. We couldn't go back the way we came, as there was no way to turn around. By then, it was pitch dark and it was obvious that we were driving in a canyon with high cliffs on either side. My reasoning was, if there is an entrance, there must be an exit—and we hoped for the best and pressed on. Eventually, the road condition improved and we found ourselves gliding up a gradual hill that opened up onto a large plateau. The sky was full of stars, but we could not see much of our surroundings, so we decided we should make camp there, to be safe. In my trunk, I had a tent, all the camping gear, and a cooler full of food and drinks.

We set up the tent in the headlights of my old car. It was difficult to pound the stakes into the rocky ground, but it was good enough for a one-night shelter. When we started to unpack, Urszula noticed a small glittering light, far in the distance, and became concerned. I told her not to worry. "You all just stay here, and I'll go check it out." I took my small flashlight and started walking through the rocky terrain. When I got closer to the light, I saw a small cluster of trees and two strange looking characters, a man and woman and several horses. They looked like vagabonds, dressed in dirty rags, and clearly had not showered in recent memory. They were obviously not tourists. The light was coming from a kerosene lantern hanging off a tree branch. I presumed that since I had walked up with a flashlight, I did not surprise them, but to make them feel that I was not intruding, I kept my distance, and greeted them by saying, "Howdy, how you all doing? I wonder if you can help me?" They gave a nod in my direction, so I continued.

I told them briefly about our miserable trip on the bumpy dirt road, and how we had been lost, with no sign of civilization for hours. I asked if they could just tell me where I was. Despite their strange appearance, they turned out to be totally harmless and were actually very nice people. They told me the road we were on was supposed to lead to a campground, but the project had been abandoned years before. They assured me that in the daylight I would have no trouble getting out of there. I thanked them for their help and headed back to my family.

When I got back to camp, everyone wanted to know what I had seen. For some reason, and I'm not sure why, my imagination took over and I started spinning a tale about the toothless, bizarrely dressed vagabonds I had just run into, who were probably horse thieves. I described their grizzled beards and hardened faces and the guns at their sides, and I admit I embellished the details just for fun, even though it was basically a true story. I could barely make out the expressions on Sława's and Urszula's faces in the dark, but I could tell they were terrified, and I secretly chuckled to myself. No doubt I enjoyed a little mischief every now and then, but before we went to bed I told them the truth that there was nothing to worry about.

We all were very tired and lay down for the night to get some sleep. It seemed that as soon as I closed my eyes, I felt someone shaking my arm. It was Urszula frantically trying to wake me up, whispering, "George, there are wolves around here!" I was instantly awake, and I could hear the sound of yapping young coyotes that seemed to be just a few yards away from where we were camped.

"Don't worry—go back to sleep," I told her. "There are no wolves in this area; those are just coyotes." Coyotes are much smaller and not as aggressive as wolves, so I wasn't worried about any of them trying to break into our tent. I immediately fell back into a deep sleep. In what seemed like the next moment, someone was shaking me awake by the knee. It was Urszula, urgently whispering, "George, there is someone trying to get inside the tent!" I listened for a moment and heard what sounded like scratching against the zippers of our tent.

"Go back to sleep. It's just the flap of the tent thrashing around in the wind," I assured her. "Besides, I have a hatchet in my bag, and I promise you are safe." I wasn't completely sure this was the case, but I knew my job was just to reassure the others. For the rest of the night I did keep a more alert ear for the sounds of the wild Wyoming night. I did hear some animals scratching at our coolers, trying to get the food that was inside them, but fortunately I was the only one awake to hear the eerie sounds.

In the morning, with the sunrise, we found ourselves among some of the most gorgeous scenery we had seen yet. We were surrounded by mountains, and just a few hundred yards away there was a beautiful, clear lake. We ate breakfast, went swimming, and even caught some fish with the pole I had in my car. It turned out that exploring the road less traveled really paid off for us, because even though it was at times a bumpy and scary ride, we all agreed that this little snapshot of the most beautiful, unspoiled wilderness was a once-in-a-lifetime experience.

The rest of the drive back to Chicago passed uneventfully, and Wojtek continued indulging in his fascination with American trucks at every rest area we pulled into. At the time, Wojtek and Urszula were running a ceramic tile business in Poland, but after they returned from the trip to Wyoming, they opened a trucking business in Poland, which they own and operate to this day, complete with over forty large semitrucks.

A few weeks after Urszula and Wojtek left for Poland, I started planning my next big hunting adventure—I wanted to repeat my bison hunting experience from two years before in South Dakota. This time I was one of the more experienced hunters among my group of hunting friends and clients, and I put a small group together. By then I had befriended a man named Russ Miller, who owned his own insurance company and had become something of a business mentor to me, teaching me about the various aspects of running my own business. As with many of my friendships, Russ started off as a client, and in return I became his hunting mentor.

Russ owned a large motor home that was the size of a big bus. This was very uncommon in those days—the interior was spacious, nicely furnished, and complete with every modern convenience. In the early months of 1980, we decided to go to South Dakota to hunt buffalo. Russ invited a few more friends, and we all set off in his luxurious motor home. I must admit this trip was much more enjoyable than the first one—it was warm inside and we did not have icicles hanging over our heads. We planned to hunt on the same property of Mr. Houck, but when we arrived, we learned that he had retired and now his son Jerry was running the operation. Luckily, Jerry ran things much as his father did and used the proceeds from hunting to maintain the conservation projects on the land.

Jerry told us they had a large herd of mature buffalo, and we were all excited to get some nice trophies. Russ insisted on hunting with a bow and arrow, which is much more challenging and requires that you be much closer to the animal. He was a very big man, over six feet, and weighed about three hundred pounds. They informed him that they didn't have a horse that would be able to carry him, but he was not discouraged and decided to go on foot. He tried for several hours with the bow, but on the open prairie there was no way he could get close enough to the animal. Finally, he decided to use my rifle and almost instantly got his buffalo, as did another member of our group at the same time. We took turns hunting, going one at a time, and alternating with another group of hunters, who were also there from Chicago and which included several policemen.

Finally, it was my turn to hunt. We left in the pickup truck, and after about an hour of driving we spotted a small herd in the distance. We left the truck, and proceeded to stalk the herd on foot. Jerry spotted a huge bull with massive horns, and I decided to take him. The challenge was to hit a one-inch target slightly behind the ear so that the bullet would sever the first vertebra connecting to the skull. This shot would cause an instant death. I had done it before, and the animal instantly crashed to the ground as if struck by lightning.

The rest of the guys stayed behind to give me my space, and I began to stalk the group of buffalo. There were only sporadic open patches of grass, as most of the ground was covered with snow, and the buffalos were on the move. I estimated my distance at about 150 yards and decided to take a shot at this giant. There were no trees or rocks for me to rest my rifle on, so I had to shoot it freehand. With nothing to stabilize my rifle on, this would be a tricky shot at this distance. Nonetheless, there were no other options, so I took it. The shot went off and the echo bounced over the rolling hills, and before the last sound faded, the buffalo was down on the ground. I took several deep breaths, and started to walk toward my trophy. When I got close, for a moment I was overwhelmed with mixed emotions. I had taken another life, but if it hadn't been me, it would have been some other hunter who did. Besides, Jerry had to harvest some of the animals; otherwise, they would starve—there wasn't enough food for all of them to survive. As I looked down at the massive body lying in the snow, I thought this seemed to be a more merciful death than a slow starvation.

After a short while, the others caught up to me and I asked one of the guys to take my picture with the trophy. I rested my foot on the back of the buffalo as he lay on the ground, holding the rifle in my left hand, and waited for Russ and Jerry to move aside so I could have my picture taken. They were just finishing up a small procedure that had to be done when an animal was shot. Jerry had to cut the cardiac artery to bleed out the meat, which was necessary because it made for a higher quality of meat. Each of us paid several thousand dollars for the license to kill one buffalo, and we were allowed to keep seventy pounds of meat from the animal to take home.

Russ had lifted the buffalo's head up by the horns so that Jerry could have better access to the throat. All of a sudden, in the blink of an eye, I saw Russ doing a backward flip in the air, Jerry lying flat on his back on the ground, and the buffalo standing on his four legs.

Before I got my senses together to put another round in the chamber, I was running for my life. Somehow, while running, I managed to load another bullet while the buffalo was right behind me. Instinctively, I made a sharp turn to the left, the buffalo slowed down, and I whirled around and took another shot precisely where I had been aiming for the first time, this time just a few feet away from him. The giant bull went down immediately. I hesitated for a moment in walking towards him, as it seemed this beast had supernatural strength, but I knew the shot was deadly. My first shot had apparently broken a vertebra in the neck, but had not severed the brain stem—it had just stunned him. I waited for the rest of the guys to recover their wits and approach the animal again. Then I saw a pickup truck driving through the prairie towards us. It was the other group of hunters from Chicago, and one of the guys shouted with excitement, "I have all this on the film!" They had seen the whole thing unfold from a distance and had rushed over after they saw the unbelievable rally the buffalo made. It was a memorable trip.

This was the second life-size buffalo I mounted in my shop, where the collection was now constantly growing. That year, in 1980, I officially incorporated my business under the name Old World Taxidermy. The studio by now was well established, and there were a number of articles written about my success and my work for the community.

My business was growing, and within two years I met more interesting people than I had met in the previous twenty years. My customers came from all different echelons of society, but they were all hunting and fishing enthusiasts with a great appreciation for the outdoors and nature. I began to do more advertising to continue to grow my business, and one of the best avenues for advertising at the time was the Chicago Hunting, Fishing, and Camping Show, today known more commonly as the Chicago Outdoor Sports Show. When I was getting started in the business, it was one of the largest outdoor sports shows in the country, and hundreds of thousands of visitors passed through the exhibits over the course of a week. I rented my first booth at the show in 1979, and I would make it an annual tradition for the next sixteen years. The key aspect of the show was that hunters and outdoor enthusiasts could get an up-close look at my work. It really wasn't that different from exhibiting paintings and sculptures—these were just pieces of art I had made with the skins of beautiful animals. Any serious hunter could tell the quality of my work by how realistic the animals seemed. I was probably one of the few people in the hunting world who had spent so many years studying at a higher institution dedicated to art, and now all of my artistic training was being put to good use in this fascinating and unique niche. I quickly gained a reputation as a skillful taxidermist, and within a short period of time found my clientele expanding throughout the US and Canada. By my second year exhibiting at the show, I already had several people working for me, and I trained them myself. Every mount that left my studio had to be of the absolute highest quality, and in the hunting world this kind of attention to detail was greatly appreciated.

It was in the early 1980s as well that the local high schools in Palatine approached me to ask if I would be willing to host local students on a type of field trip to my studio. I gladly obliged, and was happy to tell the students that I felt as though any man who can make a living from his hobby is a lucky man! It was during this time that I began to reflect on how far I had truly come in the last twenty years. I had arrived in Chicago in 1960 having just spent half of my six-dollar fortune on a small statue of the Eiffel Tower during my layover in Paris. I showed the students that little trinket during these visits, and I hope I inspired them a little bit with my story of hard work and big dreams. They were quite astonished to hear about how difficult life was in Poland in those years, compared to the luxury we lived in, in America. I told them about the shortages of food and basic supplies, and doing homework by the light of a kerosene lamp under my father's strict and watchful eye. I urged them to make use of the precious opportunities that living in this country afforded them. America had given me so much, even though twenty years ago when I arrived I barely spoke a word of English. I continued to use that Eiffel Tower in my talks to students for the next twenty years; it was certainly three dollars well spent, in retrospect. As my trophy and art collection expanded with the various travels we undertook, including numerous trips to Africa, I knew my studio made a more and more powerful impact on the young people, who were sometimes struggling to figure out what to do with their lives. I was a living example of how much America can provide you with, if only you put in the effort. Even with a basic American education, one could get so much further than the average person still trapped behind the Iron Curtain. After one of my speeches, a teacher pulled me aside and congratulated me by saying I had accomplished more in one hour than they could accomplish in six months of schooling.

I continued to participate in these inspirational and career orientation programs for local schools and organizations. Many of the students who came were from special education programs, for students that were troubled in some way. Even though many of them walked in with a chip on their shoulder and a good deal of skepticism, I could see that because of the huge mounted bison and birds and other exotic creatures, I started to at least pique their curiosity. I found myself connecting with students who normally would never have stepped foot into a studio like mine or talked to an immigrant like me. The studio became quite the attraction for many young kids, and in those years many of them would come by after school on their bikes and ask if they could sit and just watch me work. I obliged, but told them we had to make a fair trade and that they could sweep the floors in return. In those days, many kids had dreams of being trappers and hunters. Romantic notions about the American West still pervaded the culture. The *Daniel Boone* TV series was always on, and many kids were inspired by its tales of hunting and adventure. Today, sadly, that kind of lifestyle is not as popular, I think mainly because it is not politically correct to romanticize the American frontier days, or even hunting for that matter. But in the 1980s, the old notion of American exceptionalism was still in its heyday, and a business like mine was perfectly placed to thrive.

One of my favorite things to talk to kids about as well, especially in more recent years, was the positive impact hunters have on the places they hunt. The first question out of some kids' mouth was, "Why would anybody want to kill all these animals?" This was a question I enjoyed answering, because I believed hunters played an important role in the preservation of delicate ecosystems that would otherwise have difficulty sustaining themselves in the reality of today's world. In general, wherever there is sport hunting allowed, there is no poaching. Hunters play an important role in conservation of natural habitats of wild animals, and they are one of the few groups with the resources and financial ability to sustain habitats that would otherwise have fallen to development or some other worse end. Because hunting is tightly controlled, regulated, and rather expensive as hobbies go, hunters contribute enormously to the communities they frequent—both in revenue and in the dedication of local resources. For years I received letters from grateful teachers and students for opening their eyes to the fascinating world of hunting and taxidermy. Sharing my love of hunting and my respect for nature and animals was always one of the most rewarding aspects of my job.

CHAPTER 18

A *Wildlife Artist* in *His Prime*

INCREASINGLY OUR BIG FOCUS EACH YEAR BECAME THE Chicago sport show, because it generated so much business for me throughout the rest of the year. After my first small exhibit in 1979, it took me a few years to truly establish myself. In the early 1980s, the numbers attending these shows were reaching record highs—close to three hundred thousand people in one week would come through. The best part about my business was all the fascinating people I got to meet. The more interesting the trophy that was brought in, the more interesting the client usually was. People would bring me their tales of high adventure—often from vacations for which they had saved up for years to go on—and they would bring me their exotic trophies, which to them symbolized so many years and months of saving, planning, preparing, tracking, and so on. It was really an honor and a privilege to work with people in this capacity.

By 1982, my studio was well established; I had several full-time employees, and we were getting all kinds of work—big-game trophies, birds and fish, and, occasionally, we even mounted pets. The fishing on Lake Michigan was very good, so we had large numbers of fish brought in for mounting, and I truly became an expert in airbrushing. Once a fish is out of the water, it loses all its color very quickly. After the fish is mounted, the color has to be recreated, and my background in fine arts sculpture gave me a huge advantage in painting and mounting these types of delicate creatures. I took great pride in bringing these animals back to life, and I honed my skills over the years. I especially enjoyed painting saltwater fish when they occasionally came in, as they are dramatically more colorful than freshwater fresh. Despite the fact that just a few years before I had never mounted anything or even used an airbrush, I quickly developed a very good reputation for mounting all types of sea life. It was truly an art, working on this kind of three-dimensional canvas.

Increasingly my exhibits at the Chicago sport show drew large crowds. To set up the elaborate exhibits I had planned—complete with full-size buffalo, deer, pheasant habitats, and the like—was quite a big project. Also, in those early days my main emphasis was on fish, and I would bring an entire wall of mounted, colorful fish, which looked like so many paintings hanging on the wall. I was mounting several hundred fish a year at that time, so it was very big business for me. Preparing for the show was quite a project. We had a prefabricated booth with a built-in lighting system, glass display cabinets for smaller exhibits and jewelry, and a large variety of full-size mounted specimens. I spent several thousand dollars on the lighting system alone, because I knew how important this single factor was in presenting my artwork to potential clients. It took a large truck to transport all of this, and fortunately, I had many friends who were eager to help me. They were all hunters and fishermen and enjoyed visiting the show, because in exchange for their help, I provided them with free passes. At the end of the week, they would help me disassemble the booth, load everything back on the truck, and transport it all back to my studio. We would have pizza and beer, and share our favorite memories from that year's show. This quickly became one of the most important annual rituals in my and Sława's lives.

Each year preparations would start a couple of months in advance, working on new mounts to have on display. Some of them were of very large dimensions, and included dioramas of entire natural habitats. One year, I was exhibiting two bison being chased by wolves, and in the background I placed some other small mammals and birds that were indigenous to the area.

Among the group of friends that always came to help out, Roger and Kenny were the practical jokers. While they were loading the booth assembly into the truck, Kenny found a dead, dehydrated mouse on the floor. He simply could not miss the opportunity to utilize the mouse for a fantastic practical joke. There was a friend who also worked for me part time named Gary, and we called him "lover boy" because of his many girlfriends. Well, Gary wound up with that dead creature in his pocket. At the time, Gary's life was not very stable—he was between jobs, girlfriends, and homes. Needless to say he did not always live in very dignified places, and probably thought the mouse somehow got into his pocket and just died there, because while Roger had placed it there as a practical joke, Gary never made a comment about it, likely out of embarrassment.

A year later, Roger and Kenny made sure that when the day came to load the truck, they had another dead mouse ready for our friend. As we were setting up the display at the exhibition center, Gary reached into his pocket for something and pulled out the dried-out dead mouse. The memory quickly came back to him. "Son of a blip, I had one last year too," he exclaimed. Everybody erupted into laughter as if we were all in on the joke, and Gary immediately suspected everyone but had no idea who had done it. Roger and Kenny, who always operated as a team, kept up the prank, and each year one would find a way to distract Gary, and the other would get the dirty job done of putting it in his pocket. Since Gary's concentration was mainly focused on girls, he was easily distracted, and this continued for a long time. It took a number of years before he was certain that the ones guilty of this crime were Roger and Kenny. It got to the point that Gary would be checking his pockets every several minutes while we were loading up, but those two Houdinis always managed to complete their trick. Finally, after many years, Gary's attention became so sharp with determination to outwit them that during that year's preparations they couldn't get their opportunity to place the mouse into Gary's pocket. Gary thought he finally won, and the show ended that year without him getting a mouse in his pocket. Nonetheless, the guys managed to fool him once more. A few months later, winter was over, and he got into his car on a sunny summer day. As he pulled out to leave my house, the sun was blinding and he had to pull down the sun visor. Well, a dried-up mouse fell on his lap; it had been waiting for him since the January show! All of this was done in the spirit of fun and camaraderie. Everyone got a laugh out of the pranks, and we were just a bunch of grown-up guys behaving mischievously, playing childhood games to keep ourselves entertained.

Occasionally, I also enjoyed playing practical jokes on my friends. One day during the summer of 1983 I decided to clean out the garage that I had been using as storage related to my business. It was so loaded up with tools, supplies, and halfway finished projects that there was never enough space to keep the cars in it. The afternoon I began, my good friend Russ, always the reliable one, stopped over to help me straighten out the mess. He was moving things out of the garage and onto the driveway, where I was sorting everything out and deciding what to keep and what to throw out. All of a sudden he ran out of the garage, screaming, "I am getting outta this place! There are mice running all over!" He was clearly spooked by all the little vermin, which I thought was kind of funny considering what a big, burly guy Russ was. What I had learned about Russ by then was that despite his macho appearance, he was pretty much a chicken, although an endearing chicken that I always got a chuckle out of. It took me a while to calm him down, and I told him to wait for me there on the driveway. I ran into the house and got my Smith and Wesson .22-caliber revolver, loaded with snake shot rounds. These are special rounds that look like regular single-bullet revolver rounds, but actually, once fired, they explode in a spray of smaller pellets, which makes them ideal for hunting smaller prey. They are formulated specifically for small, rodent-type problems, and can be used indoors because they won't do significant damage to the walls of a house. I did not tell Russ what kind of ammunition I had loaded, and he probably would not have known the difference anyway. There is no obvious sign as to whether it is a single bullet or some other type of round fired out of a gun, unless you know what to look for.

I instructed Russ to take a long stick and move some of the stuff lying on the shelf where he had seen the mice. He hesitated for a moment and then poked some boxes. Instantly several mice jumped out. I fired two shots, one after another, and two mice were lying dead on the floor.

I looked at Russ, and he just stood there speechless with his mouth open. "Holy shit," he exclaimed. "You are a better shot than those guys I used to watch in western movies." I chuckled a bit and kept my secret to myself. Russ was neither an experienced hunter nor a shooter, and he didn't know that such ammunition existed. Snake shot rounds are very forgiving, and if you aim in the general direction of the rodent at close range, you're likely to succeed. Not wanting to spoil his experience, I didn't elaborate on that subject. Russ went on to explain himself by saying that a long time ago, when he was a small boy, he was walking towards a pond through a field overgrown with tall weeds, to do some fishing. Suddenly a mouse ran up his leg inside his pants, and he had to strip off his clothes to get rid of it! Since that time he had had a terrible phobia of mice. I told him I believed his story and forgave his fright at the small creatures.

One of the most interesting creatures I had on display in those early years was the infamous North American rattlesnake. I caught it myself in Wyoming, killing it with a club when I accidentally stumbled across its path while out hunting and made it angry. I had mounted it curled up in a striking pose, with the mouth wide open and droplets of resin made to look like venom dripping from the fangs. It was fine for people to touch and pet the larger specimens, but I specifically posted a sign next to the snake saying "Please do not touch." A small boy, about ten years old, stopped by my exhibit by himself, and became truly fascinated by the snake mount. He kept staring at it, mesmerized by the unique diamond-shaped pattern along its body. He looked at me and asked, "Please, can I touch the snake?" I considered carefully and saw how badly he wanted to touch it and said, "Sure you can touch the snake, but only the body. Under no circumstances can you touch the fangs." I figured that while the animal had been cleaned and preserved and there was no danger from the venom, fangs should nonetheless be handled with care, as I didn't want my resin droplets to break off. Just then a few new people walked in and I became busy talking with them. Out of the corner of my eye I saw the boy touching the droplets of venom I had recreated. I rushed over and pulled him away from the snake and was visibly distressed when I told him, "You just touched one of the world's most deadly venoms! You better run to the bathroom and wash it off!" I didn't really believe that he had endangered himself, because I had cleaned the animal thoroughly, but I wanted to teach him a lesson for disobeying my explicit instructions. He turned around and ran as fast as he possibly could toward the washroom.

After about half an hour had passed, I saw him walking down the aisle with his father. The father stopped in my booth and asked me some questions about mounting a fish for him. The boy meanwhile pretended to be very interested in another display, and he never acknowledged me. I figured I had done my job by teaching him to treat these animals with respect. He was probably too afraid to admit to his father what just happened. I had clearly made an impression.

Another big hit with the kids was the enormous grizzly bear I dressed up in a Chicago Bears uniform. I put a helmet on his head, painted the Chicago Bears logo on, and tucked a football under his arm. The 1980s were the heyday of the Chicago Bears, and fans were lined up down the aisle to take pictures with the Chicago bear. At one point Sława bought out all the Polaroid film at every camera shop in the entire area, and for several days we literally couldn't find any more film because of how popular those pictures were.

Later that same week my good friend Russ was working with me at my booth. It was the middle of the week and was a slow day with minimal crowds. We noticed in the distance a very tall, skinny, strange-looking man, with quite an unusual look to him, walking towards us. He was deathly pale and had very strong, sharp features that gave him an angular face. He was carrying a large bag of different brochures he had likely collected at the show, and was walking down the aisle in our direction. He stopped at my booth, and like many people who walked in, all his attention was focused on the mounted rattlesnake. A few minutes passed by while he observed it from different angles. He put down his shopping bag and in a deep baritone voice said, "There is nothing in the world that I love more than snakes." He spoke very slowly with a voice that sounded like rumbling thunder, pronouncing every word precisely. He proceeded to tell us about his collection of some of the world's most poisonous snakes, which he kept in aquariums in his basement. It was a strange encounter for sure, but you never knew who you were going to meet at one of these shows. I learned that you can never tell by the way someone looks what kinds of passions and interests they might have.

The following year, Russ jabbed me with his elbow one afternoon at the show and said, "George, the snake man is coming." The same tall and skinny man who had professed his undying love for snakes the previous year approached our counter and asked eagerly, "Do you have any snakes this year?"

"Sorry," I replied, "we sold the one we had last year, and I don't have any more." He was visibly disappointed, and I got the impression he came to the show mainly to visit the exhibits that had snakes. Every year this strange character who could speak of nothing else but snakes would visit our booth, and I always got a kick out of how happy he was when I did have a snake to show him. He never bought anything, but I always looked forward to his regular visits for years to come. One year, he just stopped showing up and we never heard from him again. We missed his quirky presence, and Russ said to me at the end of one show, "You know, George—I miss the snake guy." I told him that I agreed.

Another regular that we enjoyed visiting with each year was a character straight out of a history book. He looked like he belonged in President Teddy Roosevelt's African expedition from the turn of the century. He was dressed to perfection as a great hunter in an African safari outfit, including full khaki suit and sun hat. He even had rifle shells in the left side of his jacket, and every detail on his outfit looked historically authentic—only the rifle and binoculars were missing. He conducted himself very formally and always showed up in the exact same outfit. I'm not sure whether he had ever been to Africa, but he certainly looked the part. The Chicago sport show never failed to attract a wide array of aficionados and the occasional fanatics, and it was always one of the most entertaining weeks of the year.

Needless to say, my friend Russ was a bit of a strange character himself in his own way. Russ wasn't a hunter, but he was an avid fisherman and spent any spare time he had at my shop. He just loved hanging out, shooting the breeze, and watching me work. He was particularly passionate about bodybuilding and was as strong as an ox. He had massive biceps and an enormous chest, but was not too tall. Nonetheless, he was somewhat of an imposing figure. Russ and I had been good friends almost from the moment we met, and his loyalty and willingness to help in any situation was exceptional. The participation in the shows to promote my business and my services was not only hard work, but also very entertaining, and of course that was part of the reason my friends never hesitated to help me out. Above all, I always enjoyed meeting different people with whom I shared a passion for nature, the sport of hunting, fishing, and traveling in general. It was a great privilege for me to participate in this community, and it was an opportunity to get new clients. It was a great pleasure and a source of satisfaction to associate with people who appreciated my taxidermy work, my labor of love.

The one thorn in my side during those years exhibiting at the show was the unions who tried to meddle in our affairs. One year they came in and tried to stop my friends and me from setting up our booth, saying we needed to use certified union men for assembly and disassembly. They said I needed a union-certified electrician to plug in my lights, because it was dangerous for us to do it ourselves. I had seen this song and dance before, and I wasn't buying it. This wasn't about safety but about lining their own pockets through intimidation. I got up in the union boss's face, and told him if he or any of his guys touched one hair on my bear's head, or anything else in my booth, they might as well buy it, and it costs tens of thousands of dollars. This was a free country, and I said only my experienced employees were allowed to handle my goods, and absolutely no one else. He tried arguing with me, and I practically had to chase him out of my booth with a two-by-four because I was so angry and fed up with their charades. I wasn't going to give in to these goons and their intimidation tactics—I had been through much worse in Communist Poland.

The Chicago sport show was always in January, and my birth-day was on the thirtieth of that month. On the last day of the show, after we packed up to head home, many of my friends and fellow exhibitors would come to my booth and we would enjoy some beers and celebrate the week as everyone was wrapping up. One year after the show closed for the day and I said goodbye to all my friends, we drove home and I saw something curious in my brother Casey's driveway next door. I said to Sława, "I wonder why Casey is having so many people over at his house?" There were a few dozen cars parked in front, which seemed very unusual. She just smiled and replied, "Oh, you know how he is; he just likes to party." We pulled into our driveway, I opened the door, we walked in, and I turned on the lights. I could not believe my eyes—the house was full of people, including many of my friends I had just said goodbye to at the show. Sława had conspired to throw a party for my birthday and had invited all my friends. It was the first time in over twenty years of marriage that she had managed to keep an absolute secret from me! It was truly a wonderful surprise, and we partied with our friends until the early morning hours. To this day the hunting show and the memories surrounding it are some of my most treasured moments.

Those first several years of taxidermy work were incredibly rewarding and fulfilling, just in terms of the craft itself. Each project was a custom job and presented unique problems. There were so many aspects of the business that I had to learn about. It took some time to develop my expertise in the tanning process, which all animal skins must go through to preserve them before mounting. This process usually involves soaking the skins in chemical compounds for hours or days, which then alters the composition of the skin and prevents it from decomposing, by turning it into leather. I did not end up doing this process myself, but I nonetheless had to become an expert at it so I could outsource to the right types of businesses who would treat the skin with utmost care. When a skin arrived at my shop, it was usually dirty, greasy, and dried stiff. I had to ensure the right kind of tanning process was done to make the skin beautiful, pliable, and well preserved enough for me to work with.

Birds, meanwhile, are only preserved in a type of pickling solution, to maintain the beautiful natural texture and pliability of the feathers. This means that a bird skin, when it dries, does not have the kind of pliability that a tanned animal skin would have, making it very delicate work. I would use a mixture of wood wool, cotton twine, and cotton balls to preserve the properties of a bird's joints. There were also various tips and tricks I learned over the years to ensure that no bacteria would develop in a specimen, which can easily happen if you are not careful. Over many years I honed and perfected my skills by working with these various types of raw material.

Today, when I reflect back on my career as a taxidermist, I feel truly blessed that God gave me a talent and an opportunity to earn a living from it. I was able to support my family, and in forty years since I began my work as a wildlife artist, I have never had to work for anybody else. As the saying goes, if you make a living doing what you love, you will not have to work a day in your life. In many ways, I feel that is exactly true of the career I have had.

It is a feeling unlike any other to finish a full day of work, and to know that when you wake up the next morning, there is enough work waiting to keep you busy for the next day, the next week, and sometimes even the rest of the year. It gives you a sense of success and security, especially when customers are finding you, instead of you having to look for them.

After nearly forty years as a wildlife artist I can honestly say I was never once bored, for there is rarely a dull moment in my line of work. I relished the opportunities to solve difficult cases that required all of my professional skills and expertise to work out. Solving these predicaments, fixing cases that seemed lost beyond hope and turning them into something beautiful, was a great source of satisfaction for me.

A large part of my job was truly understanding the wildlife and its behavior, which meant I also had to have a deep famil- iarity with different habitats. I pored over books and technical materials to make sure that every specimen that left my office was completely realistic and reflected the true beauty of the nature that God created. It is enormously important that a wildlife artist be intimately familiar with the anatomy of animals, and be familiar with their behavior to capture a lifelike appearance. To truly perfect this art required years of study as well as real-world experience. Only after becoming close to and studying animals in their natural habitats in the wild was it possible to faithfully replicate their movements. In addition, I had to become an expert with extensive knowledge of flora and what naturally occurs in different habitats, including in aquatic scenery, which also often included geological structures. To be truly faithful to the natural universe, every detail must be accurate down to the tiniest blade of grass and pebble included in a work of art.

Every hunter and fisherman who visited my shop with a trophy for mounting wanted to first and foremost preserve the memories of his adventure. For me it is always a pleasure to see a beaming client walk in and eagerly tell me their stories. I loved listening to the people I worked with, as each story was special and unique. When the client would come back to pick up the finished mount, it was deeply fulfilling to see how much they appreciated my work. I observed the excitement reflected in their faces as they remembered the hunt or the fishing escapade. Regardless of the age of a client, I could always see a childlike glint in their eyes in those moments and I knew I had made their day. To be able to make a living from this kind of work, honoring the give and take between man and nature, is one of the greatest blessings of my life.

CHAPTER 19

Poland During
the Cold War

I N 1986, THE SOLIDARITY MOVEMENT WAS IN FULL
swing, and we were all watching the developments in Poland
with great interest. Sława and I hadn't been to Poland together
since we had first met twenty-two years before. That summer, we
decided it would be a good idea for us to go visit our family again.
One of the other main reasons we wanted to go was because
Henry had not been to Poland since he was forcibly drafted into
the German army in 1943. He and his wife, Margaret, decided it
might be time to visit their old homeland again. Margaret had not
been to Poland since she was deported to a German labor camp
when she was just a very small child at the start of the war.

As we were planning our trip, one of the great disasters of
that era occurred—the Chernobyl nuclear plant exploded, and
we knew the nuclear fallout would affect some parts of southeast
Poland. We weren't sure what was going to happen, but since our
trip was planned for the fall and by that time it seemed the area
of Poland we would be visiting was safe, we went ahead with our

plans. We wanted mainly to go to Lubocheń to visit our sister Henrietta and see our hometown again. In those days it was very hard to keep in touch with people overseas—phone calls were prohibitively expensive and connections were very bad. I had lost touch with my aunt who lived in Gdańsk, my mother's sister, whom Sława and I had stayed with in the summer of 1964. Her children were by now fully grown, but no one in our family had a phone number or address for them, so I had no way to get in touch with them. We also knew that my cousin Casimir, who had been instrumental in helping me get my car fixed in the ship-yards all those years ago, had passed away just before Solidarity got its footing.

Nonetheless, we stopped in Gdańsk for a day just to take in the sights of this historic town. We were walking down one of the main drags, called Długa, or Long Street, enjoying the art galleries and jewelry shops that it was famous for. In one particular shop we were admiring some beautiful amber pieces—the kind that Poland is most famous for. The cities in northern Poland in particular were famous for the artisans that worked with these precious materials. I took a closer look at a necklace I was admiring, and was completely shocked when I saw the artist's name on the tag: Lech Małkowski. This was my cousin's son! I knew his name, although he had been a small boy last time I saw him; there was no doubt in my mind that this was my family member. I knew some years ago he had enrolled in the Gdańsk Art Academy, and in some of the last letters we had exchanged with his mother years ago, she told us of his great painting talent.

I asked the shop owner if he knew Mr. Małkowski, and of course he did. I explained the situation and said I was his uncle. The shop owner took sympathy with my cause and gave me Mr. Małkowski's address. I couldn't believe our good fortune that out of all the shops in Gdańsk, we found one where my family's artwork was on display. We went to Mr. Małkowski's house, and through him I was able to find my cousin and my aunt. It was a joyful reunion and everybody was very happy to see us. We visited with them the rest of the night and got caught up on everything that had happened in the twenty-two years since we had last been there.

On this trip, we had a Betamax video camera with us. It was one of those huge pieces of equipment that needed to be carried on your shoulder—it looked like what today would be a professional movie film camera. We had one because we were passionate about photography, of course, and wanted to document everything around us. I think because of that equipment and the fact that we were Westerners, we were very conspicuously followed by a small military jeep wherever we went. This jeep would always be about a half block behind us as we drove around the city.

Solidarity was happening at the time, and we arrived just shortly after the Communist police forces, known informally as the "Zomo," had attacked some of the workers who were striking in the shipyards. Our relatives told us stories about how the government brought in police from different cities so that they wouldn't know any of the locals and wouldn't be soft on them. Several people died when they were run over by the Soviet-issued tanks. We knew tension was high, and it was no joke to mess around with the authorities. Nonetheless, our only true purpose in having the camera was to film our family and friends and to preserve our memories from the trip, which is exactly what we did. After only three weeks of being followed around gray Communist Poland, we were excited to head back home to America.

CHAPTER 20

The Arctic

JANUARY 1989 WOULD BE OUR EIGHTH YEAR EXHIBITING at the Chicago sport show, and by now we were a staple of the community there. Most of my friends in the industry also exhibited at the show, and so each year was the equivalent of a big family reunion. When things got a bit quieter at my booth, I would leave Sława to watch over things, and I would go walk the floor and visit with all the friends I'd made over the years.

Upon returning to my booth one afternoon I found my good friend Dr. Don Kettelkamp, his wife, Clemmy, and Sława engaged in a conversation. It looked as though I might be interrupting something serious as I walked up, but they all turned to me with big grins, and I could tell that Sława had some sort of surprise that was just ready to burst out of her. "You are going on a musk ox hunt in two months!" she exclaimed triumphantly. I didn't know what was going on, so I turned to my friend and said, "Don, what is this all about?" It turned out that Don, a serious hunter, had a musk ox hunt booked with a Canadian outfitter, but an important conference had come up and he was unable to go on the hunt after all. Don was the director of the American Orthopedic Surgeons Association, and he was suddenly required to be in New Zealand at that time for a conference that most English-speaking countries participated in. There was no way he would make it back in time, and he had already paid the substantial sum of $2,000 as a nonrefundable deposit (the equivalent of almost $3,800 today). He had been telling Sława how unfortunate it was that he was not going to be able to go on the hunt, and Sława told him he shouldn't cancel it—that instead he should transfer it to me and I would go in his place. Of course, Sława didn't have to twist my arm to go on such an adventure. The only thing I wasn't sure of was whether she had forgotten that we had a family trip planned to Hawaii at the end of March. Sława was always so encouraging and supportive of my hobbies and interests, and she assured me that we would find a way to make it work.

Musk ox are one of the most exotic and expensive animals you can hunt in North America. For many years they had been on the endangered species list, but now the herds in the Arctic had recovered and the area was being opened up to hunters and the dollars they brought. One can imagine there is precious little tourism in the far northern reaches of Canada above the Arctic Circle, so the locals there were eager to invite hunters into their community. Up until then the largest animal I had hunted was bison, and that was in a relatively tame environment on a South Dakota farm. Going to the Arctic to hunt an exotic animal like the musk ox would be unlike any other experience I had had. I knew it would be an enormous challenge, and that I had to be prepared for temperatures that were regularly at minus forty degrees. I had never considered that I could afford such a trip, or even had the slightest thought about planning one—it had seemed so far beyond the scope of my imagination, but thanks to my friend and the timing of his conference, I was able to capture this opportunity. I had always been confined to continental hunting, and thought that people who booked big trips with outfitters to hunt exotic animals in faraway locations were just way out of my league. Here Don generously told me if I just reimbursed him the $1,000 for the deposit and paid the balance of what was due, the trip was mine. Before I knew it I was off on the adventure of a lifetime.

In early March, as we were packing for the family trip to Hawaii, I was simultaneously packing for my Arctic hunt. We re-arranged our itinerary so that I would return to Chicago just long enough to change suitcases, and be off again for the Arctic in less than twenty-four hours. Canada North Outfitters, the company organizing the trip, sent me a long list of items I would need for the hunt. One of the most important aspects was that I would need to winterize any mechanical equipment I had, most importantly my rifles and cameras. I had to completely clean the gun from any oil and grease, and to do this I had to wash it thoroughly in gasoline.

In the Arctic the air is very dry—there is actually less precipitation there than in the Sahara desert—and I would encounter sustained temperatures from thirty to forty degrees below zero. The information the company sent me certainly was trying to prepare me for the worst, but I wasn't too worried about it. I was forty-six years old, was in good shape, and had a strong constitution that was also very resistant to the cold. The harsh conditions alone would have kept some people away, but I knew this would be the trip of a lifetime.

On March 27, 1989, less than twenty-four hours after we returned from Hawaii, Sława dropped me off at O'Hare airport once again. I had packed four large suitcases, one of which was a gun case for the one rifle I traveled with, which was very reliable. Then I had two big duffel bags with clothes, and one photo equipment bag. In those days there were no high-tech materials like Gore-Tex, so instead I had packed things like silk underwear and socks, which do not retain moisture either. I had everything in duplicate, including cameras, batteries, and my rifles. I had a 35mm Canon QL Pellix single-lens reflex camera that operated by wind-up mechanism and required no battery, so I knew that would work well in those conditions. I was also bringing my 16mm Bolex Swiss-made professional video camera, which cost as much as a Chevy Impala in those days. Its main advantage was that it didn't need a battery, which would have been useless in those subzero temperatures, and instead could be manually wound up with a crank to provide enough power to shoot short clips of video. I knew the Bolex would work in those conditions as well, and I was determined to document this trip.

The itinerary before me was insane—I would end up taking five different airplanes. I flew through Minneapolis, Edmonton, and Yellowknife (the capital of the Northwest Territories), and then Coppermine, a small village where I caught my first glimpse of the Arctic Ocean. From there I flew to Cambridge on Victoria

Island, the final stop before we flew into the wilderness to reach our tents. We were higher than the northernmost point on Alaska, the town of Barrow—and I had never been to such a location.

Almost forty-eight hours after I left home, I finally arrived at my second-to-last stop for the night, and I was starving. I had gone from the eighty-five-degree heat of Hawaii to the forty-below-freezing temps of the Arctic in less than three days, and I have no doubt this intensified my period of adjustment to the subzero temperatures. It was brutally cold, and the wind cut your skin when you walked outside. Cambridge would be the home base for our hunt, and it was here that a representative from the outfitter met me, along with the three other hunters signed up for the trip. This was unlike anything I had ever done before—none of my friends were with me, and we were clearly doing a high-caliber level of hunting. These were serious people who invested serious money in their pursuit of hunting.

The first stop was the local Inuit co-op, a kind of general store only for locals. Next door to it was a smokehouse where they served us smoked sockeye salmon, bread, and coffee. I shouldn't say they "served" us, because in this environment, no such luxury existed. You could help yourself from the slabs of smoked fish resting on the ice. I was starving after two days of eating crackers on a plane, and I think I ate half of a sixteen-pound fish all by myself. After that we checked in to a small motel to catch some rest for the night.

The next morning one more plane trip awaited us—our crew of four hunters and the guide from the outfitting company boarded a twin-engine Beaver aircraft, the workhorse of the Arctic. We flew another four hours to arrive at a place right on the shore of the Arctic Ocean called Bay Chimo, an area rich with musk ox. Local Inuit guides had already set up our camp here and were waiting for us, and I managed to capture a few shots from the air. Everything was white ice in every direction—it looked like the most pristine no-man's-land I had ever seen. We landed just a few hundred yards from our tents, and four Inuit guides and a cook greeted us at the plane with snowmobiles ready to transport us to our tents. I later learned that it took these Inuits almost a week to travel by snowmobile from their village to our hunting area. They were truly hardy people who could survive in these conditions. They informed us that minus forty degrees was a bit of a heat wave for them—that this was "not so bad," compared to how things can get. For me, coming from Hawaii, this was a difference of almost 125 degrees!

I was fascinated as I watched the Inuits finish building our camp. They were using a carpenter's handsaw to cut blocks out of the snowdrifts in shapes and sizes very similar to big cinderblocks. The snow was light, but at the same time very dense. They were just finishing constructing the outhouse, which was a hole in the snow with three waist-high walls around it for protection from the Arctic wind. I noted there was no fourth wall, and no bench to sit on, but this was a luxury they put together for us hunters. Later on, it turned out it was a nightmare to use these "facilities"—squatting with all those layers of clothing, including the caribou-skin pants on top that the Inuits gave us. Nonetheless, I can confirm that throughout the week, nobody crapped in their pants. I would know, because five of us shared one tent. The five of us consisted of a chiropractor from Ontario named Peter; two husky guys named Randy and Larry from Washington State; the guide from Canada North Expeditions, named Jack Donning; and me—originally from Poland and presently living in Palatine, Illinois. Jack was in charge of coordinating all the logistics for everybody. Each hunter had his own Inuit guide, sled, and snowmobile. My guide, Philip Kadlun, appeared to be a very likable person, and we hit it off from the start.

The next morning the cook prepared breakfast for us from dried potatoes, powdered scrambled eggs (which tasted awful), bread, and Jell-O. I was now starting to get really excited; I knew we were going to see the musk ox soon, and I had never before seen one in the wild. In fact, I had never seen one alive! They are generally only found north of the Arctic Circle. Immediately after breakfast we took off on the hunt—I was amazed to see that our guides were able to start the snowmobile engines in these temperatures without any problems. I'm not sure what kind of magic they used, but in no time we were off on the hunt. Each snowmobile pulled a sled that was approximately sixteen feet long and built entirely out of wood, and was held together with either leathery straps or caribou sinews (which are even stronger) instead of nails to ensure the most flexibility of the joints of the sled. This ensured that as we sped over the frozen ground, the sled would not break apart if we hit a chunk of ice or rock. As we sped through the barren land, only thirty feet of rope separated my sled from my Inuit guide's speeding snowmobile in front of me. The first day of travel on the sled was a nightmare. With all the bumps and snowdrifts, there were sudden drops of three to four feet. After several hours of travel in a seated position on this sled with no support behind me, I began to feel a pain in my back. It was torture for my spine and tailbone. That first day we spotted an Arctic bird called a ptarmigan, a member of the grouse family that is indigenous to the Arctic, but we did not see any musk ox. Nonetheless, the ptarmigan were an interesting sight, as they are known for the fact that during the short Arctic spring and summer they grow brown plumage that then turns completely white for the winter. We returned to camp cold and tired after almost half the day spent on the search. We ate some food and had one cup of hot tea before crawling into our sleeping bags for the night.

The tent the five of us shared had a tarp on the floor, and the snow underneath it began to pack up in odd shapes from all of us moving around. This would cause the surface to become very uneven, and of course it was dangerously slippery. Whenever one of us would stand up to get something from his duffel bag, he would usually slip and fall on another man who was trying to sleep.

In the morning, after a breakfast of more dried scrambled eggs, bread, and Jell-O, we took off to hunt. After the previous day's painful sledding experience (which had undoubtedly aggravated the slipped disc I had had surgery on a few years prior), I decided to improve my traveling accommodations. I loaded my duffel bags and other gear onto the sled. I was now able to ride in a semi-kneeling position, like a cowboy riding a bull. I used a rope to tie the whole pile in place, and then I hung on to the rope segments as if they were reins. Just as the day before, four sleds took off—two teams of two, in case a snowmobile broke down or there was an accident. If a team was caught alone in such a situation in that unforgiving terrain, it would likely end in death. I rode with my Inuit guide, Philip, and we were paired with Peter and his guide (also named Jack). While traveling over the frozen land, we kept a distance of several hundred yards between us, but we always kept visual contact with the other team. Occasionally, we stopped to talk and deliberate our hunting strategy. There were no natural land markers—only white, barren land, whipped by the wind as far as you could see in every direction—and one could easily get the impression that he was just traveling in circles. At times it seemed the horizon melted together with the sky, and it created a flat wall of white in the distance. Beneath us the ground alternated between slick ice and patchy snow, but none of it was easy going. The only natural features we could sometimes make out were rocks and boulders covered with Arctic lichen, a type of moss that grew here and was a favorite food of musk ox. Every few hours we would stop to break some ice, melt it on our mini propane stoves, and drink some warm tea while we stretched our legs and surveyed the featureless horizon.

We were well into our second day and still there were no signs of musk ox. The Inuits must have sensed something different was coming in our direction, and they had us continue a little farther until we reached a large snow embankment that we could sit against and make ourselves comfortable. No sooner had we gotten some ice in our little stoves to make tea than a thick fog suddenly descended on us. In an instant, we found ourselves in the middle of a whiteout the likes of which I have never experienced before or since. I could hardly see the men sitting just a few feet to my left and right, and yet I was completely entranced by this remarkable experience. Anyone who travels to the Arctic has been fairly warned of the extreme dangers of whiteout—countless travelers and explorers have lost their lives in these conditions, which can sometimes last for days. This particular phenomenon only occurs in the Arctic when particles of water in the air freeze, and it creates conditions that are many times worse than the typical thick Pacific fog. Normally this would be the height of fear and anxiety for a traveler in these parts, and yet oddly I felt a feeling of extreme serenity come over me. All of a sudden there was absolute silence and I heard not even a rustle of wind from any direction. All of my senses should have been completely disoriented, and yet I felt completely safe in the company of my experienced local hunters, who just leaned back against the snow and calmly closed their eyes. I felt like I was suspended in the clouds, serenely floating through the heavens. There was no horizon, no sky, and no ground. It was as though I was inside a bubble, and even my voice sounded different—all sounds were muffled as if everything was being absorbed by big cotton balls. A feeling came over me that if I were a child, I would have believed that this was the place where Santa Claus lived, and I smiled at my good fortune to be having the experience I was having. Meanwhile, I could tell my chiropractor friend was not handling it as well as I was, but I was too busy enjoying a feeling of otherworldly tranquility. This was especially interesting since whiteouts are usually one of the most frightening and dangerous conditions you can encounter in the Arctic. Every one of us had heard stories of hunters who died less than fifteen feet from their tent, and who couldn't find the door that was right in front of them in the whiteout conditions.

While we waited in these conditions, the Inuits told us hunting stories that had been passed down for generations in their families. I was curious about one unusual feature I had seen a handful of times as we had been speeding across the land. Every other hour or so, we would come across a rock formation that was clearly man-made. They were piles of rocks that looked like they were carefully arranged to hold their shape and height, and they looked like they had been there for a very long time. I was fascinated by these piles since I knew we were hundreds of miles from any place that humans inhabited. Philip explained that these were markers placed there by their ancestors and were used as orientation points. They varied in height and the number of rocks, and all Inuits had them memorized from generation to generation so they could always find their way home. There was no GPS in those days, and a compass would not have worked very well either so close to the North Pole. After a few hours the whiteout cleared up and we continued on our way.

After the beautiful and yet somewhat unsettling experience of the whiteout, we all decided to travel back to camp. We felt relieved to be on our way back. After riding for what seemed like several hours, our two guides stopped, got off their snowmobiles, and walked towards each other. Peter and I waited on our sleds, and watched with a twinge of unease as they stood there and pointed in different directions. I was actually preoccupied with watching the most beautiful, dancing aurora borealis, which had just appeared in a mesmerizing sky full of stars. I stared at the gorgeous colors dancing back and forth, and eventually I noticed out of the corner of my eye that the guides appeared to be arguing with each other in their Eskimo language, which didn't sound like anything I had ever heard before. It had a characteristic clicking sound to it, which there is no equivalent to in European languages. The sound came from snapping the tongue against the roof of the mouth, and didn't even sound like language to me. I was convinced we were lost, but Peter and I felt it prudent to stay on our sleds and remain silent. I had grown up in the vast black forests of northern Poland, and had been lost many times and yet had always found my way. I didn't think we had anything to worry about. After all, these hunters had their piles of stone markers built by their ancestors, and a sky full of stars they knew how to read. I figured at worst we'd be a few hours delayed getting back to camp.

At this point it was quite difficult for me to look around because a big block of ice had built up on my long beard and frozen up together with my parka. I could not turn my head and was confined to looking straight ahead, hoping I would soon see our camp in my sights. Finally, after several more hours of traveling, I could suddenly make out two small dark spots on the horizon. They were our tents! In a few minutes we were pulling into camp and were informed it was ten o'clock in the evening. If we had been even a couple hundred yards off in either direction, we would have likely missed the tents, and continued with a very unpleasant experience for several more hours. I had not seen any piles of stones since the whiteout, and yet we pulled directly into camp as if we were pulling into a driveway at home. I was extremely impressed by the Inuit's sense of direction, and I gained a tremendous respect for our guides.

It was a jubilant arrival as everyone ran out to greet us. My partner, Peter, was visibly shaken up by the time we pulled into camp. It was understandable because he had been raised in a city and had likely never been truly lost in the wilderness. By now, our friends had been getting ready to take off with the two other snowmobiles to look for us. Inside the tent my beard finally thawed and I was able to take off my heavy parka. Everyone had a lot of questions about what had happened to us, as we were the only ones caught in a whiteout and had been nearly lost. It seemed like the two other hunters were almost envious of our otherworldly experience in the whiteout, and they peppered us with questions. Before we turned in for the night, I asked Philip what he and the guide had been arguing about. "We were reading the stars," he said, not arguing, and I felt satisfied with that answer.

After defrosting and a little rest, I decided to put my heavy parka on and head outside to smoke my tobacco pipe. I wanted to take another look at the spectacular aurora borealis. It seemed as though I could never get enough, and I don't know how long I stood there in the middle of the Arctic night just to get a view. It reminded me slightly of the rhythmic movement of a water ballet I had seen at a fancy casino in Las Vegas. There, hundreds of water jets shot streams into the sky, and the entire performance was lit with dozens of colored spotlights. The aurora borealis moved in a similar way to me, although it was on a much grander scale. It seemed to spread over the entire sky, glowing with millions of different colors. Every now and then I would see a meteor coming down. Some would burn up in the sky and others seemed to disappear beyond the horizon. It was a lucky thing for me that the Arctic wolves we had been hearing every night were silent tonight, for I was too preoccupied to have noticed them if they were there. They were attracted to the frozen fish the Inuits left lined up headfirst in the snow, tails up. They resembled a picket fence on a Wisconsin farm in the winter, and no doubt the scent attracted some predators, but lucky for me, I peacefully returned to my tent that night, danced over the slippery floor, found my sleeping bag, and zipped myself up to my chin with my woolen ski cap pulled low over my ears.

We were now on our third day of hunting and no one had yet spotted a musk ox. To make matters worse, my Hawaiian tan started to peel, and it was difficult to scratch my itching back under all those layers of clothes. I was eager to fulfill the purpose we had come here for. After breakfast Philip had the snowmobile warmed up and ready to go. I checked the bolt on my Weatherby .300 caliber to make sure it had not frozen up. At the camp, we always left our weapons and anything mechanical outside the tent. If you took them inside, they would attract moisture and then would freeze up instantly when taken back out into the frigid air. Despite all the exposure to the elements, my weapon was fine. I loaded my shells and we were on our way to look for the musk ox. We quickly put dozens of miles of barren ground between us and our camp. Only the ptarmigans, with their white plumage, were dodging out from under our snowmobiles. Once in a while, we would see small groups of caribou, and it seemed they did not pay any attention to us, as if they knew that we were after musk ox. In the late afternoon of that third day, just after we stopped for our afternoon tea and biscuits, Philip finally spotted a group of musk ox in the distance. Our spirits soared with this good news, and our hearts raced as we sped in their direction. Since my guide and I spotted the musk ox first, it would be my turn to hunt.

The group of musk ox was in a long valley about five hundred yards away. Philip concluded that the nine oxen were heading into the valley for protection from the frigid Arctic wind for the night. We decided to leave the snowmobiles behind and to flank them on foot. We ran for several hundred yards to find a suitable position to wait, presuming that they would follow the direction we had anticipated. This was difficult and slow going, considering the many layers of clothing we were wearing, along with the dense caribou-fur overalls. We got into position on the side of the valley and lay down. We lost sight of the oxen when we were on our stomachs, but we stayed down and hoped luck would keep them moving in the same direction. We waited patiently, and it seemed like forever. I had left my caribou-skin mittens on my sled, not anticipating that this was going to be such a long wait, and I began to feel the pain in my fingers from the cold. The run from the snowmobile in heavy clothes had left me drenched in sweat, and now I was hot for the first time in the Arctic. After close to twenty minutes of lying in the snow in minus-forty-degree weather, I began to feel as if I had just taken a shower of ice water. The only thing that overpowered this uncomfortable feeling was the adrenaline pumping in my blood. Even the peeling skin on my back stopped itching, and I was solely focused on the task at hand.

All of a sudden, the musk oxen appeared on the horizon, moving in our direction! Philip gauged that they were about three hundred yards away, and asked whether I thought I could take the one nearest to us. "No problem," I replied. "I will take the one on the left side." I took aim through my scope and realized in that moment that I did not have any feeling in my shooting finger. I could not feel the trigger, and I couldn't feel my finger squeezing it. I'm not sure how, but the shot managed to go off anyway. It felt as if I had squeezed it with my mind. There was a loud bang, and a large pile of fur dropped down to the frozen ground. We stood up, and Philip slapped me on my back so hard he almost gave me whiplash from all the excitement, and shouted, "*Good!*"

I walked up to the enormous musk ox lying in the snow, and I couldn't believe my eyes. There it was—the most unusual trophy I have ever seen, with massive, curved ivory-colored horns. The long hair on the sides of its body looked like drapes that wrapped around its frame. The rest of the herd was long gone beyond the horizon, and unfortunately, my partner, Peter, wouldn't get a chance to hunt that day. He and his guide pulled up alongside us, and we all just stood and admired the beautiful animal and took pictures. Both guides pulled out their knives and started to skin the animal. To my amazement, they were done in about fifteen minutes, which was incredibly fast for such a large animal, weighing probably over six hundred pounds. It was necessary to skin the animal as quickly as possible to take advantage of its body heat. Otherwise, your hands would freeze in this frigid cold. As a taxidermist, I was very impressed with their skill. I thanked Philip for doing such an excellent job as my guide, and especially for finding such a beautiful trophy. We bundled up the hide, quartered the carcass, packed it all on the sled, and took off back to the camp. By the time we reached our camp, it was dark and very late. Billions of shining stars were above us in the sky, and the aurora borealis was doing its performance for all to enjoy. When we got back, we saw that one of the hunters from the other team had also gotten a trophy that day, so there were now two musk ox in the camp.

The next day Peter and his guide were going out to hunt. Since my guide, Philip, had to go with them for backup and safety, I decided to join the group even though I could have just stayed back and relaxed at camp. It was a lucky day for Peter. He got his musk ox early in the afternoon, and I had the opportunity to witness his joy of bagging the great trophy. When we returned to the camp, it was still daylight. Later that evening, the fourth hunter in our group came back happy with his trophy, so now each of us had gotten our ox. We had to wait two more days for the twin-engine Beaver plane to pick us up. We had time to rest, take pictures, talk, and socialize. The four hunters and our guides truly enjoyed each other's company. We had become like a brotherhood by the end because of all the harsh conditions and intense emotions we had experienced together. It's hard to imagine, but those few days in one of the most desolate places on earth, hunting one of earth's most unusual animals, were some of the most enjoyable days I could remember.

I spent a lot of time with my guide, Philip, who appeared to be very interested in hearing my stories about the outside world. Having heard that I'd returned home from Hawaii barely a week ago, Philip was eager to hear all about that strange place. I told him about the tropical wonders, the different colors of sand beaches, the spectacular flowers, the green mountains, the ocean full of colorful fish, the exotic fruit, and the hot climate. He had never even been near such a place, and was fascinated by my details. "If you could have an opportunity to leave the cold Arctic," I asked him, "and live in this warm, colorful, exotic place, would you want to do it?" He paused for a moment. He looked around at the vast colorless horizon around us, gazing far off into the distance as if he was truly contemplating leaving this frigid place. Then all of a sudden he snapped back into place and with a serious expression on his face replied, "I would like to see it all. But to live there? No, I don't think so."

The last morning in our camp, we packed our gear and waited for the same twin-engine Beaver to arrive. All of a sudden, the plane appeared in the sky, circling above us, and I took the opportunity to take pictures. I tried to catch the plane as it was flying low above our tents, coming in to land. I was lucky enough to catch it in just the perfect spot, so that our entire camp, the horizon, and the plane were in view. To this day, over twenty-five years later, I still have an enlarged, twenty-by-thirty-inch copy of that picture hanging in my office. It takes me right back to the memories of this grand adventure and the journey there and back to this no-man's-land above the Arctic Circle.

The plane made a few circles above us and gracefully landed on the frozen Bay Chimo ground. We loaded our gear and trophies, boarded, and took off. Everyone was jubilant and anxious to get back to civilization. As the plane took off and circled around to gain altitude, I watched our four guides waving goodbye to us down below. I watched through the windows until they became small dots on the vast horizon. For some time I felt sad to leave Philip, with whom I had developed a great camaraderie, and who above all was instrumental in helping create this unforgettable adventure. I knew this hunt had been a turning point in my life, and from now on the small-time hunting in my backyard would take second place in my mind because I now set my ambitions much higher.

The three-hour flight to Cambridge on Victoria Island was very exciting. The view of the frozen ocean below was truly spectacular. There were glaciers that had cracks in the ice that looked like they stretched for miles, and that from the sky appeared as canyons with no bottom. We stayed in the one small hotel in Cambridge, and to this day I can remember what it felt like to walk into that warm room after a week with no heat, and feel the softness of the carpet under my feet. I was so glad I didn't have to worry about keeping my balance on a slippery, uneven ice floor. All I had to do was take a hot shower and crawl into my bed, and that was exactly what I did.

Before I could fall asleep, I heard the howling of wolves nearby. I thought I was dreaming, and then I realized what it was. In Cambridge, every other household had a team of sled dogs to help them get around, and apparently it was time for their evening concert. The neighborhood dogs communicated with each other through their evening howling. One group started to howl at one side of the town, and when finished, the other group would respond, and then another. The sounds were coming from all directions. Finally, I fell asleep to the choir of howling dogs, which seemed to last a long time. The next morning, it was time for the long journey home: from Coppermine to Yellowknife and on to Edmonton, where I stayed overnight before my flight to Minneapolis and finally O'Hare airport in Chicago.

In Chicago, I went through customs and collected my bags, my musk ox skull with horns, the full musk ox hide, and a couple hundred pounds of meat. Sława was waiting anxiously for me at the arrivals area, and I was eager to tell her how grateful I was to her for arranging this adventure of a lifetime for me. I was so happy to be home with her. I recalled what Philip, my Inuit guide, had said in response to my question about moving to a place like Hawaii and leaving his frigid homeland behind. I felt the same way about coming home—I was glad I had experienced all of the serenity and adventure of that remarkable land, but the only place I wanted to be was home in the Midwest with my wife and daughter. I couldn't imagine living anywhere else. Shortly after I returned from the Arctic, I found a quote by Teddy Roosevelt that resonated with me strongly: "Far above the Arctic Circle, on the frozen tundra of Northwest Territories, lives one of the most unusual animals, and it offers one of the world's most unusual hunts. The musk ox—the buffalo of the tundra." That quote hangs in my office to this day, and the full mount of my musk ox still stands proudly in my trophy room.

My entire extended family in Chicago 1960

With my parents after arriving at
Midway airport at 4 a.m. 1960

Christmas with my parents 1964

Studying

Henry, his wife Margaret, and their daughter

My first car, a 1959 Ford Galaxy

My second car, my beloved
white 1960 Thunderbird

Polish military insignia I made in honor of Polish WWII
aviators at the Sherman House exhibition 1962

1966

Camping with boy scouts in Wisconsin 1962

The first picture Sława sent me 1962

The MS Batory

On the MS Batory enroute
to Poland 1964

The first picnic Sława and I had on the side of the road the day we met

Thunderbird stuck in the mud
in the Polish countryside

A horse pulls us out

A church in Drzycim, not
far from Lubocheń

On the veranda we rented for two weeks in Piławki 1964

Visiting a memorial to the
1410 battle of Grunwald

Skansen open air museum in western Poland

During our time in Piławki

Copernicus library in Toruń

800-year old Malbork castle we visited when leaving Piławki

The Wrocław town
hall exterior, 1986

Newlyweds

The "starlet" on her honeymoon in Zakopane

Getting married in the Wrocław town hall

Sława's paternal grandfather's family. Top row second from left is Sława's grandfather (Sława is the 5th generation)

Henryk Partum, Left, with his brother before the Bolshevik Revolution of 1917

Albin and Gabriela Szafranowski, Sława's maternal grandparents

Sława's maternal grandfather (second row, center) during the war between Russia and Japan 1904

Sława, her sister Urszula and their mother in Wrocław 1951

Sława as a baby with her mother

Sława's father Henryk Partum

Miroslawa Szafranowski, Sława's mother,
before she married Henryk Partum

Sława's maternal grandmother,
center, with her sisters

Sława's maternal grandmother at
the turn of the century

Chicago church wedding 1966

George and Krysia 1969

Krysia helping her dad at work

Krysia's second Christmas 1970

Our house in Palatine in 1972

George and Krysia

George's mother working in
the garden in Palatine

George's father working in the yard 1975

Sława and Krysia 1975

Krysia with a friend, both her
grandmothers, and Sława, 1976

My father and Krysia

George, Henry, Mom, Dad, Halina, Casey

My father and his three sons

Hunting with my father in Wyoming

Old World Taxidermy 1992

Taxidermy workshop in Palatine

First showroom at OWT   Bison hunt in South Dakota

Mounting elephant for a client

My parents circa 1971

Family reunion in Poland 1986

Special needs children sponsored
for medical treatment by the Polish
charity organization "Dar Serca"

Sława's sister Urszula and her husband
visiting Chicago July 1993

The lake we woke up to when we got
lost in the western wilderness

Children of Polish Consulate staff in
Chicago attending school in America
during their parents' tenure

My taxidermy display at the SCI convention in Las Vegas

Boy scouts touring the studio

Plane flying over our camp to pick us up

With my guides and my Musk Ox

Protective gear

My hunting sled

Some examples of my oil paintings and artwork

Self portrait with Sława

Lighthouse   Stormy Sea

The Universe   Profile   Flowers For My Mother

Chaos

The Ecstasy

Artist's Studio

The Monk

Praying Monk

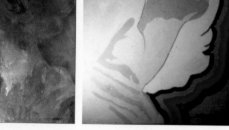

Sława

Jayne Mansfield

"Marlena" pencil drawing

Chicago Harbor   Fishing Village 1960s   Church in Bydgoszcz

Vietnam War   Lake Michicagn

Tophat   Lonesomeness   My Model

War Memories 1966   Still Life

George in the studio in the 1960s

Self portrait 1968

Etching of Sława

Mother and Child   Woman Resting   Bydgoszcz, Poland

My favorite model—Sława

PART III

Africa, Art, and the American Dream

CHAPTER 21

First Safari in the Land of Dreams

THE 1980S WERE AN EXCITING TIME FOR OUR FAMILY. My studio was growing, and I was gaining a good reputation as a taxidermist. Sława had an excellent job at a prestigious photography studio in downtown Chicago, managing an entire photography division for them. We felt like we had arrived—we were making a successful living doing things we loved, and we had plenty of time and resources to travel, have adventures, and spend time with our friends and loved ones. Little did we know that the 1990s would bring an even more exciting chapter to our lives, something I would have hardly believed if you had told me when I was starting my taxidermy business.

After I came back from the musk ox hunt, I regaled my friend Don with the stories of my adventure. It was thanks to him, of course, that this whole trip had even happened. Don first came to my studio as a client in the mid-1980s. He was one of the most avid and dedicated hunters I had ever known. He was an orthopedic surgeon, but he spent most of his free time traveling on faraway trips to hunt game I had never even seen before. While I had done a few exotic mounts in the past, he was one of my first clients and friends who kept bringing me some truly unusual trophies. At first I was even a bit intimidated because I had little experience mounting animals like impalas, baboons, Cape buffalo, and wildebeest. I wasn't familiar with their habitats and behavior, and felt I was a bit out of my element mounting species like these. I studied as much as I could from books, and trusted my instincts on the rest. Don, and a few other clients who went on exotic safaris, had utmost confidence in me and kept bringing me their unique mounts to work on.

After I came back from the musk ox hunt, Don saw how enthralled I was with it, and he started trying to talk Sława and me into accompanying him and his wife, Clemmy, on their next safari to Africa. When I thought of Africa, the first things that came to my mind were Lady Rose and her manor full of African trophies. It had always been in the back of my mind that her wealthy and illustrious family had traveled to Africa a hundred years ago to partake in adventures in a completely foreign world at that time. I still had pictures in my head of her hallways lined with exotic heads that I had never seen since. Yet for some reason, even now, I didn't truly believe that Africa was something that was within my grasp. It still seemed too exotic, too far, and undoubtedly too expensive. It had always been a luxury far beyond my reach, something which only well-to-do aristocratic families and rich surgeons could do.

One Saturday afternoon in the late spring of 1990, Don and his wife were sitting in our garden telling us about their planned trip to South Africa at the end of July. I listened with great excitement as Don talked about his preparations.

"George, why don't you just come with me?" Don said finally, as I peppered him with questions about how everything worked. I was taken aback slightly, because to be honest it had never occurred to me that I could actually go. Don quickly ran down the details and convinced me it would be affordable, if we planned properly. At a certain point I said to myself, why not? This certainly was within my reach. It wasn't cheap, that's for sure, but it was also the kind of sum that a middle-class family with two good jobs could save up for in a few months if they set their minds to it. Sława and I conferred, and despite additional financial obligations we were facing at that time, such as sending our daughter, Krystyna, to Ohio State University, we decided we would take the plunge and commit. The next week Don called his friend in South Africa and booked an additional safari for one hunter, as well as for one observer and photographer, Sława. We were going to Africa!

Once we realized we could go, we started the preparations in earnest with Don and Clemmy's help. We were over the moon with joy. We were at an age where we had resources and time on our hands, and yet were still full of energy and enthusiasm. It was absolutely the best time in our lives to take on a new adventure like this.

On August 1, 1990, we flew to Houston, Texas, to begin our journey. It feels like only yesterday that our friend Chester was driving us to the airport in Chicago. I was so excited I could hardly believe this trip was finally happening. From Houston we continued on through London, and then finally to Johannesburg, the largest city in South Africa. It was a long trip flying over the entire African continent, but our excitement pushed aside any feelings of discomfort. I couldn't wait for the sun to rise on my first African morning so I could at last visually experience the fact that I had actually arrived in the exotic land of my childhood dream. When we passed the equator, the sky above began to turn spectacular colors. It's possible there were some sandstorms over the Kalahari Desert, and the sand in the air created spectacular sunrises and sunsets.

I began to realize that I would soon be walking on some of the most ancient soil on this planet, the place where all human life had sprung from, and where the great abundance of nature first flared forth in this world. It was one of the most indescribably exciting moments. Finally, early in the morning two days after we had departed, we landed at our destination. Our guide, Adam Boshoff, met us at the terminal. Adam is what is known as a professional hunter, or "PH" for short. Westerners would consider him a guide, but in his country, he was part of an elite occupation. He was a typical South African guy, dressed in khaki shorts and a button-up khaki shirt, topped off with a baseball cap, and he walked with a laid-back, macho gait. We cleared our rifles and baggage through customs, and made our way to the expedition-equipped Land Rovers that were waiting to take us to our camp. I think Adam was a little taken aback seeing a woman carrying a rifle, because at the time it was still an uncommon sight, and he was doubly surprised when she got in the Land Rover behind the wheel. She thought that she was getting in the passenger side, but because they drove on the left side of the road in Africa, she ended up in the driver's seat. It was a moment of comedy seeing his hesitation, but Sława took it all in stride and just cracked a joke about how she didn't mind wearing the pants in a relationship, gave him a wink, and moved over to the passenger side. Sometimes I think that Sława, being a typical, liberated American woman, was too much for the South African guys, who probably still thought a woman's place was in the kitchen.

Adam was a young guy, a bachelor in his midthirties, and as we started driving, we were making small talk and he admitted to us that he had had a bit too much fun the night before and had a slight headache from the alcohol he had consumed.

"Oh here, take two of these," Sława said, handing Adam a bottle of Tylenol she had in her purse. He picked up the bottle curiously, raised an eyebrow, and tried to open the top. I think Sława purposely let him fumble for a moment, trying to force it open, before she reached for it again.

"Oh, I can help you with that," she said, taking the bottle out of his hands. "It's childproof," she said, looking right at him as she pressed and opened the top in a second, and somehow managed to keep a straight face. Adam laughed, and the ice broke—I think Sława's gentle ribbing had made him let his guard down, and we were on our way.

From the airport we headed due north, towards the vast Kalahari Desert, which was on the border with Botswana. It was a full day of driving to get there. The journey through South Africa via car was a great experience for both of us. The countryside was unlike anything I had seen before. Sława had her camera aimed outside the window the whole time, taking it all in.

"When we had to read *In Desert and Wilderness* growing up, I never in a million years imagined I would actually be in Africa," Sława told our group as she referred to the classic novel by Polish Nobel laureate Henryk Sienkiewicz. It was a book all Polish children read in school.

"I can't believe I'm seeing the same things Sienkiewicz described," Sława said, as she smiled and shook her head in wonder. I was amazed to see people wearing heavy, woolen coats, with caps on their heads, but Don explained that for them it was the middle of winter. It still did not make any sense to me, because the temperature was above eighty degrees Fahrenheit, but they seemed to be chilly. We crossed the Tropic of Capricorn and were getting close to our destination, and we finally arrived in the small town of Madibogo, where our hunting lodge was, and this would be our home base for the next three weeks. The place we were staying at here in the Kalahari Desert was simply gorgeous. Our camp was situated on a large, flat plateau, surrounded on three sides by tall green mountains. Our accommodations were round, white buildings made of earth and straw, with thatched roofs, and located not far from a generous watering hole. There were tall bougainvillea bushes that climbed the tall trees around our temporary homes. We were situated on privately owned property that was hundreds of thousands of acres, and the nearby African village and families that inhabited it were all part of this property, which was part of a private game reserve for hunters. We settled into our accommodations, and were greeted warmly by our hosts as we sat down to a delicious dinner and we talked about preparations for the next day.

I could barely get any sleep that night because I was so excited about the next day's hunt. First thing in the morning we sighted our rifles, which means that we practiced shooting at a target at a set distance to make sure our scope and sights were aiming accurately and ready for the hunt. That early in the morning I was amazed to see white frost on the ground in shady spots, which I never expected to see in Africa.

After making all the preparations, I finally set out for the hunt that afternoon, with Adam at my side as my PH. We had seen several beautiful oryx antelopes, which have black and white marking on their faces and long straight horns with sharp tips.

"That is a nice trophy," Adam whispered in my ear as we stalked quietly through the bush. "Take him." The shot went off from my .300-caliber Weatherby; the antelope ran for a short distance and fell to the ground in an area covered with thorny bushes and tall dry grasses. Sława had been waiting in the vehicle with the driver while Adam and I were stalking the antelope. When they heard the shot, they drove to join us. I was already by my trophy, admiring the beautiful horns. We took dozens of pictures, for this was a momentous occasion. I had just fulfilled a major lifelong dream of mine—I had successfully hunted a beautiful trophy on the very first day of my African safari. I felt like I was the happiest man under the sun. We loaded the animal on the truck, and drove back to our camp.

That evening the cook prepared supper for all of us, and we spent some time enjoying a few drinks around the bonfire and getting to know the other hunters staying at the lodge. Wally Zollman and his wife, Brenda, were both passionate hunters, and had been on many safaris. For Don's wife, Clemmy, this was also her first safari in Africa, although she had hunted deer in the US. Sława was the only nonhunter in our group. We were enjoying the evening, the drinks, and the fire, and Sława excused herself to her room for a short while. While she was away, Clemmy whispered in my ear that because Sława's birthday was in two days, on August 5th, she and the other ladies had decided to improvise a celebration for that occasion. They had conspired with the cook to have a surprise party for her and a birthday cake. I smiled and was happy that Sława would have an especially memorable time on her birthday.

The next morning, we all went hunting in different directions. Sława went with me and was taking a lot of pictures. I bagged a blesbok antelope, and I slowly began to feel as though I belonged there, in Africa. It was my kind of place. We returned early to camp after my second consecutive successful hunt, and Sława said she wanted to take a nap, as she was a little tired from all the activity. She said she would join us later by the bonfire. Brenda and Clemmy took advantage of her absence to get busy preparing the birthday cake for the next day's celebration. With limited provisions of some flour, jelly, and fruit, they created a very impressive concoction. That evening we again reconvened around the bonfire with the other guests at the lodge, enjoying gin and tonics, and sharing hunting stories. We took in a sunset that had some of the most gorgeous hues of red, orange, and pink—and then suddenly it was completely dark. At this low latitude there was virtually no dusk. Soon the bonfires of the villagers around us lit up, and we could hear their rhythmic chanting in the distance. It was at this moment that the owner of the property came to greet all his guests for the first time. He was a fine gentleman, a typical South African of Dutch descent. He was born and raised in South Africa, and had grown up working his family's farm. He spoke fluent Afrikaans and English. We offered him a drink and asked him to join us tomorrow evening for a small birthday celebration for Sława. Unfortunately, he said he wouldn't be able to since he had some business to attend to.

"I regret not being able to celebrate your birthday," he said, turning to Sława. "But please accept a present I have prepared for you." Sława sat up and gave the gentleman a surprised look. "Tomorrow, you will go to hunt the springbok antelope with a professional hunter," he explained. "And this is all on me, free of charge, as my birthday gift to you." Sława was speechless. She had never hunted before in her life. However, she was familiar with weapons and had been with me to the shooting range many times. She was a good shot and I knew she had it in her, even though she may have hesitated. She felt it would be impolite to decline such a generous birthday present. She gracefully accepted and no doubt was thinking to herself, "I will worry about the rest tomorrow." I had asked her a few times while we were back in the States whether she wanted to join me for a hunt, but she always declined and said she preferred taking pictures. In those days very few women hunted, and it was generally just me and a group of men chasing down our trophies.

Secretly I thought to myself that she must be very glad for the opportunity, and since the other two ladies were hunting, I was glad she wouldn't be left behind. I think I was more excited than she was! It was a new page in a new chapter of my life because my partner and wife would now be sharing my great passion, hunting. That night, we could hardly fall asleep, and Sława was stressed and worrying about how she would do on her first hunt. I assured her she would do fine and encouraged her to get some rest. While she drifted off into a fitful sleep, I lay awake staring at the ceiling and taking it all in. Africa was already in my blood—it was during this trip that I began to fully realize that Africa had been in my subconscious as long as I could remember, and now that I was here, all those thoughts and dreams from years past were bubbling to the surface. I had always thought of it as a land of warriors and beasts—a place where men went for great adventures and great accomplishments, and now I felt like I was joining their ranks. Sława and I were making a living as artists back in the US now, and we always gravitated towards the more colorful side of life. I lay in bed and took in all the sounds of the wild African night. I heard loud roaring that sounded uncomfortably close to our hut (we didn't find out until the next morning that it was bull ostriches, which we could have sworn were lions). I also heard loud herds running up and down the plateau around us, but as we discovered the next morning, it was just donkeys that were kept on the property that were responsible for the noise. I wished more than anything that my father could be there. I also thought of Rose Plehn's brothers—Friedrich, Rudolph, and Albert—and I tried to imagine what their experience in Africa would have been like one hundred years ago. The most prominent thought, however, was how lucky I was to live in America, and have the opportunity to experience the adventures I had dreamed about since I was a small child in Lubocheń. Within a few days, I knew this was the beginning of a new chapter in my life. I was already planning when I would return to the mysterious African continent, even though I had several more weeks to go.

After breakfast we decided on a final strategy for Sława's hunt that day. We would drive deep into the Kalahari Desert to where we thought we would find the springbok. The terrain did not look very inviting as we cruised along; there were some sand dunes but mostly there were thorn bushes and plants from the cacti family. It was rocky terrain and everything seemed covered in thorns. It would not be an easy hunt. The springbok congregate in herds, usually in areas that are wide open, providing no place for the hunter to hide and stalk quietly. In these conditions the animals would see any threat from far away and would run off. It would be quite a challenge to get close enough to take a shot before you would be discovered.

Surprisingly, the professional hunter did not have much experience in this terrain either. He had just recently graduated from a professional hunters' school, and we could tell he was trying hard not to show his concerns about guiding an inexperienced hunter under such difficult circumstances. The tracker working with us was a local Kalahari Bushman. His tribesmen call themselves the San people, and they live in one of the most inhospitable places on earth, surviving in a desert where water and food are very scarce.

I was fascinated listening to their language because it was full of clicks. It reminded me of the sounds of the Inuit language I had heard just the year before from my friends in the Arctic. They make the sound by pressing their tongue against the roof of the mouth, and each click has a different tone and meaning. I could hardly believe that even though the Arctic Inuits and Kalahari Bushmen lived worlds apart, their language and method of communicating strongly resembled each other. It was a sign for me of the interconnectedness of all humanity.

Sława was hunting with my .30-06-caliber Browning, which she was familiar with from the shooting range. For the first time, I stayed back in the vehicle, which was not easy for me to do. I would much rather have been with her to offer encouragement and support, but a group of four stalking through the wilderness would only make the hunt more difficult. The herds of springbok are always on the alert for any danger, as they are a favorite prey of lions. In open spaces like the one we were in, they could easily spot any danger. I watched from the vehicle and followed them with my binoculars, but soon I lost sight of them. Time passed incredibly slowly for me, and I waited hour after hour with no sign of them. I kept hoping to hear a shot, but the only sounds were distant calls from zebra stallions and some strange bird calls, and occasionally, I would see vultures circling in the sky.

I began to feel apprehensive about the whole thing. I realized this was a particularly difficult hunt for someone who had little experience. I sat and wished with all my heart that she would be successful, for I so much wanted her to have the experience I had had so many times. Despite my best efforts, I couldn't wait any longer and decided to start driving the vehicle in the direction that I believed they must be. I drove around for some time, circling behind acacia trees and outcroppings For some time I could not catch sight of them, and by now the sun was about to drop below the horizon, plunging us into darkness. I paused for a moment and took in the overwhelming beauty of the African sunset over the desert. In those peaceful moments in which I was caught up looking at the sky, I heard a distant rifle shot! I quickly started the engine and drove as fast as I could through the bushes in the direction I believed the shot came from. At the same time, I was hoping I would not hear another shot, which would mean the first shot had missed the target.

I plowed through the Kalahari bush searching for them when suddenly in the far distance I could see the two figures standing next to a white spot on the ground. I was quickly upon them, and could see the professional hunter and the tracker positioning a beautiful springbok for a picture. Sława was standing next to it, her arms full of scratches from the thorns and a big smile on her face. When she saw me she ran towards me, screaming, "I did it!"

It was a moment that I will never forget. I knew from then on I would have a hunting partner for the rest of my life. I was overjoyed for her. It was pitch dark by the time we got back to the camp. Everyone was eagerly awaiting news of how the hunt went. We cleaned up and joined the rest of the group around the campfire. The celebration that night was extra special because not only did we surprise Sława with a beautiful cake, but she was also riding high after completing her first successful hunt. That night, she was a celebrity and everybody was congratulating her.

I couldn't remember ever being more proud of her and happy for her than I was that night.

On one of the last days of hunting, we had an experience that was also unique for hunters on safari. One of our Bushmen trackers noticed a cloud of dust rising in the distance. When we got closer, we saw a pack of jackals attacking a baby eland antelope that was probably just several days old. The eland is from the antelope family, but an adult can weigh over 1,200 pounds. They are also known for their distinctive, tightly spiraled horns that grow from their skull in a V shape. As we got closer, the jackals abandoned the baby, but she was badly hurt. We gently picked her up, put her on the truck, and brought her to our camp. Despite her unfortunate encounter with jackals, this was the baby eland's lucky day. She would have two doctors and a nurse attending to her wounds. Our friend Don, the orthopedic surgeon, immediately got to work, as did fellow hunter Wally Zollman, who was a plastic surgeon, and his wife Brenda, who was a registered nurse. Considering the poor creature's injuries, it was a good thing she had an excellent medical team to take care of her. They performed surgery and stitched her back together. In just two days the baby eland was running around making friends with the domestic animals on the farm. She was well on the road to recovery when we set off for our next adventure, which was about a four-hour drive away in an area in the northernmost part of South Africa, known at that time as the Transvaal Province. It was split into smaller regions following the end of apartheid in 1994. This area was much more wooden and dense than the Kalahari bush we were just in, and presented an opportunity to hunt different types of game.

"My goal is to hunt a leopard," said Don to our host, Dion, who was an old friend of his and a professional hunter as well. "With a muzzleloader," he added, a comment at which Dion raised an eyebrow in his direction.

"That's a dangerous animal," said Dion slowly. "And that's a dangerous weapon. You have only one chance and you cannot afford to miss." Don knew the dangers of course, but he wanted a real challenge, because he had experienced almost everything else the hunting world had to offer him. There were six trackers available to our group, who worked with Dion to find the game, and none of them wanted to go with Don and his primitive weapon. They knew there was nothing more dangerous than a wounded leopard in the wild, and so in the end, they had to draw straws for who would accompany Dion and Don on the hunt.

The camp we stayed at was near a village where many local families live, and there was also a school for their children. Every evening when we sat by the bonfire, we enjoyed listening to the sounds of people singing and kids laughing. The people of the village had their own bonfires that we could see sparkling in the distance, and we would occasionally hear their baritone voices chanting and singing around the fire, and all this mingled with the occasional roars of lions, hyenas, and jackals. As our trip wound down, I took extra time each night to savor these incredible moments. I had been fascinated by Africa my entire life; read countless books about the place, starting when I was a boy; and watched movies filled with wonder. Now that I was finally here, I could hardly believe it. This safari was one of the most extraordinary experiences of my life; I was absolutely charmed by this

exotic land and the enchanting people and animals that inhabited it. Our friend Don didn't end up getting a leopard with his
muzzleloader, but the seed was already planted in my mind that I
would hunt a leopard one day. I felt like I was living a life beyond
my wildest dreams. Every night after the rest of the guests had
gone to bed, I would go outside and light up my pipe and let my
imagination take over. I knew that this experience was a turning
point in my life, and my visions for what the future would hold
started changing and growing with each passing minute.

CHAPTER 22

Africa in Our Blood

W HEN WE RETURNED FROM AFRICA, IT WAS ALL WE could think about. We developed the hundreds of pictures we had taken, and mounted the trophies we had shipped back from halfway around the world. In a certain sense, we were changed people—we had now been to Africa to hunt! It was all we could think and talk about for weeks. I felt I was in the prime of my life, and I had just experienced what to me had always been the "holy grail" for hunting enthusiasts. All I could think about at that time was when I would be able to return to Africa.

The early 1990s were an extremely interesting time because of all the changes that were happening when the Soviet Union collapsed and Communism came to a peaceful end. We were overjoyed at the news, and the emergence of a free and democratic Poland once again. This period brought a new level of prosperity to my business. As formerly inaccessible areas of the USSR became open to the West, hunters flocked to remote places like Tajikistan to hunt exotic animals such as Marco Polo sheep, and argali sheep. The tag, or permit, to shoot a Marco Polo sheep in Mongolia or Tajikistan could start anywhere between $20,000 and $30,000, and only went up from there. This was an enormous sum, especially in those days. My studio became very busy, as I was receiving work from hunts that had taken place in all kinds of remote corners of the world—Mongolia, Kyrgyzstan, Tajikistan, the Kamchatka Peninsula in the far northeast of Russia, and various places in Africa and North America. The studio was so busy that I had a one-year backlog of work, which was very uncommon in my profession. I was employing five people, and sometimes we worked seven days a week. I was also licensed by the US Fish and Wildlife Department and the State of Illinois Department of Natural Resources, and also by the US Department of Agriculture as what was known as an "inspector in field." Any incoming shipments of animal skins from foreign countries had to be soaked in a chemical compound to disinfect them before they could be cleared through customs. The local fish and wildlife department at the customs office would only release untreated skins to someone with this certification, and I received many calls from hunters at the airport desperate to get their skins released out of customs. My job was to make sure the proper procedures were being used and that the skins were safe for import into the US. I inspected shipments not only for my own studio, but also for various taxidermy studios around the country, as Chicago was a main port of entry through which many of these international shipments came. Hunters would not be permitted to travel throughout the rest of the country with the skin and horns until they were disinfected, and more often than not, hunters would leave them in my studio for the taxidermy work as well. Sometimes I would even have to travel to the airport twice a day, especially on weekends, to conduct the inspections and pick up goods destined for my shop.

A year and a half had passed since we returned from South Africa, and Sława and I were itching to go back. The business was flourishing and I knew my employees could manage in my absence, so Sława and I decided to take the plunge and book another safari. We had kept in touch with our friend Adam Boshoff, who had guided us as our PH during our first safari, and he informed us that he'd now struck out on his own and started his own outfitting business. We liked Adam a lot. He was young, smart, and good at his job, and we welcomed the opportunity to support his fledgling business and hunt with him again. He was employing two skinners and one tracker, and that was good enough for us. We told him we would be coming to visit that very spring, in April of 1992.

In the less than two years since we had returned from Africa, Sława had become an accomplished marksman, going to the range frequently for practice. I bought her a beautiful .30-06 Browning Gold Medallion rifle, trimmed in a gorgeous black walnut grain. On our upcoming trip to Africa, she planned on pursuing wild game with her trusty rifle, in addition to her usual photography pursuits. I would travel with my Weatherby .300, which was my favorite firearm and had been with me both in the Arctic and during the last African safari. I also had with me an additional rifle, which was a gift for Adam from a client of his in Michigan whom I was also friendly with. We had a much larger gun case with us on this trip than previously, and we were excited to get on our way.

Once again, our friend Chester drove us to the airport, and we felt like two little kids starting on a grand adventure. It is possible we were even more excited the second time compared to the first, because now we had some idea of what to expect and we knew how absolutely wonderful it would be. We had completely fallen in love with Africa. It felt like it was in our blood.

In Johannesburg, Adam was waiting for us at the terminal, and we quickly cleared customs and were on our way. We felt right at home. Our plan was to spend our first week sightseeing around Johannesburg, and then the following two weeks hunting in the northern part of the country, which was at that time still known as the Transvaal Province. The town we headed to was not far from Messina, which is one of the northernmost points of South Africa and borders Zimbabwe. We were excited to head to this side of Africa, because we had been much farther west before, in the sandy expanses of the Kalahari Desert. The scenery in this part of Africa was greener, and was notable for one particular feature we had never seen before: the baobab trees. Baobabs are a striking feature of the landscape because they are so enormous. The width of the trunk can reach sixty feet, while they only grow to about seventy-five feet in total height. Radiocarbon dating has confirmed that some of these trees are over two thousand years old. These massive trunks can store up to twenty-six thousand gallons of fresh water to endure the arid conditions of the region. People and animals look to these trees as a source of precious water in a drought.

These trees also have a spiritual meaning for African people. They are sometimes described as "upside down" because of the short branches that look like the roots of a tree. Legend has it that the baobab tree looks like it does because the devil yanked the tree out of the ground and shoved it back into the earth upside down, leaving the tree's roots sticking up in the air. Their grayish-brown bark is typically smooth, and its medicinal uses range from treating fever to preventing malaria. They are an imposing sight in these parts of Africa, and completely breathtaking when seen in person.

After a week of sightseeing, among both these natural wonders and some important historical sites in South Africa, it was time for us to leave for the hunting grounds. We waited for Adam to arrive in the morning. He was already a half hour late when the phone rang, and he was on the other end of the line explaining the problem on his hands. His partner had taken the Land Rover on a hunt the previous day and the engine had had a blowout. It turned out that he and his friend actually shared ownership of that Land Rover, and that there was no backup plan, as Adam did not own an expedition vehicle for safaris. I was a little surprised by this, and we were now facing a big dilemma. We had traveled thousands of miles and paid a deposit to go on a hunting safari. Now we had no way of getting there. I inquired about the possibility of renting a vehicle, but there were few such options, as the vehicle took quite a beating traveling through the bush in pursuit of game for several weeks, and the only people who would rent to a hunting party would charge an exorbitant rate. My next question was about the possibility of buying another vehicle, and before I finished asking how much it would cost, Adam came back with the answer—about $4,000. He said he had been late this morning because he was checking into exactly that option. He'd found a used Land Rover for a reasonable price, but he still didn't have enough money to buy it.

At this point my mood improved, and I told him I had a solution. I would pay up front for the safari, which was very unusual, and he could come to the hotel and get the cash right then and there. Then he would have enough money to buy the vehicle. He was overwhelmed and surprised by my offer. While we had bonded on our first trip, we still didn't know each other that well. He hurried over to the hotel, and I handed him a wad of cash. Some people might have thought it was a little crazy to just hand over all that money before any services had been rendered. He could have easily made off with it and we would have never seen him again. I always had a good instinct for who was trustworthy, and I knew Adam wouldn't do us wrong. In the meantime, Sława and I enjoyed a stroll in the gardens while we waited for Adam to return with the goods. Sure enough, about thirty minutes later he arrived in a good-looking white Land Rover with a custom roof rack that looked exactly liked it belonged in old safari movies from the 1960s. I was happy I was able to help him purchase his very first vehicle. We were ready to go, and everybody was happy with the arrangement.

In 1992, this region of Africa was in the middle of a drought that had already lasted six years. The owners of large hunting properties were glad to see hunters arriving to thin out the herds of animals, since food was scarce and the animals were starving. Selective hunting is healthy for maintaining balanced populations, and it also generates revenue for further maintenance and conservation of animal habitats. Over the past few decades, as hunting became a major industry in Africa, many species that were on the verge of extinction came back in large numbers and were now off the endangered species list. This is due in no small part to the role hunters play in these communities. For years now, land that had traditionally been used to raise livestock for meat was being turned into game preserves for hunters. In the 1950s, when the land was used only for ranching, there was almost no wild game there, but as soon as ranchers realized that the tag for a kudu antelope would bring them $1,000 versus the $200 they might receive in meat for a cow, they started converting their land into hunting preserves. In addition, legal, controlled hunting prevents poaching. The average foreign hunter spends thousands of dollars while on safari in Africa and employs many local people during his stay. When the hunt is over, he also leaves the meat behind for the natives and keeps only the horns and the skin. Traditional communities, for the most part, welcome and support foreign hunters because of the commerce they bring, and for that same reason they shun and condemn poachers, making it much less likely that a poacher could succeed in their regions. In some African countries where sport hunting is illegal, the animal populations are in decline because there are no resources available for preserving their habitats. To make matters worse, in economically weak areas, some people who live in poverty turn to poaching to feed their families because there are so few options for work. By comparison, in lands where selective hunting is allowed and encouraged, the herds of animals are flourishing and there is almost zero poaching. The local people are the best guardians of the wildlife, and in these areas they consider poachers criminals who are stealing their national resources.

As the son of a European forester, I had always considered the hunting culture to be one that cultivates a great appreciation for nature and camaraderie among fellow citizens to support that natural wonder. I saw this exact same principle at work among the African communities I visited, and it no doubt contributed to why I felt so at home here. To me, even though hunters selectively take the lives of some animals, we are part of the greater circle of life, which is in a delicate balance as part of the modern ecosystem in troubled places like Africa. A hunter studies his quarry and its habitat in immense detail. His job is to know every habit of the animal in its natural surrounding—where it finds food, water, shelter, and mates. He must understand the psychology of the animal, and in a sense put himself in the mindset of the animal he is stalking. A truly proficient hunter can see the world through the eyes of the animal. To me this was always the epitome of being close to nature. Only when you have spent so many countless hours studying animals in their natural habitats, and also learning and reading about them and their environment in all your spare time, can you begin to truly consider yourself a naturalist. By contributing to communities that helped preserve wildlife habitats, we always felt we were doing our part to honor nature's great abundance. Some people would rather not see animals die in any manner at all, but the truth is that this is not realistic. There is a saying in Africa that nothing dies of natural causes or old age. The weak and sick are always killed by some predator. Hunters never hunt females or young, and mainly go after old males. Also, hunting is a more humane way for an animal to die, and a true hunter never lets an animal suffer, because he aims to bring it down with one clean shot, whereas poachers often cruelly harvest an animal's precious horns while leaving the beast alive and mutilated. Many local communities would be desperate for work and a means of survival if it weren't for hunters. In many circumstances, the animals would not thrive, and the land would become barren under the strain of supporting herds that were allowed to multiply indefinitely. I had always known all of this intuitively. Even while hunting in Poland so many years ago, I felt as though the act of hunting brought me closer to nature than anything else. Now, in Africa, the same principle applied, and we felt we were doing our part to honor the nature that God had provided on this earth.

After driving for many hours in the Land Rover that Adam bought, we finally reached our destination. The camp was located in a beautiful, remote area by the Sand River. We unpacked our belongings and the provisions we had brought. We made ourselves comfortable under a large fever tree to relax and enjoy a cocktail. Adam's wife joined the party to help prepare the meals during our stay. Our trackers stayed in a nearby rondavel, a type of traditional circular African building with a thatched roof. It was an incredibly peaceful setting, especially with the occasional sounds of wildlife reaching us from the distance. Suddenly, we heard loud splashes of water, and my first thought was that there were crocodiles in the river. The sun had already set, so we grabbed a flashlight and carefully made our way to the shore to investigate. When we got close to the shore, we did not see any crocodiles, but we instead came upon a very unusual sight. The river was dried out because of the drought, with the exception of a few small pools of water where fish congregated. Huge catfish were grouped up in an organized hunt for smaller fish, and were chasing them from one end of the pool to the other. This was the commotion we heard, and it was quite a sight to see. This would be repeated every night at the same time during our stay; we could set our watches by it. We enjoyed spending the evening with Adam and his wife; they were kind and pleasant people. Adam's biggest dream was to visit the USA one day and see the car races at the Indianapolis 500 in person.

After a good night's rest, we came up with a plan for our hunt in the morning. During this trip, I made it a priority to hunt an animal I'd never hunted before—a leopard. Hunting such an elusive animal is much more complicated than hunting herd animals, of course. The first step was to set up some bait, and so first thing in the morning I shot two impalas that would hopefully attract the leopard. We spent the rest of the day working with our trackers to build two large blinds that we could hide behind in a tree, and tied the impalas to a tree nearby so that the leopard would not be able to drag them off into the bush once he came upon them.

Now there was nothing much left to do but wait. We spent the next day hunting antelope in the plains, and quietly checking the leopard bait location every few hours. One morning Sława took a shot at a large waterbuck antelope, but she missed. She was quite upset because it was a large animal and not a difficult target. She was absolutely sure of her aim and tried to convince me that there was something wrong with her rifle. I didn't take her too seriously, and chalked it up to simple inexperience, despite her insistence.

We tracked the waterbuck all day hoping for another shot. Finally, after many hours, she had a good opportunity to take another shot. It seemed very easy; the animal was less than one hundred yards away, and I knew she could easily hit it. I had seen her do it many times before. I positioned myself in front of her so she could rest the rifle on my shoulder as a support rest, which would increase her accuracy. She took aim, squeezed the trigger, and—to our mutual shock—missed again.

She was devastated, and I was dumbfounded. I could not understand how she could miss such a big target at this relatively close distance. I wanted so badly for her to succeed, to be my full-fledged hunting partner. I worried that this bad experience would make her lose interest in the sport of hunting.

We walked through the bush, sullen and quiet on our way back to our vehicle. In these circumstances, no one had any good words to say. I tried to offer some support and told her not to be discouraged, but she knew it was a shot she absolutely should not have missed, and she was inconsolable. As we were getting back into the vehicle, I took her rifle from her hands to put it in the back, and I instantly noticed there was something wrong with it. Suddenly, I remembered how she had complained about it earlier in the day. After a quick inspection I discovered that the rifle was loose in the stock. The portion that connects the long barrel to the stock, which rests against your shoulder, was completely loose! This was a brand-new weapon and it was unusual that after just a few shots the screws would have come loose to such a degree. Under these circumstances, the rifle would never shoot accurately. I immediately showed her what was wrong, and it was with great relief that Sława and everyone in our party realized there was in fact something wrong with her rifle that was making her miss her shots. I felt terrible for ignoring her complaints, and apologized to her profusely. If I wanted her to be my partner, I knew it was my job to ensure she went out for the day with proper equipment. From then on I always checked and double-checked our rifles to make sure they were functioning correctly and to prevent the kind of heart-wrenching scenario we had experienced that day. After I tightened all the screws, she never missed again, and every animal she aimed at she took with one shot. Through the remaining days of our safari she bagged a warthog, a steenbok antelope, a large impala, and an impressive zebra stallion. It was her most successful hunt yet. I was fortunate to get a warthog, impala, waterbuck, and bushbuck antelope. The leopard I wanted so badly never even came near the bait, so it just wasn't meant to be on this trip.

When the hunt was over, we had one more item on our agenda before we headed back home. Wally Zollman, whom we had become friends with on our first safari, had given us the address of an art dealer in Pretoria that he did business with. We had visited Wally's home in Indianapolis several times over the past two years, and we were incredibly impressed with his collection of unique African art. We asked Adam to take us to see Wally's art dealer, Fritz Van Zyl, because we were interested in starting our own collection. From the moment we walked into Fritz's shop, there was instant chemistry between us. He had excellent taste, and employed some of the best artists and craftsmen in southern Africa. There were talented sculptors of semiprecious stones and leadwood, and many experts in the iconic African art of scrimshaw. Most of his employees were from the Shona tribe of Zimbabwe. We took a grand tour of his galleries and were incredibly impressed by the quality of what we saw. We only bought a few small pieces from him at the time, since we barely had any more room in our luggage to take anything back. Nonetheless, we knew the seed of a great friendship and partnership had been planted. After we returned home, I had a tremendous amount of work to catch up on, and I was anxious for all of our African trophies to arrive so I could get to work on them. During this time I frequently called Fritz, and we discussed my plan to start importing African art to the US.

With my background in fine arts, I was naturally drawn to this aspect of the rich African culture. Fritz was my first supplier, but I quickly made contacts with other independent artists and began working with them directly. For me, this kind of work was pure enjoyment—it was at the intersection of all my passions and talents in life, and I was able to bring unique art to America, and share prosperity with my African friends in my home away from home. I started an aggressive nationwide advertising campaign in many art- and hunting-related magazines, such as the *Wildlife Art Journal* and *Sporting Classics*. I started having many inquiries about the unique products we were offering. I officially opened the Old World Gallery as my art-dealing venture, and our business expanded even more.

CHAPTER 23

Unusual Hunts,
Unforgettable Scenes

THE EARLY 1990S WERE BOOM YEARS FOR MY
taxidermy studio. Despite having several taxidermists
working for me, I usually worked long hours, seven days a week.
Sława continued working in the photo laboratory, and Krystyna
had finished college in Ohio and had started her first full-time job
in the "real world." Sława's mother would stay with us for long
periods of time, and because she could watch our beloved golden
retriever, Caesar, we were afforded the opportunity to travel on
extended trips. After our second trip to Africa, I became more
active in my local chapter of Safari Club International. I attended
all the fundraising banquets, and gave donations for the auctions.
The proceeds from these events went to good causes that I wanted to support, in particular for nature conservation and political
action to protect the hunters' rights. At one of the fundraising
banquets in Chicago, Sława and I were seated at a table with an elegant woman named Stella Low and her son, George Marx. Stella
was born and raised in South Africa, and was old enough to be

Sława's mother, but she looked like she could have been Sława's older sister. The two of them hit it off tremendously. Stella was sophisticated, well mannered, and well versed. She reminded me of a Victorian lady, and she commanded respect and admiration with her appearance and behavior. We had just returned from Africa less than one year ago, so we had many interesting topics to discuss, and we passed the evening in pleasant company and enjoyable conversation.

After the meal, the live auction began. I didn't stay for this part, because I didn't think there was anything I wanted to bid on. Instead, I bought some raffle tickets, hoping to win a Weatherby .375-caliber rifle, which was an excellent, American-made rifle for hunting big game. The raffle would come later, and so I excused myself from the table to use the restroom while the live auction was going on.

Upon returning, I had to pass by the auctioneer's pulpit, and one of the auctioneer assistants approached and congratulated me on the trip to Africa. At that point, I had no clue what he was talking about. I'd returned from Africa a few months ago, and I thought somehow he had gotten the dates mixed up, and was congratulating me on my past trip. I sat down at my table, not paying much attention to the ongoing auction, as I did not plan to buy anything after spending so much money on our last trip. I was a bit puzzled by the atmosphere—everyone was quiet and looking at me.

"Congratulations, George," Stella finally said to me. "You are going to Africa again." Now I was really confused—first the guy at the podium and now Stella were congratulating me on my trip to Africa. I looked to Sława for answers and she gave me a wry smile.

"Well," she started, giving me a mischievous look. "I just bid on the last item up for sale. And I won the auction. I bought us a hunting safari trip in Africa!" I could hardly believe my ears! It turned out the hunt that was up for bid was a donation from our new tablemates, Stella and George, to hunt on their private game reserve. Sława took it upon herself to make sure she won the trip, and I could tell she was happy at the thought of visiting Stella in Africa. *Holy cow,* I thought to myself. *I've just come back from Africa and in another six months I will be going again!* I was thrilled, and not least of all because I couldn't be accused of spending money foolishly, as it was all Sława's idea. Apparently she liked it there, and that was just fine with me.

I was really happy and excited, already making plans in my head as to what I would like to hunt. I was so preoccupied that I didn't pay much attention to what else was happening the rest of the evening. All of a sudden, I was called to the table where the raffle ticket for the rifle was being pulled out. I was the winner of the Weatherby .375 caliber I wanted so much to have! It was a truly lucky day for me. Sława bought a safari to Africa at the auction and I won my coveted rifle. I felt beyond exhilarated. An African safari was the dream of a lifetime for many people, and here I was about to be going for the third time in three years.

Four weeks before our departure, I started to make plans. We knew we would do the weeklong safari with George and Stella, who owned Thabazimbi Safaris, which was about a five-hour drive north of Johannesburg in the Transvaal. I decided that since we were already going to be in Africa, we should book a few more adventures. We decided to spend the first week with Dion Goosen, who was the outfitter we had used three years ago on our first safari in the Transvaal Province. I also called Fritz Van Zyl, the art dealer I had been working with, and asked him to arrange a fishing trip for us on the Indian Ocean. I'd heard him talk about it many times, and it was always a dream of mine to catch a marlin. Fritz owned a twin-engine Cessna airplane, and he also had some property on a small island in the Bazaruto Archipelago, which was part of Mozambique and just fifty miles off the coast. One day Sława came home with a travel magazine that had a gorgeous picture on the cover, featuring Bazaruto and a title saying, "Paradise at the End of the World." We could hardly wait. Everything was arranged for an epic five-week adventure, and we could barely sleep in the days leading up to it.

When we arrived in Johannesburg early in September of 1993, we were already quite familiar with the routine of the customs process and the formalities required to obtain firearm permits. We were quickly on our way. Dion picked us up and we traveled to the northeast part of the country near the Botswana border and the Limpopo River, where we had already been two times before. It was a long drive, but we truly enjoyed the scenery and occasional stops on the way to stretch our legs and get something to eat. As we drew closer to our destination, the scenery became incredibly beautiful. The lowlands by the river were forested, with tall trees and patches of tall grass growing in between. The place was teeming with all kinds of birds and game. The Limpopo River was partially dried out, but in some areas there were large pools of water full of hippos lying there motionless and occasionally displaying their temper by showing off their impressive ivory teeth. At the top of tall trees, small, black-faced vervet monkeys were scrambling around and expressing their unhappiness at our presence with loud cries. These monkeys live near areas inhabited by people and can often become pests, stealing food and other items from houses, and raiding crops.

I stood there and took it all in. I felt like I was in my home away from home among all these sights, sounds, and smells. Observing the various scenes before me, many old memories from my childhood flooded my mind. I thought back on the book I received as a Christmas present when I was five years old and living in Poland just after the war ended. The book's hero, Bambo, was in my thoughts, and I settled in for the night on the bank of the Limpopo River. As a child I was so completely fascinated by the word "Limpopo"; it always sounded so exotic to me. I had never heard anything like it. All I had at that time was a few illustrations of a half-naked black boy playing in an exotic wilderness, and my imagination had, for years, carried me away with thoughts about Africa, Limpopo, and Bambo. It was a feeling of great satisfaction, and I felt some divine providence, that now I was in that exact same place, on the banks of that very Limpopo River that had fascinated me as a youth. Best of all, I had a feeling this place was becoming my second home. The memories of the Christmas when I received that one specific book were very strong in me. I could remember it as though it were yesterday, the joy I felt getting presents as a child, the colorful tree, singing carols with my family and our neighbors. It all felt so fresh in my mind as I stood there in Africa almost fifty years later. That Christmas when I received the book was the one holiday from my childhood that stuck out more than any other. I only wished that my parents were still alive so that I could share my joyful memories with them when I returned home from the safari. I wished I could tell them that the childhood dreams triggered by the book they gave me had now come true.

We slept in large gray-green canvas tents, with improvised showers nearby. The accommodations were not luxurious, but were very comfortable, and it all enhanced the atmosphere of the traditional African safari. During the week we spent with Dion, we left very early every morning, driving through the bush and looking for game. The week flew by, and we felt we were in our element hunting various animals. I got a very impressive kudu, a large antelope from the spiral-horn family. To this day it has one of the largest sets of horns in my trophy room, and I'm very proud of it. It was a difficult shot because the animal was in a full run several hundred yards away, but I still could not resist. I took the shot, and the kudu ran for a couple hundred yards and went down. Another day it was Sława's turn to hunt. We were walking through the bush in the area where the Limpopo River ran along the border between South Africa and Botswana. We spotted a nice bushbuck antelope and the hunt was on. We followed his tracks for a while and finally got close enough for Sława to take a shot. The animal did not fall down instantly. It ran away and crossed the Limpopo River and then dropped in the shallow water on the other side. We had a dilemma on our hands. Her trophy was lying dead in Botswana and we were in South Africa. What were we to do? There was only one solution: we crossed the border without a visa to retrieve Sława's trophy. The borders were patrolled by guards, and if someone had seen us dragging an animal across the river into South Africa, they might have shot us on sight. Luckily, we got our trophy without any incident.

Our seven-day safari with Dion in the Limpopo Valley came to an end, and we were on our way to Bazaruto, Mozambique, for the second part of our adventure. It was a long drive to get to the airport in Pretoria, and on the way there, Dion proposed we stop to rest at a camp where he had previously hunted with clients. I was happy to make a stop after several hours of driving, and it sounded like a great idea to have breakfast in this beautiful hunting area of the Northern Transvaal that we had never seen before. I thought that I might have a chance to shoot a big warthog, an accomplishment which had eluded me during our week in the Limpopo region. I felt optimistic and thought that perhaps luck would be with me this time.

The terrain was sculpted with hills covered by acacia trees, and on the vast open spaces in between them grew leafy mopani trees, which are a favorite of kudu antelopes looking for shade. It seemed that Dion knew the area very well, and my excitement surged, as I thought I might actually get the coveted warthog here. Dion stayed behind with Sława and I set off with our native tracker, Samuel. We walked several miles through the bush exploring the surroundings, and we decided that sitting by a large watering hole that was frequented by all kinds of animals would be our best bet. It was hot in the early afternoon and Samuel suggested that we sit under a tall termite mound, about seven feet high, that was located in the shade of a massive leadwood tree. On the ground in front of us was a fallen tree providing good camouflage and also serving as a perfect resting bench for my rifle. We relaxed in the cool shade and kept our eyes on the watering hole.

About half an hour passed and a small group of warthogs came by for a drink, followed by a group of impalas. We sat and waited and then saw four young kudu antelopes show up to quench their thirst. I watched them through my binoculars as they scouted the area to see whether it was safe. Only the birds were around. Finally they took their drink of water without interruption and slowly withdrew back into the thick bush.

As we were sitting at the base of the termite mound, I was constantly offended by a very obnoxious stench. It smelled like dirty old clothes saturated with perspiration and worse, as if the person wearing them hadn't taken a bath in months. I could not figure out where this horrible stench was coming from. Sitting next to me was Samuel, a very humble and pleasant man from the Shona tribe in his late twenties. He appeared very civilized, and I had also found him bright and well mannered. While his clothes were not exactly Banana Republic issue, you could tell they were quite worn out from frequent washing.

I started thinking to myself, how can he not smell his own body odor? Despite the fact that his tribe lived in primitive conditions, I thought they would be able to at least take a bath in a stream every couple of days, especially in this hot climate. As I was mulling over his way of life, I suddenly felt an extremely hot burning sensation on my butt. It felt as if someone put out a cigarette on that part of my body. I was wearing shorts, and instinctively, with my hand, I touched my behind, and I felt on my skin a hard, crunchy bump. I rubbed it between my thumb and the tips of my fingers, but it was not letting go. Whatever it was, it had largely disintegrated and the rest was stuck to my skin. That horrible stench I had smelled before now intensified many times over. It smelled like a concoction of body odor and rotten meat. I tried to focus my vision when, at the same time, Samuel nudged me with his arm and silently pointed to the other side of the waterhole.

A group of baboons was cautiously emerging from between the mopani trees towards the waterhole. Instantly a thought flashed through my mind. If there was a big male among them, I would take him instead of the big warthog that hadn't shown up. I took another look at my hand to see what I was holding between my fingers. To my surprise I was holding a black insect that looked like a cross between a large ant and a termite, and a yellowish secretion from its body was smeared on my skin. If I thought the smell was offensive before, it was nothing compared to the rancid odor that threatened to knock me over now. I almost felt I should apologize to Samuel for my thoughts, but I had bigger things to concentrate on and turned my attention to the baboon.

"Wait for the leader," Samuel whispered in my ear. "He will be the last one to come out." That is the way a troop of baboons behaves. When they go on a mission, they first send out the youngsters; next are the older adults, then the females, and at the end, when the dominant male leader decides that it is safe, he cautiously emerges from hiding. That was exactly what happened. The whole parade came before him, and there he finally was. A big black male almost as large as a gorilla, with a flowing mane draping around his shoulders, slowly came out to join the rest of the group. As I watched him, I was thinking how much the kids back home would enjoy seeing him during a field trip to my little museum in Palatine.

The shot went off from my .30-06 Browning rifle and hit the leader about 150 yards away. The sound traveled across the pond and the echo bounced back from the mopani trees. In an instant all the baboons were gone, and all I could hear was their alarmed, loud screams of "Wa-hoo, wa-hoo!" coming from all directions.

Samuel shook his head in disbelief, and we looked at the animal lying on the ground, motionless.

"Man, this is one big bobyjan," he said, using the local term for baboon.

I asked Samuel to go get the vehicle where we had left it a couple miles back, and then meet me on the other side of the pond where the baboon had fallen. The animal hadn't moved since I shot him, but as I crossed the distance between us and approached him, he suddenly got up on all fours and darted off into the woods. He moved so quickly, I didn't even have a chance to take a second shot at him, and I realized that I now had a serious task ahead of me. I would have to go into the woods to track the wounded animal. The entire troop of baboons was harassing me from a safe distance in the trees as I started trailing the blood of their wounded leader. Their screams were coming from all directions, and it seemed like I was alone and surrounded from all sides.

I began to worry that Samuel would not find me in the place we agreed to meet, and I knew that the farther I went into the woods, the more dangerous it would be for me. By now some of the baboons were becoming uncomfortably bold and were coming out of the shadows and surrounding me, trying to charge at the intruder in their territory. I remembered reading stories about how these animals worked in packs and could devise strategies to hunt prey with almost human-like intelligence. I pushed the danger out of my mind, for I knew there was no way I could abandon my pursuit. The animal was wounded, and I had an ethical obligation to find him, dead or alive. As I walked, I kept finding traces of blood and knew I was on the right trail. At one point I lost his tracks, and I walked around in circles until I picked them up again. In the meantime, the rest of the baboons were just a few yards away from me and were getting bolder, and more aggressive. They threatened me by displaying their wide-open mouths and sharp, two-inch-long canines, close enough that I could see their wet, glistening menace. I only had two rounds of ammo left in my rifle, and I had to use them wisely. The baboon troop was closing in on me so much that I couldn't properly concentrate on tracking my wounded bobyjan; my situation was getting more dangerous with every passing minute.

I had no choice, and finally I decided to aim a warning shot above their heads in the area where they were concentrated. Fortunately it worked. They stopped their hollering and scattered into the woods. As I walked, I entered a clearing, and now I was totally exposed if they should try to attack me again. The area was spotted with several termite mounds, but there was no sign of the baboon and no tracks. The only resource I had left was my intuition. As I looked around, I saw from a distance a tall termite mound surrounded by a cluster of small trees that cast a shadow over it.

Instinctively I thought that a wounded animal might choose to hide there, as it seemed like a secluded spot perfect for taking refuge. My adrenaline shot up and my heart started to pound. For the first time in over an hour of tracking this animal, I thought this might be the moment when I finally would come face to face with him. I imagined that he could be waiting to pounce on me just as I rounded the corner of the termite mound, and my heart raced. Cautiously I began to circle the base of the mound, and suddenly, when I was about halfway around, there he was. He was in a semiseated position, leaning against the mound, one arm hanging limp at his side and the other over his lap, staring at me with his dark brown eyes and baring his enormous, two-inch-long canines. I stared at him, and he stared at me. He exhaled deeply, and after a few seconds stopped breathing.

For a moment I forgot I was still holding a rifle in my hands with one round of ammunition left, and a strange emotion of sadness came over me as I looked at this massive, strong animal and felt as though I regretted taking the life of the leader. I knew that probably by the end of the day there would be another, younger male to take his place and that such was the way of nature. If I hadn't taken this baboon's life, another male would have fought him to the death for the leadership role. As they say, nothing ever dies of natural causes in Africa.

Total silence fell over the bush, and then, after a few seconds, as if by some mysterious way of communication, the loud "Wahoo, wa-hoo!" of baboon screams filled the air as if they were expressing their sorrow over the passing of their leader.

After a short while I came out of the haze of my meditations, as I heard the sound of a vehicle approaching. Samuel had been looking for me since he heard the last shot, and I started to walk towards him. He brought the truck around, and I was very happy to collect my trophy. The whole experience was truly exhilarating, and it wasn't until we were safely driving away that I truly was able to comprehend the extremely precarious situation I was just in. While it was happening, I was completely in the moment, doing what any respectable hunter would do—tracking down his wounded prey. It was all a grand adventure for me, but I realized that being in Africa, alone, in possession of only one bullet and surrounded by injured and angry animals, would probably be considered insane by normal standards. For me, it was just one of the most powerful memories from my time there, and one that I will never forget.

We got back in our vehicles and started heading towards Pretoria again, to meet our friend and art dealer, Fritz Van Zyl, who would fly us to Bazaruto Island in Mozambique in his plane. By this time we had become good friends with Dion and his wife, Betsy, and so we invited them to join us in Bazaruto since we were covering the costs of the entire trip. We had room for two more, and we all happily set off for our paradise at the end of the world. Fritz and his business partner, Mark, a retired fighter pilot who had flown Harriers for the British Air Force, flew us to Bazaruto in their twin-engine Cessna 421 Golden Eagle. The plane could seat six passengers, and was appointed very luxuriously with leather swivel seats, a top-shelf bar, and hors d'oeuvres. Best of all, for the first time in my life I could smoke a cigar during a flight!

Our first stop was Maputo, the capital of Mozambique. We had left South Africa with a significant delay and hadn't had time to get the required visas before arriving. Instead, we arranged for a representative from the Mozambique Ministry of Tourism to meet us at the airport to take care of the formalities. It was puzzling to me why such a high dignitary would have to meet a bunch of tourists who just wanted to go fishing, but this was shortly after the civil war ended and the Marxist government had fallen. We probably were some of the first visitors to fly in on a private plane, so they assumed we were big shots. I had my video camera ready to go the moment the cabin door opened, and I started filming the scenery around the airport. Suddenly, there was a hand blocking my lens, and a few uniformed soldiers surrounded me. Despite the fact that the Communist regime had officially ended, the paranoid behavior I knew so well from my youth still remained. The memories of my life in Communist Poland instantly flooded my mind, and I noticed the signs everywhere prohibiting taking photographs of any structures, railroads, bridges, and government buildings. I put my camera away and we were escorted to the terminal. It was a grim-looking building, and the only people there were some workers mopping the floors. It was a long gray room with no windows and nothing decorative except for a few old propaganda posters and a row of hard plastic chairs along the wall. In the corner there was an antiquated machine that looked like it might have been used for checking luggage. We sat and waited in that dreary room for a long time, while the workers kept endlessly mopping the floor back and forth, all the while watching us from the corners of their eyes. We walked back and forth to the plane a few times to get snacks and sodas while we waited.

After about two hours, our dignitary showed up, dressed up in a fancy black suit that was probably two sizes too large on him. He apologized for being late, but said this is the African way, and that nothing happens on time. We got our visas without much fuss and arranged to stop back in Maputo on our return from Bazaruto so he could take us on a tour of the town. We were excited to be on our way. We passed through the customs gate and stated we had nothing to declare, because all of our possessions had been left on the plane anyway. Our passports were stamped, and as we walked towards the plane, a lady called us back to the terminal, ordering us to go through the X-ray machine. It was rather comical considering we'd been walking back and forth to the plane for the past two hours, and if we had wanted to smuggle anything in or out, no one would have been the wiser. Nonetheless, we complied with the bureaucratic procedures, and were soon on our way.

We were quite late leaving Maputo, and there wasn't much sunlight left for the short, thirty-minute flight. We didn't know what kind of landing accommodations were on Bazaruto, but no one was really worried, because we had our ex–fighter pilot in control of the aircraft. The atmosphere on the plane was very relaxed, and we were all excited and looking forward to fishing in the Indian Ocean. I could not wait to see the "paradise at the end of the world" I'd read about in my travel magazine. As happens at these low latitudes, the sky rapidly became dark almost the instant the sun dipped below the horizon, and suddenly we saw brilliant stars sparkling in the sky and below us only a dark, narrow island, barely lit from the glare of the ocean. Bazaruto is a sandy strip that is only five miles across at its widest point, and barely twenty miles long. It is located about fifty miles off the shore of Mozambique in the Bazaruto Archipelago, which is all part of a large national park. Everyone stopped talking and the atmosphere became tense. I tried to ask Mark a question, but he just replied brusquely, "Hold on, I have to concentrate now." He circled the island to signal our arrival, and we came down for the landing in total silence and almost total darkness. The landing strip was not lit, and I could not even see it from the air and wondered whether Mark could, but I decided to keep quiet. As we got closer to the ground, I could see the landing lights of our aircraft shining on the grass strip in the direction we would land. I don't know how he did it, but while all the passengers held their breath, Mark found the unmarked grass strip and brought us safely onto the ground. As the wheels touched down gently, I hoped there were no termite mounds in the vicinity that would catch the wheels of the plane and likely make us flip over, but luckily we came safely to a gentle stop. It was a moment of total exhilaration among us. We all vigorously congratulated Mark on his aviator skills and expressed how happy we were to be alive.

As we lowered the door and exited the plane, there was a group of people waiting for us in a pickup truck. They were people who worked at the one resort on the island, and they saw our plane coming in to land.

"We do not appreciate these kinds of surprises," one of them remarked seriously, as this grassy strip was obviously not intended for use after dark. "We do not have medical facilities here and we do not look forward to picking up dead bodies," another added without a smile. We could tell by the grave looks on their faces that things could have ended very badly for us, but it just made us all the more exhilarated to have arrived in such a manner. They rounded us and our belongings up, and we checked in to our surprisingly luxurious accommodations, where we were the only guests for the rest of the week.

When we arrived at our resort, we were welcomed like royalty. A gourmet meal was waiting for us that included fresh seafood, giant crabs, kingfish, a roasted goat, and a load of exotic fruits. It was enough to feed a small army, and the six of us dug in with great enthusiasm. The tables were exquisitely arranged with African motif tablecloths, and the napkins were folded to mimic birds of paradise, and were set in our wineglasses. I almost felt guilty disassembling that artistic creation. After spending two weeks "roughing it" in the African bush, sleeping in tents and eating simple meals on tin tableware, this welcoming meal was an overwhelming, unforgettable experience.

We partied late into the night after our precarious arrival. Our host, Luigi, was a Mozambican of Portuguese decent who had married a beautiful local African woman. He was very friendly and had a fantastic sense of humor. Our beverages were cocktails of exotic fruits mixed with alcohol and were continuously served throughout the evening. After having a few too many of these concoctions, Mark and Fritz decided to arm wrestle. Suddenly both chairs collapsed under them and the two big men were flat on the floor. Fritz began to apologize and offered to pay for the damage. Luigi didn't want to hear any of it, and just kept repeating "No problem, don't worry," with a smile on his face. After our exciting day and celebrations late into the evening, Sława and I finally retired to our chalet by the ocean and got a good night's sleep under our mosquito net.

Early the next morning we jumped right into the main reason we had come to Bazaruto—fishing. The Bazaruto Archipelago is world renowned for its superb white sand, alluring golden sunsets, and tall palm trees. It is one of the most spectacular destinations on earth. The wildlife includes small antelope, flamingos, pelicans, otters, dolphins, humpback whales, and crocodiles. Best of all, hundreds of species of fish have been recorded as native to these waters, making them one of the world's premier fishing locations. We immediately started catching a wide variety of fish, but no marlin—the main reason I had come. Sława and Dion experienced a bit of seasickness, and so they spent most of their time snorkeling. When I returned from fishing, Sława was so excited to tell me about how much she had enjoyed her day on the white sand beach, swimming in the warm turquoise water and enjoying the excellent visibility with an amazing variety of marine species and exotic, fragile coral reefs. The boys running the boat were a little surprised to hear where she had snorkeled, as this was a favorite spot of great white sharks, but apparently they had not been too hungry that day, lucky for her. The island of Bazaruto was even more beautiful than I expected, and it seemed the pristine beaches, which stretched for miles, had never been disturbed by humans. Closer to the shore there were high dunes, and in the lower elevations tall trees grew. There were no roads—only sandy trails around the island. We rarely saw other people, but one day as we drove our jeep on the trail to the interior of the island, we came across a small group of women, one of whom was carrying a small child wrapped in a blanket on her back. She approached our jeep and turned to Sława, asking whether she could cure her child from the severe scabs the baby had all over his body. She believed that a white woman with blonde hair must have magic powers, and she was not completely wrong. Sława had in her bag some antibiotic ointment, which she applied to the baby, and then she gave the woman the medication to continue treatment.

For the next few days we enjoyed catching fish, including many different varieties of dorado, yellowfin tuna, and about ten different species of kingfish. On the third day I caught the most interesting one of all—a bull shark, known in these areas as a Zambezi shark. They thrive in warm coastal waters and are among the most aggressive species of shark in the world. I fought him for almost two hours, and when he got close to the boat, I got a good look at him, and let him go. The men running our boat estimated he weighed close to three hundred pounds. The next day I hooked an even larger shark, but before I cut him loose, he broke the line himself.

Near our resort there was a sandy peninsula that would become exposed during low tide and stretch far into the ocean, sometimes as far as three miles when the moon was full. Every evening thousands of flamingos would congregate there for the night. One late afternoon we were fishing along its shore, and as the sun began to set, thousands of flamingos and other birds began to settle down for the night. It didn't seem that our presence in their resting ground disturbed them at all. We slowly wrapped up our fishing poles and gently made our way through the throngs of birds back to the shore. They weren't at all perturbed by us, and it was a magical experience walking through them. The next morning I walked out by myself along the peninsula, and was enjoying my solitude here on this peninsula a few miles from shore. The tide was coming in, and the water level was about at my ankles. It was an unforgettable experience to walk on the bottom of what was the ocean several hours ago, among the variety of seabirds feeding on crabs and other sea creatures along the peninsula, all of them ignoring my presence. I can still remember the feeling of this ocean floor's warm layer of gray mud under my feet, squishing between my toes as I walked through this pristine nature and soaked it all in. I felt like I might have been the first person on earth to have this experience, and it was a moment of pure bliss.

Sadly, our excursion to this paradise island came to an end, and we packed up for the flight back. Luckily we had one more leg of the journey before us—the safari Sława bought at the SCI auction. The idea of visiting with Stella and George made it a little easier to bear leaving this paradise. We made a quick stop in Maputo to visit with our government official, as promised. He was waiting for us when we arrived, surprisingly right on schedule. He was very friendly and accommodating, and took us on the ride through the city. During the colonial days it was called Lorenzo Marks, and it was considered the French Riviera of Africa. We drove along the ocean's coast, where the dilapidated villas stood as a reminder of past wealth. The Marxist regime had managed in two decades to destroy what had taken a century to build. Our official government guide took us to the market to do some shopping, but it was an impossible task. We were the only tourists around for miles, and the local vendors were crowding us trying to sell their products. Homeless children begged for money, and we were quickly overwhelmed. We headed back to the airport, paid our guide, and took off to Johannesburg. After reaching a higher altitude, we flew over Maputo, and from the air we could see a once-busy harbor now completely blocked with sunken ships from the war that had just ended. We had about one thousand miles to fly to reach South Africa, and it was now evening. The ground below us was dotted with thousands of bonfires to spread warmth during the African winter, and we settled in for the flight.

CHAPTER 24

A Wounded Leopard in the Dark

FOR THE LAST LEG OF OUR TRIP, WE DROVE FROM Johannesburg to a place called the Leopard Lodge in the Northern Transvaal province, where we would be reunited with our friends from the Safari Club banquet, Stella and her son, George. I was also extremely excited because with their outfitting company, Thabazimbi Safaris, I would finally be able to hunt a leopard, which was one of my priorities on this trip. When we arrived at the lodge, Stella, her husband, Gerrit, and Stella's son, George (who was her son from her previous marriage) greeted us warmly. They received us with a formal dinner, and we spent the evening getting acquainted with Gerrit. He was in his late fifties, a small guy and very skinny, but he had a thundering voice. If you were in the other room you would think he was six feet, six inches tall and weighed 350 pounds. He had owned a small tobacco farm in this region, and he and Stella had gotten married after her previous husband, George's father, passed away several years before. Since then they had bought this land and set up an outfitting company for hunters. Even out here in the African bush, Stella had her usual sophisticated look about her. She was tall and blonde and had a soft, almost angelic voice. She and Sława were by now the best of friends.

Gerrit and George had hired a very well known professional hunter named Bossey, who specialized in hunting leopards. The following afternoon, after we had gone for a swim in the pool, this man came and found us lounging around and enjoying the sun.

"Hi, I am Bossey," he said, introducing himself. "I understand you want to shoot a leopard." It was not a question, it was a statement.

"You bet I do," I responded. "I'm George. What's the plan?" He explained we would drive to a place about an hour away where he had a blind set up on the ground between some trees and bushes in a densely wooded area.

"From my experience, donkey is the preferred meat for a leopard to feed on," he said, "and I have a donkey tied up to the tree there." I was dumbfounded. The last time I hunted for a leopard, unsuccessfully of course, I had shot two impalas, which we tied to several tree branches up in the air, and I thought that was the way it was always done. It didn't seem very professional to just tie a donkey to a tree and hope to attract a leopard, but Gerrit assured me that Bossey was the best hunter in the area, and knew what he was doing.

"There are plenty of donkeys around here," Bossey explained. "Everyone has them, mostly for transportation, but once they get old, they get rid of them. So I tied a dead donkey to the base of the tree," Bossey went on, saying this worked much better than tying impalas up in the tree branches. I was relieved to hear the donkey was not alive, and I decided I would just trust his judgment.

That night it was time to go. Leopard hunting is done in the dark, and so I got my rifle and my safari jacket, as it would probably be cold at night. Gerrit joined us with a thermos full of hot coffee, and we were on our way. We arrived at the blind just after the sun set. We found ourselves in beautiful mountainous bush country that was sparsely forested and dotted with huge boulders, some of them as large as a house. All three of us got inside the blind, which was basically a small hut on the ground constructed of branches and surrounded by bushes. It was so well camouflaged that I only noticed it right as we were about to walk into it. Inside, there was a board installed that would serve as a bench for all three of us to sit on. I was instructed to sit in the middle with Gerrit on my left and Bossey to my right. In front of me there was a narrow opening with a solid branch at the base that I could rest my rifle on. Bossey had brought a car battery and a floodlight, because it was standard procedure to shine a bright light on the animal when it appeared to make it freeze for a moment before you shoot, but I told him I didn't want to use the light, because it would be against my hunting ethics, and I wanted the conditions to be as natural as possible. Hunting leopards is completely different from hunting any other game; it is not possible to stalk these animals, as they are almost silent, and nearly invisible in their natural environment. The only way is to lure them in and hope they come to you. The bait was set up about seventy yards from us, and while it was not visible to the naked eye in the dark, I could see it through the scope of my rifle and knew I wouldn't have a problem shooting the animal when it came near.

I worked out a strategy for myself. I memorized the top of the tree that stood out against the sky above the bait, so that I would be able to aim at the target in just a couple of seconds when he appeared. I would aim at the top of the tree and then drop my rifle down vertically. This way I could see the target very well through the scope. It was a dark, cloudy night, with only a quarter of the moon showing. The wind picked up and the clouds started to move very fast. When they covered the moon, we were in total darkness, but as long as there was a glimmer of light, I could make out the top of the tree. Suddenly, I noticed Bossey picked up his binoculars and was very intensely observing something. I implemented my system—aimed at the top of the tree and came down. Looking through the scope, I could see an animal feeding on our bait, but from the silhouette I knew it was not a leopard.

"A brown hyena is feeding on our donkey," he whispered in a resigned tone. "Now that a hyena contaminated the bait, a leopard will not come." We were all incredibly disappointed, and knew we would have to start over again the next day. Suddenly, there was a loud rumbling sound in our blind, and we chuckled when we realized it came from Gerrit's stomach. In the past, he had had some intestinal problems, and part of his stomach had been removed.

"Would you like to have some coffee now?" he asked. I nodded, and just at the moment when Gerrit was opening the thermos, there came a loud, blood-freezing, gurgling roar that sounded like it was an arm's length behind us. It was a ferocious sound that broke the silence of the night and made all the hairs on the back of our necks stand up. The powerful roar echoed across the canyon, and we sat there frozen. We realized a leopard had been right in the area circling the bait, and that the sound of opening the thermos had alerted him to our presence, and he had run off. We sat speechless for a while, looking at each other, the dark clouds passing over the moon, the wind swirling.

"Let's have that coffee," I said finally, but the thermos was on the ground and the coffee had spilled. Bossey suggested we leave in case the leopard decided to sneak up on us again. When we got back to our vehicle, Bossey said that there was no sense returning tomorrow because the leopard would not come back. He had been disturbed by us and by the hyena, its mortal enemy in the wild, and it would be a waste of time to come back to that same spot. I, however, did not agree with him. "I want to come back tomorrow," I said emphatically. The whole experience had gotten me so charged up that I would rather stay up all night for even the slightest chance to get that leopard. We finally agreed we would come back the following day, and we returned to the lodge just after midnight. I couldn't wait to tell Sława about my close call with the leopard.

We spent the following day hunting warthogs with our favorite tracker at Thabazimbi, Alfred. But all I could think about during the day was trying again for the leopard that night. Finally, in the late afternoon, Bossey arrived, and again the three of us drove to the leopard blind. Bossey still did not believe that the leopard would come back after being spooked by both the hyena and our presence. I didn't know what to think, but I'm just a naturally optimistic person and was hoping the cat would not be able to resist fresh donkey meat. We parked our vehicle far away and walked to the blind. I already knew the routine. Gerrit put his coffee thermos under the bench, Bossey put his car battery with the spotlight on one side, and I stuck the barrel of my rifle through the opening of the blind and hoped for the best. The weather conditions were the same as the previous night; right after the sun set, the wind picked up, and the scattered clouds were fast moving through the sky. I repeated my strategy from the night before, taking aim at the top of the tree and lowering the barrel of the rifle in a straight line down to where the donkey carcass was tied at the base of the trunk. For three hours, nothing happened, and not even a hyena appeared. I began to think Bossey was right and that we were wasting our time here in this same location.

Then all of a sudden Bossey picked up his binoculars. Instantly I pointed my rifle at the top of the highest point of the tree and followed it down. There, to my amazement, I clearly saw a spotted cat standing over the dead donkey, seemingly contemplating which parts he should devour first. I looked at Bossey, and he looked back and gave me a silent nod. I pulled the trigger, and the shot from my .300-caliber Weatherby went off. There was a loud, blood-curdling roar that bounced off all the surrounding boulders, followed by silence.

Bossey and Gerrit congratulated me, and I lit my pipe and waited. It would be too dangerous to approach a leopard that could possibly be hurt, as a wounded leopard in the African bush is one of the most deadly things you can encounter. After about ten minutes passed by, we left the blind and waited a few minutes while Bossey got his spotlight working so we could get a view of the scene. Slowly and cautiously we approached the bait. We were positive we would find a dead leopard lying by the donkey, and yet there was nothing there when we arrived—only the carcass of a dead donkey. We stood there speechless. I thought if he did not drop on the spot, we would surely find him nearby, because I was positive I had hit exactly where I was aiming; I had tested the scope on my rifle just the day before. We looked around and didn't even see a sign of blood. Even with all their combined years of hunting experience, Bossey and Gerrit had no explanation.

I decided to conduct a little investigation. I stood precisely where the leopard would have been on the bait, and I drew an imaginary line to the opening in the blind from which I had taken the shot. I continued the trajectory of the bullet from behind the leopard and carefully inspected every twig and tall blade of a grass. Finally I found a tiny fragment of flesh, slightly smaller than a thimble, stuck to a clump of grass, and now I was convinced that I had shot the animal slightly behind the shoulder, exactly where I had been aiming. Still we had no idea how far he could have gone with that kind of injury. Some very unpleasant scenarios entered my mind, such as the animal lying dead under a bush somewhere that I would never find him. To lose a trophy, especially a leopard, was unthinkable. It was now a question of going after a wounded leopard, one of the most dangerous situations one can encounter in Africa, but what is unquestionably the right thing to do, ethically. I continued with my shooting trajectory and found my bullet wedged in a tree. The puzzle was resolved to some degree because we knew the bullet had gone through the animal, but where was he? I imagined him wounded and hiding somewhere, waiting for his chance to get even.

Every hunting manual on the subject always comes with a dire warning: "Never track a wounded leopard at night. Wait for daylight before proceeding." Bossey, however, had a different opinion; equipped with his big battery and the spotlight, he said, "Let's go and look for him. He could not have gone too far." I started thinking to myself that this is getting to be a very dangerous game. Bossey was holding the light, and I didn't have much confidence in Gerrit's shooting skills. Even a man armed with a rifle would not stand much of a chance if he was attacked by a wounded leopard in the dark.

In these kinds of situations it is recommended to track a wounded leopard with a shotgun, because if a leopard charges at close range, he could reach his nearest victim in one leap. There is no time to aim, and so a shotgun is best if you hope to survive a big cat attack in close quarters. I only had the rifle and my .38 magnum revolver, but if Bossey and Gerrit were willing to look for him, I would certainly not object. He was my leopard. I shot him, and I took on the responsibility of taking him out of the bush. There was no option to back out of this situation, no matter how dangerous it was.

I decided that Gerrit should carry the rifle and I would walk beside him holding my revolver with both hands. If the leopard attacked me and knocked me to the ground, as long as I didn't lose my revolver, I would still have a chance to put some lead in him. This tense situation lasted no more than half an hour, but to me it seemed like it was forever. Finally Bossey said we should call it a night. We agreed we would come back early in the morning to resume the search. Back at the lodge I could not close my eyes, and it seemed like the morning would never come. I was lying wide awake, devastated by the thought that this magnificent animal might go to waste if I didn't find him tomorrow.

When Bossey came to pick us up at dawn, we were ready and waiting. Sława drove with George Marx, and we stopped on the way at the nearby village to pick up eight trackers, who followed us in a pickup truck. This kind of situation called for reinforcements. We soon arrived at the familiar spot, and Bossey assembled the whole crew in a clearing to give us a briefing. I could tell by the way he was talking that he was not happy. Clearly something besides the missing leopard was bothering him.

We all stood around him in a circle as he began to speak. I didn't understand what was going on with all the formalities, because I knew all these locals knew each other and knew what it takes to track a wounded leopard.

"We are here to look for a wounded leopard," Bossey said to the group. "Hopefully we'll find him and hopefully he will be dead. However, there is a possibility he still might be alive." He paused and looked directly at Sława. "I must emphasize that a wounded leopard is the most dangerous animal in all of Africa. If the leopard attacks and tears somebody's face off, I will not be responsible for it." At that point Sława's blue eyes grew bigger, and she started to back up slowly towards the truck. She got inside and rolled up the windows. Actually I was glad that Bossey helped me out in this situation, and drove home the point to her of how dangerous it was. I knew she would want to be around to take pictures, but it simply was not safe for her. A moment later George Marx approached me and offered to take Sława with him, assuring me he would walk in front of her with a shotgun. I felt she would be safe this way, and I agreed to that.

We started our search at the point where I shot him and followed the best local trackers. Not very far away, on a big boulder, a tracker found several leopard hairs sticking to a bloodstained leaf, but obviously the animal had abandoned that spot and moved on. My imagination really began to take over now. I knew a leopard could maul his victims by holding them with his front paws and canines while disemboweling them with his back paws. Even if one could survive the attack, the wounds would be infected with bacteria that are very difficult to treat. Terrible scenarios were passing through my head, that someone in our tracking party would get hurt because of the leopard I had shot.

As the search continued, I tried to keep my hopes high, but as time passed, even my natural optimism started to fade. We covered every square yard of an area half a mile wide and almost one mile long. I knew he could not have gone far; I believed my shot had been well placed. We had been searching for over four hours and everyone seemed ready to give up, except for me. I was hoping they would not give up and leave me alone, because I was still determined to find my leopard. I saw some of the men packing up and getting back into their vehicles, and I felt disheartened and annoyed. I had promised them a good reward if the leopard was found, but they seemed to think it was a lost cause. Now it was just me and one tracker left. Even Bossey had given up.

Suddenly I heard the tracker calling in his local Tswana language, which I could not understand, but from the sound of it I knew it had to be good news—and it was. He had found the leopard! He was in a spot we passed by several times. It was close to the edge of the canyon where there was a steep embankment. I had searched that area several times, holding on to roots and branches because of the steep slope. The leopard had lodged itself under one of the deep crevasses in the canyon, and died there just out of view. The previous night when we attempted to look for him, we were, in fact, very close to where he was, and we were very lucky that, for whatever reason, he had not attacked us then, because it's likely we would have been grievously injured.

Everyone gathered around in a jubilant mood. I was the happiest man around. The trackers carried the leopard to a nearby boulder, where they laid him down and I got my first look at him. He was enormous, and beautiful. We positioned him on top of the boulder, and Sława had the opportunity to take many pictures. For me it was the experience of a lifetime, something I would remember forever. The African leopard belongs to the group of animals called "the African big five" or "the dangerous five," and is among the most difficult animals to bag. Back home, I mounted the leopard in a large landscape scene just at the moment he kills an impala. He is captured forever in his impressive role as one of the most powerful African animals, and I have displayed this African diorama many times and always get the most compliments on it.

We still had a few days left to hunt, and I was very satisfied with my experience. Now it was time to focus on Sława. The next day she was going for a blesbok antelope with George and a couple of local trackers. She was making good progress with her hunting skills, and by now was able to recognize many different species of African animals, and she was able to follow their tracks, which is a very important skill for a hunter. Late in the morning we spotted a nice blesbok, and Sława took a shot at him. Her marksmanship was excellent, and the animal fell down on the spot. Of course, there is a tradition to take a picture with a trophy. It was important for Sława to look good, but after walking through the thorn-filled bush in the heat and dust, she was not very happy with her appearance, so she decided to go back to the truck to fix herself up a bit.

The trackers positioned the animal in a proper spot for a picture, and we waited for her. Time passed by and she was not coming back. In the hot sun the internal gases of the animal started to blow up, and the stomach of the blesbok began to resemble a blown-up balloon. Finally one of the trackers went off into the bush to go find her. Shortly thereafter they came back and Sława was all made up and ready for a photo session. The tracker had a puzzled expression on his face. He said something in his native Tswana language; I asked George to translate: "I do not understand the white people. Our ancestors painted their faces before they went to war or to hunt, yet this white woman is doing this after she killed the animal. Then she keeps the useless parts—the skin and the horns. She gives away the best part, the meat. This is a very strange behavior."

And so our epic African safari wound down, and it was time to go home. We were exhilarated. We had hunted a total of twenty-two trophies—an impressive number for a single hunting trip—and were bringing home some of the most exotic specimens we had gotten yet. We traveled back to America filled with the wonderful memories of high adventure, excitement, and all the new friends we had made in Africa.

CHAPTER 25

The Doberman

IN ADDITION TO MY PRIMARY CLIENTELE OF HUNTERS
from around the world wanting to have their exotic trophies
mounted, my clients are occasionally people who were very attached to their pets; when their beloved animals die, the owners
sometimes wish to have them preserved for all time by a taxidermist. When such clients arrive at my doorstep, they are usually
in a deeply troubled emotional state. They are upset, grieving,
and under tremendous emotional strain. In such situations, I always make it a priority to try to talk them out of having their pet
mounted. I truly understand and can sympathize with their situation, but such work is very expensive, and takes many months
to complete. There is something uncomfortable about making
a business deal with a person for a costly memento under such
sorrowful circumstances. The other problem is that owners are
intimately familiar with every expression on their beloved pet's
face, and it makes the work of the taxidermist that much more
difficult to do in these circumstances. To most people all German

shepherds, golden retrievers, or poodles look alike. For pet own-ers however, their pet is always unique and has nuanced facial expressions recognizable only by their masters. To do a good job of making a pet owner satisfied, I have to carefully study dozens of photographs or even videos, and I also have detailed conversations with the owners to learn as much as I possibly can about the char-acter of the pet. I must have a sense of the animal's personality if I am to faithfully recreate him for his owner. Cats and dogs are the most difficult to do exactly because of the intimacy the person had with the pet. I often try to point out to clients that given the amount of money that they would spend preserving this one, they should consider buying another animal. At the very least, I tell them that keeping the departed pet frozen for some time to let the first wave of emotional stress pass would allow them to make the decision about preservation when they are not in the throes of the immediate grief of the death. The truth is that I rarely persuade a person not to have his pet mounted, and yet sometimes they do change their mind. One time I received a thank-you letter from a woman I had successfully convinced not to mount her pet. She said that, in truth, she could not have afforded it anyway, but that at the time her emotions were overpowering her reality, and in the end she was happy with her decision.

One time I mounted a pair of service dogs who had faithfully spent their lives working for a woman who suffered from mus-cular dystrophy and was confined to a wheelchair. Surprisingly, she and her husband were not as emotional as most people are in such situations. Both of them were highly educated people and made it clear they were making a rational, thoughtful decision to honor the service dogs that had been their constant companions.

I worked with one dog at a time. After I removed the skin from the dog for tanning, the couple came to my studio with a small coffin to pick up the dog's body for burial. The coffin was lined in satin and decorated with the usual burial regalia. They put the remains inside along with some photographs, and then sealed the coffin permanently with special tape designed for that purpose. As they were walking slowly to their car carrying their precious cargo, my neighbor across the street was mowing his lawn and observing the funeral procession out of the corner of his eye. He pretended not to see anything unusual, but the next day he could not contain his curiosity. He came over to ask what the coffin at a taxidermist's studio was all about. I was amused by his inquisitive nature and kept him guessing for a while, before I finally revealed it was actually an old service dog, and not a human in the coffin.

Some years ago I received a phone call from a Colombian man inquiring if I would mount his pet, and I gave him my usual spiel about the cost. He had a very old, terminally ill Doberman that had just been euthanized to put it out of its suffering and was now kept in the freezer at his veterinarian's office. I recommended that the man wait several days before making a final decision. The next day he called to let me know he was on his way over with the dog, and hung up. When he arrived, I thought there was something peculiar about the situation. First of all, the man seemed completely detached and unemotional about the animal. There was no trace of anguish or grief on his face. He walked in, cool as a cucumber, wearing an Armani suit, a silk shirt, ostentatious jewelry, and shiny dress shoes, and with a leather attaché case under his arm. He was curt and to the point. In our brief conversation I found out only that he was from Bogotá, Colombia. We stepped outside and walked to his flashy Mercedes to get the dead, frozen dog out of the trunk. I wrote the invoice and took a 50 percent deposit, which he paid on the spot with hundred-dollar bills.

Most people in this situation would postpone their departure, and display a difficult time parting with their beloved pet. This character, however, appeared to be totally unemotional and impassive, and wanted to leave in a hurry.

"Just do a good job," he remarked to me before he took off. I assured him that when I was done, the animal would look as young and healthy as ever, although the man specified he wanted to have him mounted curled up with his eyes closed as if he were asleep.

After six months the job was finally completed, and I was very happy with the result. It was striking how peaceful and alive the dog looked lying there. The only thing missing was the movement of his belly; otherwise, you would have believed he was taking a nap. I hadn't heard from the customer since he dropped the animal off, which was also unusual, so I gave him a ring to let him know that his dog was ready for pickup. He said he would come by in a few weeks, because he was currently out of town. I was happy to keep the dog for a little while to show off my masterpiece to my friends and other customers. It truly was one of the most lifelike pieces I had ever created, almost like a *Mona Lisa* of taxidermy work. I put the "sleeping Doberman" on the floor in my trophy room, where I kept many mounts as samples to show customers. It turned out that many people were afraid to walk into the room, because they could see the sleeping guard dog behind the glass door to the gallery and didn't want to rouse him. I chuckled and assured clients that there was no danger because the animal was deaf and very old.

I had been a professional working taxidermist for over twenty-five years and had mounted lions, bison, birds, pets, and any number of exotic species you could think of. But the Doberman was truly something special, and many people who had known my work for years told me I had outdone myself on this job. A month passed and there was no sign of the owner, so I called him again. He apologized and mumbled an excuse, saying he would come by in one week. Another month later I called again, and was given more excuses, but again he promised he would come in one week. The man in the Armani suit had given me four different phone numbers, but eventually all of them became disconnected and I was unable to get in touch with him. I must admit that although I wanted to be paid for the job, the fun I had with hesitant guests and customers who were afraid of my "sleeping" Doberman was well worth the wait.

A year and a half had passed since I finished the animal, and the Doberman was now a fixture in my house. One day my friend Robert, who is a private investigator, stopped by. He and his wife had a collection agency, and Robert asked whether I had any bounced checks from clients and said he would help me collect the money. Fortunately, I never had any such problems with my customers, but then I remembered the Colombian man who never picked up his dog. I felt that I was stiffed for the 50 percent balance on this job, and by now the fun with a "sleeping" dog was getting old.

I told Robert the story. He took a copy of the invoice and said, "I'll see what I can do."

Another six months went by and I had just about forgotten my conversation with Robert, until one day I received an excited phone call from him.

"Listen carefully. I found the guy with the Doberman," he began. "He is staying in a motel in Franklin Park. I have him on hold on a three-way phone line. I will switch over and talk to him, but he will not know that you are also listening to the conversation. Listen, but do not say anything unless I tell you to." I was excited and intrigued by this bit of mystery and listened in eagerly. Robert got back on the line with the Colombian, and I heard him explain that he was representing me and just wanted the man to pick up the dog and pay the balance.

The Colombian replied to Robert curtly, "I do not owe you any explanations. I have already made an appointment with George to pick up the dog Monday morning." This conversation was happening Saturday evening, and the man had made no such plan with me. At this point Robert asked me, "George, are you meeting this guy on Monday?" I spoke up and answered, "This is news to me, but maybe he's planning on coming by my studio after all and I just missed the message?"

The guy must have been shocked to hear me, but I tried to sound as naïve as possible. The mood changed quickly, and our conversation became quite friendly. We wished each other good night, promised to see each other on Monday, and hung up the phone. After we ended the conversation, Robert called me back and said, "Get ready. I'm picking you up in fifteen minutes and we're going to pay this guy a visit." I didn't know what Robert had in mind, but this was just another adventure for me, so I was eager to play along.

As I hurriedly carried the "sleeping" dog and waited for Robert by the front door, I thought I might miss having this masterpiece in my house. "You overstayed your welcome here," I said to the Doberman. "You scared enough of my friends and customers, and now you are going back to your papa." I had really gotten used to thinking of this dog as a sleeping guest in my studio. I had barely gotten to the front door when Robert pulled into my driveway. He jumped out of his car and opened up the trunk. For a moment I considered taking a handgun with me, but I decided it wouldn't be a good idea. At the time I did not have a permit to carry a concealed weapon, and besides, I knew that Robert always had on him a Colt .45 pistol.

We were on our way with our special delivery. It took us about half an hour to get to the motel, and I was extremely curious as to how Robert had found the guy after such a long time. But first, we had to make sure we covered the details about how we would handle the situation once we arrived at the motel. It was a long, one-story building with about a dozen or more doors, but there was only one car parked in front of one of the doors. It was not a fancy Mercedes but rather an old beat-up Ford of some sort, and it was clear that this was our man, as he was the only guest. We parked a little ways down from the room and got the dog out of the car. "I hope the door is not locked," said Robert, since we had agreed our plan would be to waltz right in instead of knocking.

"I will open the door and you will walk in with the dog," Robert instructed me. "I will stay by the open door, and you conduct your business."

"Okay, I got it," I replied, my heart beating a little faster, not knowing what we would find on the other side of that door.

Robert was in his early fifties, a bold, heavily built man with massive shoulders, about five feet, ten inches tall. He was wearing an open leather bomber jacket, and the grip of a Colt .45 was visible just underneath. Both of us knew that we were facing a bad, shady character and that if anything went wrong, it would not be worth the balance that he owed me for my job. At this point it was a matter of principle, and I enjoyed the challenge of going into an unknown situation.

According to plan, Robert swiftly opened the door for me, and I walked in, carrying the curled-up dog with both of my arms stretched out, as a waiter would carry a tray with plates on it. Inside the room there were two men. One was my delinquent client, sitting on the sofa, and another man sat in a nearby chair, both just watching television. They jumped when the door was flung open, but luckily nobody reached for a gun or reacted too hastily to the situation.

I calmly walked across the room, placed the dog on my customer's lap, and said, "Here is your dog. You must be very happy to see him after such a long time. By the way, you owe me the balance for this job."

As long as I live, I have never seen two people with such dumbstruck looks on their faces. Both men seemed shocked into silence, looking incredulous and stunned as I walked in. I'm not sure if he was more surprised that we had found him, or that we had the guts to just waltz into his room unannounced; but either way, we made quite the impression.

Just to his left on the couch where he was sitting was his fancy leather briefcase. After silently placing the dog on his right side, he put the briefcase on his lap and opened it. It was filled with "bricks" of one-hundred-dollar bills. I stood there silently and was glad things seemed to be going according to plan. My customer hadn't said a word to me; he just counted out what he owed and handed me the money. I didn't bother to recount it. I just rolled up the banknotes, put them in my pocket, and thanked him for his business as I backed out of the room without turning my back.

Robert moved to the side to let me pass, he closed the door behind us, and we quickly walked to our car and took off. I couldn't believe what we had just done, and I felt exhilarated. I was still wondering how Robert had managed to find this guy with just one invoice and a few phone numbers. All Robert would tell me was that the man lived in Texas, and that he was only staying in this obscure motel for a short time. I wanted more details but all Robert would say was, "It is a long story, but I have my ways."

Robert dropped me off at my house and we celebrated the happy ending with a beer. My curiosity has never been satisfied, and I don't think I'll ever know the secrets of Robert's trade. Nonetheless, thanks to his ingenuity and gutsy plan, I was able to recover the substantial amount of money this man owed me. For a long time after that day, I would continue to miss the "sleeping" Doberman guarding my studio.

CHAPTER 26

Art and the African Wilds

BETWEEN ALL THE AFRICAN MOUNTS AND THE interesting work I had from local customers, my business continued to flourish. After those exciting three African safaris in the early 1990s, I realized I had outgrown the Chicago hunting and fishing show. In 1996 I decided to join the big leagues and exhibit my work at the Safari Club International Expo, which took place usually in Las Vegas, but occasionally in Reno, each year. By now I had a tremendous number of exotic trophies to exhibit, and I wanted a larger audience. The SCI show was the natural next step, and it was like going from a rowboat to a yacht in the world of hunting. By now I was also gaining a reputation as a dealer of fine African art, and many people would seek out my Old World Gallery just to see what treasures I had imported from Africa this time. With each trip, and with my continuing partnership with my good friend Fritz Von Zyl, I selected the best pieces of African carvings, paintings, masks, scrimshaw, and the like, and I soon became one of the largest dealers of African art in the USA. My list of art clients was growing, and I would regularly receive large containers that included everything from carvings in leadwood and hippo and warthog ivory to semiprecious stone sculptures crafted out of exquisite materials such as verdite, bloodstone, and African opal.

Some years the trip to the American southwest would be a very difficult undertaking. The show always took place in the winter, and we had to drive a big truck through the Rocky Mountains. At times it almost seemed suicidal because the roads would be covered with snow and ice, and we thought we would never make it in time to set up, therefore losing the money we spent on our prepaid booth at the show. Even Sława learned to drive the big truck, and we would alternate so I could rest. I always felt so fortunate to have her by my side as a partner in everything we did. She would drive the truck on those open stretches of road in the West where the speed limit was eighty miles per hour like a pro.

Exhibiting at the SCI shows brought a new level of recognition to my business, which now included a truly international clientele. It gave me tremendous self-esteem and confidence to be a respected and recognized leader in my field. Often our new friends Stella, Gerrit, and George from Thabazimbi Safaris would exhibit in the booth right next to us, and we always looked forward to our annual reunions with them. I enjoyed the hundreds of people I met each year and felt I was the luckiest person in the world for being able to make a comfortable living doing something that I enjoyed so thoroughly.

One year there was an extremely obese man in my booth, and he was dressed rather sloppily, in baggy sweatpants and a sweatshirt. He didn't seem like the normal type of attendee at this show. I watched him cautiously every time he turned around in the tight quarters of my booth. I almost had a heart attack when he bumped a pedestal which supported a large, top-heavy bust of a woman made out of some very expensive butter jade, and the whole thing started to wobble dangerously. I grabbed it just in time, and I was about to say something to the man. There wasn't a lot of space, and while I didn't want to be rude, I was concerned for the safety of my art! I was just about to go up and ask him to please be careful or to leave my booth, when Sława kicked me in the shin and pointed out that this man had a security detail with him—men dressed in dark suits who were shadowing his every move. On closer inspection I saw his name tag, which said he was a sheik from Qatar! I chuckled to myself and quickly learned the lesson that you can never judge a book by its cover, especially in the world of hunting. This man was a passionate collector, even if he didn't look like much of a hunter himself.

I truly enjoyed meeting all the new people who came into my life because of my line of work. I always made it a point to respect everyone, regardless of their status, because I believe that you can learn something new from just about anyone. I knew that I had gotten to where I was in life because of the help and support of my family and many friends, and I always tried to extend that same helping hand forward. Many people would come to me to ask my advice and opinions on various matters, and I was always happy to help inspire other people, young or old, and to encourage them to expand their horizons. "If you can dream it, you can live it" became a kind of motto of mine. I always avoided people who were pessimistic, dishonest, or envious, as there were those in the business as well. I believed deep in my heart that anyone who worked hard enough at what they loved could become successful in America, and all the various people I met in my line of work just proved my point. I was making my living as an artist selling high-end, luxury goods to clients who appreciated them tremendously, and it was something I never could have imagined growing up.

I increasingly devoted my time to the Safari Club because their main purpose was to promote hunters' rights, and to work for increased nature conservation. When, in the 1950s, African ranchers began converting their land to hunting safaris, many animals, like the white and black rhino, were saved from the brink of extinction, because it became a profitable business for ranchers to have these animals around. Ranchers began reintroducing indigenous species so that they could be hunted, and their numbers increased and they flourished. Over time, the original wildlife that had inhabited these ranch lands made a strong comeback under the strict government control and regulations that surrounded the sport of hunting. Today, both the black and white rhino have come back from the brink of extinction in large part thanks to conservation efforts from hunters' groups. Safari Club International played a role in this conservation, and that is the exact kind of work that most hunters are proudest of.

For many years I was president of the Illinois chapter of the Safari Club, and today I hold the position of vice president. Sława is a board member, and together we have been recognized many times for our work in conservation and hunters' rights, something we are both very proud of. Of course the Second Amendment, which protects the right to bear arms, is also a large focus of our lobbying efforts, and it is a cause I believe in deeply. For me, it was always about more than just hunting. I had experienced how Communists in Poland had taken away the citizenry's weapons first, and then implemented a terrible socialist state once the people were powerless to change it. To me, taking away a man's weapons was the first step towards disempowering the public and enabling a dictatorship. I always had that history in the back of my mind when I thought of protecting our Second Amendment rights, and I knew disarming the public was the first step towards enabling a corrupt government to rule. In Communist Poland, people were promised many things for free by their government— including food, jobs, and housing. What they didn't realize at the time was that when the government offers you something for free, you later pay for it with your freedom. I learned that lesson firsthand, and was determined not to let that happen in America. I knew America was a strong country first and foremost because it was a free country, and I worked with organizations like SCI to keep it that way.

Deep down, I realized the Safari Club was primarily a patriotic American organization, and that was what I loved about it most. We were members who believed in the genuine American virtues of hard work, self-reliance, and liberty for all. In recent years we've raised money for soldiers, and sent wounded warriors on specialized hunting trips. We stood for anything that was truly American.

In 1999, Sława and I decided to build a large addition to our home that would become our art gallery and wildlife museum. We built an enormous room complete with twenty-foot vaulted ceilings, and three thousand square feet of display space. We actually situated our new master suite just above this exquisite museum, and we would pass through our beloved collections each day on our way to turn in for the night. We enjoyed being surrounded by all of these beautiful artifacts on a daily basis, and we loved sharing them with everybody who came to visit. The addition of the museum to our humble Palatine estate garnered quite a bit of interest locally, and several journalists came by to take pictures and do a story on our thriving local business. Our clientele continued to diversify and now included not only hunters and fishermen, but art collectors as well. I interacted daily with people from every walk of life, and this was one of the best aspects of my job. From plumbers and carpenters to professors and business owners, we were united in our passion for the art and sport of hunting, and I enjoyed spending time with each and every one of the people who came into my shop.

My life was busy, but still, I longed to return to Africa. It had been several years now, but I would smoke my pipe and gaze out my window and think back on all my African memories. One Sunday afternoon I was sitting in my new study and marveling at the exquisite stone and leadwood carvings representing African animals and native people that filled my home. Just then I got an idea for a piece of more functional art, and reached for a piece of paper to begin drawing. It would essentially be a large wooden bar that would also have a carved wooden roof with a canopy over it, so that the whole thing would give the effect of looking like an African hut. The base would be an ornate wooden cabinet decorated on all sides by raw leadwood logs that would be carved into various wildlife scenes. The countertop would be made out of one huge leadwood trunk, cut in half and polished to a high shine to reveal the beautiful grain of this tough wood. I knew it would be a gorgeous piece because it would be surrounded on all sides by the natural leadwood bark, while the parts carved from the inside of the tree would darken with age and would shine like polished stone. I had never seen such a piece in America, and knew it would be a hit.

I faxed the drawing to Fritz and asked for his opinion. He loved the idea, but wondered how such a massive piece could be shipped. I thought we could ship it in parts in smaller containers, just like everything else. One of my clients immediately commissioned the piece when he saw my drawing, so we struck a deal, and Fritz hired some of the best artists in Africa, Norman Chapoterera and Robert Nzali, to get started. The two of them worked for over a year to finish that leadwood bar, and the results were absolutely exquisite. It came with carved barstools that I later upholstered in my studio with skins of African antelopes. When the container arrived at my studio, it took eight strong men to unload and assemble it. It weighed close to four tons and was by far one of the most ambitious projects I had taken on. It was spectacular. The artists had used large leadwood logs that had collapsed and lay drying in the African sun for many years. Now those twisted, ornate logs became parts of anatomically correct African animals in the scenery, and the result was absolutely magnificent.

The scope of my projects was getting larger, and clients were clamoring for African art. I invited the talented sculptor David Mudede, from the Shona tribe, to visit me in the US to work on some custom pieces for one of my clients' trophy rooms. David stayed in our house for six months while working on this project. I was very impressed not only by his incredible artistic talent, but also by his knowledge of philosophy and culture that had all been passed down orally from his ancestors. He had an amazing work ethic, and he would send all the money he earned working for me to the people in his small village in Africa.

During these years I traveled to Africa three more times with Sława to hunt and collect more art. We became quite close with Alfred, our favorite tracker who worked for George and Stella. He became a good friend of ours and we would often talk about African art together. One day while we were returning from a hunt, Alfred suddenly stopped the vehicle and turned to look at us.

"Today I will take you to a place that you will greatly enjoy seeing," he said with a mischievous grin. We had spent so much time with Alfred driving over all of this terrain that I couldn't imagine what new scenery he had in store for us. I was curious, but he refused to elaborate and just kept driving. Eventually he got off the main road, so our progress slowed, and we entered onto a rough trail that seemed to be heading absolutely nowhere. When we finally got to a spot where the car could go no farther, the three of us continued on foot, climbing over big boulders and rocky cliffs in some places. We had no idea where he was taking us, but after about an hour we reached a small canyon that had a large cave on one side, just off the ground. We climbed up onto the overhang that led to the cave, and once we entered, Sława and I both gasped when we realized what we were looking at. There before us was an enchanting, prehistoric "art gallery." The stone wall was decorated with ancient Bushman paintings of animals, as well as figures hunting with bows and arrows in beautiful red ochre pigments. We were completely mesmerized—we could not believe we were seeing authentic, original paintings like this out in the wild, and not behind a piece of glass in a museum. I felt like I was one of the most privileged human beings on earth, to have an opportunity to see this kind of work up close, where it was originally painted. I looked around and tried to imagine what this place would have looked like thousands of years ago. Who was this Bushman artist? Why did he take the time to create these images for the next generation? I felt an incredible connection to those ancient artists, and their love of African scenery. I felt in a small way I was contributing to their perpetuation through my work as an art dealer and avid hunter, and I felt it was a moment of deep connection with my beloved second home, Africa.

During this time I accumulated quite a large collection of scrimshaw art as well, which is one of the most iconic forms of African art. It is made by making hundreds of fine scratches on the surface of ivory. Then the scratches are dyed with pigment, and the image, which had previously been invisible, comes to life. It took an enormous amount of skill to be a successful scrimshaw artist, and these etchings became one of my favorite items to collect. There were two brothers in particular who were experts in this form of art, and I commissioned many pieces from them. Sadly, one of the Messina brothers passed away from AIDS, as did so many of my African friends and artists I had worked with over the years. It was a terrible epidemic, and it seemed no one in Africa was untouched by this horrible disease. It was a great shame to see so much talent disappear from the world at such a young age. I felt a tremendous connection with many of my African artist brothers, and was privileged to know them and to collect their works of art.

In 1999, I also planned to expand my activities in Africa in one other way, and that was to invest in land development. In the 1990s there were many interesting investment opportunities as corrupt governments collapsed, and one in particular in Mozambique came to my attention. Stella's husband, Gerrit, called me one day with news of a great new deal related to something we had casually talked about for a few years—running our own game concession. After the collapse of the Marxist regime in Mozambique, the new democratic government was seeking foreign investment to boost the economy and bring in capital and development expertise. These ventures were subsidized by the United Nations and the World Bank, and from the sound of it would provide an excellent opportunity for us to invest in one of our favorite places in the world. By now we had known Gerrit for almost ten years, and he had frequently stayed at our house, usually for several weeks around our annual SCI shows. I trusted him, and he worked to put the deal together. We decided to seek a long-term land lease in Mozambique, which would total about 702,000 acres, about the equivalent of 1,100 square miles. The land was designated as a natural park, but there were options to develop it along certain guidelines provided by the government. In return for the lease, we would be under obligation to build infrastructure like roads and bridges, and provide employment for the native people there. The investment would require several million dollars, to purchase the forty-nine-year lease, and we decided to start legal proceedings to make it happen. The three main investors were me, Gerrit, and a retired Mozambican general who was a friend of Gerrit's (by law we were required to have at least one native partner). Gerrit was a good asset to have because he was Afrikaner, spoke several tribal languages, and had excellent local contacts. I would be responsible for getting other investors together to make up the rest of the pool of money, and I would also be in charge of procurement of the large equipment necessary to develop this barren land. We planned to develop some basics quickly, and to start offering hunting safaris within a year. We figured with our combined expertise and knowledge, we would be able to run a profitable hunting business in no time. I had many customers and friends who were ready to sign up for safaris with our proposed outfitter, and four in particular provided substantial financial reinforcement so that we could go ahead with our proposal. Frank was an international industrialist, Ron was the owner of a large electrical company, John was a prominent surgeon, and David was a veterinarian and owner of a large animal clinic.

We worked quickly with Gerrit to secure one of the plum pieces of land that was being offered as a game concession, and bordered an immense national park. This land had not been hunted in almost thirty years, and we could only imagine that the experience of setting foot there would be like hunting on virgin African land, just like people did over one hundred years ago. Our first safaris would just be outfitted with the basics—tents, jeeps, and meals cooked over a fire. We also had plans to set aside ten thousand acres strictly as a Cape buffalo breeding area. We could hardly wait to get started, and couldn't believe that soon a small piece of Africa would have our name on it. One cold February day we had a board meeting of our small investment group of six people in downtown Chicago, and Gerrit flew in from South Africa for the event. Gerrit had been staying at my house for several days before the meeting, and I had seen him staying up late into the night preparing papers for this meeting. He seemed to be going over everything again and again, and I started to become a little curious about his behavior. At the meeting we all had our attorneys present, including one who was fluent in Portuguese (because that is the official language of Mozambique, and all the government documents were written in it). The meeting should have been a simple one. We were just going to review and approve the points of the contract between us that we had already discussed. The investors had already handed over their money; we just needed to sign the papers. Gerrit was fumbling around at the meeting, and couldn't seem to find certain papers despite all his preparations the night before. I was probably the only one who thought he was acting strangely, because I knew him so well, but I wasn't sure what to do. Gerrit was acting nervous, and handed his lawyer the wrong set of documents to sign. Things seemed to be a mess, and I didn't understand where the confusion came from, but we adjourned the meeting until Gerrit was able to get the paperwork in order. I was confused but didn't suspect anything just yet; I assumed he just hadn't brought everything he needed from South Africa, and that he would get it straightened out shortly after he returned there.

By now, I had over twenty safaris booked for hunters who were eager to hunt on our land in Mozambique the following year. They had already paid their deposits, and the money was supposed to go toward development of the land. The *Chicago Tribune* even wrote a large article about me and this project to develop a part of Africa. Of course, Gerrit was the main partner in South Africa, and was controlling everything. Just after he returned to Africa, there was a raging typhoon in the Indian Ocean that hit Mozambique hard and created several weeks of distraction while the country was consumed by floods and destruction. We waited patiently for Gerrit to get back to us with the final papers and notes on the progress, but then we were suddenly not able to reach him. A week or two went by and we realized it was not just the typhoon; Gerrit was avoiding us, and we started to get nervous.

Finally, Sława made the horrible discovery that the banking accounts set up for our investment had been cleared out, and all the money my partners and I had poured into them was gone. This was absolutely devastating news, and we could hardly believe what we were looking at. We tried to call Gerrit but were unsuccessful. When we spoke to Stella, we realized the worst of it. Gerrit had also stolen substantial amounts of money from her and Thabazimbi Safaris, and had disappeared. No one had heard from him for weeks. He had also sold hundreds of safaris to various people all over the world, and then disappeared with the deposits, as well as the money that was intended for our land lease. Sława and I were absolutely devastated. Not only had we truly grown to love the idea that a piece of Africa would soon be ours, investing almost two years into putting this deal together, but now we were out an enormous amount of money. The worst part was that my friends and fellow investors had put in their money because I asked them to, and the shame of losing their money was the hardest part to bear. I decided I would personally reimburse everybody's investments, because I felt responsible for getting my friends into the mess with Gerrit. Everyone was terribly sorry to see the project dissolved and appalled that Gerrit had disappeared with all of our money. I assured them I would reimburse them for every dime, and within a year I had done just that. The most important thing for me was that I be able to walk away from this situation honorably, and hold my head high among my friends and colleagues. It was worth the struggle and effort to pay back those dollars. Later I heard whispers from third parties about what people said about me, that my word was worth more than gold. I felt proud knowing I had kept my honor intact.

This dramatic swindle by one of my close friends was one of the most earth-shaking experiences I've ever had in my life. For years now I had been riding high on my white stallion of success, proud and triumphant and heading towards greater and greater horizons. Now I was knocked down and completely blindsided in a way I don't know that anybody could have foreseen. Even Gerrit's own wife, Stella, was a victim and did not see it coming. My biggest reward was that I kept the friendship of all the people whose respect mattered to me most.

Stella passed away in 2011, and we have not been back to Africa since. We are almost afraid to go back to a place where we spent so much time with our good friends over the past twenty years, now that she is gone. I know things will not be the same without her dignified presence filling the place. The deal with Gerrit certainly tainted us, but I never lost my ability to trust people. I knew from experience that there were more decent and honest people in the world than there were thieves and liars. Through all my decades of doing business I can count on one hand the people I would not want to do business with again, and sadly, my old friend Gerrit is included in that small group. Nonetheless, the experience of negotiating for a piece of the African landscape was one I will never forget. I had to meet with a local tribal chief under a sacred marula tree so that he could decide whether I should be allowed to strike this deal with the Mozambican government. During that meeting he would go off into the bush to consult the spirits of his ancestors, and he returned to announce that the deal was on. The spirits had advised him that this white man was sincere and trustworthy. I savored those moments, instead of focusing on the bad. Despite how things ended, I always felt I should count my blessings rather than brood on the past, and that was exactly what I continued to do.

CHAPTER 27

Buck Fever

CONSIDERING ALL THE UNPREDICTABLE HUNTING and often hazardous tracking I had done in exotic spots on three different continents, I never would have imagined that the most narrow escape I would have with wildlife would happen in my own backyard. Every year the hunting season in Wisconsin opens on the weekend before Thanksgiving and triggers a "buck fever" among hunters. They spend millions of dollars buying hunting clothes, new rifles, bows, and all kinds of gadgets related to hunting, as well as shelling out thousands of dollars for hunting licenses. Hunters are famous collectors of gear, and I certainly was not exempt from this phenomenon. Although all my closets and my garage were stocked with hunting gadgetry, I would always think of something new I needed to buy that season. When the bag I took on my hunting trips got full, I just bought another bag, like any hunter would.

That year I planned to hunt with my friend Gary. He was one of the first people who came to work for me when I first opened my taxidermy studio in 1978. He was excellent at mounting birds, and was very fast and accurate in his work. For years Gary had been inviting me to join him on his annual hunting expeditions to the property of a local farmer he knew in southwest Wisconsin, which bordered the Mississippi River. He always traveled with a group of friends, and since I am not a big fan of group hunting, especially with people I don't know, I always declined this offer. This year, however, we agreed that just the two of us would go, and I was looking forward to spending time in this beautiful area of rolling hills, valleys, and ravines.

We left at noon the day before the season opened, and after three hours we arrived at the motel where Gary had already made a reservation the previous year. We had plenty of time to go to the local shooting range to check our rifles and make sure our sights were right on target. As usual, I had with me my favorite Weatherby .300, which I had not parted with for the last thirty years. We went to bed early since we had to be out in the woods well before daybreak.

At four o'clock in the morning, we got dressed and headed out. A flurry was coming down, and half an inch had already accumulated in the first snowfall of the season, creating perfect conditions for deer hunting. We drove to the woods and walked another fifteen minutes to reach our designated positions at the edge of a large wooded area. I chose a spot under a huge oak tree facing two large, hilly open fields. To my left was a runoff area from a small ravine where water drained during storms. Gary chose to walk several hundred yards to my right and positioned himself on the edge of the woods overlooking one of the hills.

I situated myself at my cozy spot underneath the wide trunk of the oak tree. The branches were so large they almost touched the ground, and while it was good camouflage for me, some of the leaves were still clinging to the branches and obscuring part of my view of the hills, where I expected to see deer on the horizon returning from their nightly feeding grounds in the soybean fields. I had with me a folding hunting seat, some candy bars, and a thermos full of hot coffee. I was very content. After a few hours a chilly, damp breeze started to pick up, letting me know that winter was on the way, and I had to zip up my parka. Several times I observed does returning from the feeding grounds over the hill to my left, and I anticipated hearing a shot from the spot where Gary was hunting at any moment, but there was total silence.

I began to wonder what the heck was going on with me. It was not even freezing outside, and yet I felt the breeze going right through to my bones. Fifteen years ago I slept in a tent in the Arctic for a week, when the temperatures were forty below zero, and I never remembered being as cold as I was now. I thought either the dry Arctic air was very different from this damp breeze, or the years must be getting to me. It was getting close to 11:00 a.m., and since I did not hear Gary's shot and I did not see anything worthwhile to take a shot at, I thought it was probably time to call it quits. I ate my candy bar and got my pipe out, and since nothing was coming my way, I decided to go to the pickup truck and wait for Gary. As I was packing my pipe, out of the left corner of my eye

I saw the branches moving in the thickets less than seventy feet away, right by the little ravine.

I slowly put the unlit pipe back in my pocket, and looking closer, I realized that the moving branches were the tips of a buck's antlers. I could not see the body, not even the head. I couldn't even tell which direction he was facing, and looking through the scope was not much help. All I could see was the tips of the antlers as he moved slowly through the woods. All of a sudden, the buck apparently got wind of me, and he bolted out into the field and started racing up the hill away from me at about a thirty-degree angle. He was in a perfect position for me to take a shot as he moved to higher ground, but the dried leaves on the oak tree branches were obstructing my view. Finally, when he was about 250 yards away from me, I was able to see him clearly through the opening between the branches, and I decided to take the shot. I squeezed the trigger, and the shot went off as the buck was running at full speed. With the sound of the shot still echoing through the woods, he dropped on his behind. A second later, as the buck was struggling to get up, I frantically chambered another round and took another shot, but my gun misfired and the shot didn't go off. A moment later he disappeared over the hill about 350 yards away. It all happened in just a few seconds. I was devastated. This was a huge buck, with a big rack. I had wounded him, and there was a possibility that I would now lose him. If he crossed the hill to the other side, where we did not have permission to hunt, I would not be able to track him and would have no hope of finding him.

As all of these thoughts were flashing through my mind, I was still holding up my rifle and gazing at the spot where the buck disappeared. What happened next was astonishing. Apparently, the buck made a U-turn about a hundred yards behind the hill and started coming back. At first his head appeared beyond the horizon, and in a split second I could see his full body coming down the hill straight towards me at full speed. He was getting larger by the moment and was producing a bellowing sound, which sounded like a roar and a bark combined, and it was getting louder by the second. I'd never heard or experienced anything like this before.

I was frantically trying to get him in my sights to take another shot. It is very difficult to shoot a target coming straight at you, and the damn branches with dead leaves were obstructing my view. I had been trying to take the shot from a standing position, and I dropped to one knee to see if there was a better opening. He was now about one hundred yards away and was approaching me with his head down, as if ready to spar with another rival buck, and all the time the bellowing continued without letting up.

When he was about 150 feet away, I found an opening for a clear shot. I squeezed the trigger, but the shot did not go off. I heard an empty click, and my heart skipped a beat. I thought my trusty Weatherby rifle must have misfired a second time, since I believed that I still had one more bullet in the chamber. In the meantime the buck was plowing through the shrubs that separated us. With his head down, the prongs on his rack were aimed at me like white ivory spears. His bellowing was one incredibly loud, continuous sound, and he was thrashing the shrubs in his way, which mixed with the aggressive sounds he was making. The last image I had of him consisted of two black eyes focused directly on me when he was maybe ten feet away. At the last second, I jumped to my left, behind the huge trunk of the oak tree, and at that very moment, the beast passed by me with the speed of lightning and in another second disappeared into the woods.

As I tried to regain my composure, I noticed blood all over the trail the buck had cut through the bushes as he passed by me. My clothes were also splattered with his blood, and the wet snow that still stuck to the tree trunk from the morning's snowfall looked as if someone had poured a full cup of blood over it. Less than five minutes had passed since the moment I first saw the buck.

I was dumbfounded. I had hunted countless animals and dozens of different species on three continents, and never in my entire hunting career had I experienced anything like this. It was unthinkable to me that a deer, after being shot and wounded, would run close to a mile (in my estimation), and then turn around to charge the hunter. Sure, some species in Africa, like a leopard, would do that, but I was in Wisconsin, heartland of the USA, and only hunting "harmless" whitetail buck. I picked up my folding seat, which the buck had knocked over, and it too was covered in blood. I took a seat, and got out my pipe to rest and catch my breath for a moment. I knew the animal was too dangerous to track right away. I lit the pipe and sat down, still a bit shaky, and tried to soak in everything that had just happened, and how close I had come to being impaled on that buck's impressive rack.

After about fifteen minutes, I felt calm and collected and was ready to start following his tracks. I was certain that by now he would have bled out, and I could approach him safely. The light dusting of snow showed a clear blood trail, which I had no problem following. It started to thin out, and just then led me to a clearing covered in dried, fallen oak leaves where the snow had melted. I concentrated on picking up his tracks, and noticed a large fallen tree lying just to my left at the entrance to the clearing. There was my buck, lying beside it with his head on the trunk, still breathing. I recalled how he looked as he was coming at me with his head down and shiny tines pointing at me, and I put another bullet in him from a safe distance. I immediately got to work dressing the animal and removing the organs, and I tied my tag to his antlers. When the buck first bolted, I had taken a so-called Texas heart shot as the animal sprinted away at 250 yards. In hunters' jargon this means a shot to the hindquarters, and while it is not an ideal shot, if done properly, it can sever a major artery or the spinal cord, resulting in instant death. My shot had indeed severed his femoral artery, but had missed any vital organs. He had begun to bleed to death as he ran away. After I was done, I stood back and admired my work, wondering how Gary (who, as I would later find out, was not feeling well) and I would be able to get this three-hundred-plus-pound buck out of the woods. He was a six-pointer, with massive widespread beams—a beautiful old buck.

I left him there and walked back to my oak tree. I sat down again and tried to figure out what had happened with my rifle. I saw two .300-caliber bullets lying on the ground, one indented from the firing pin and the other without a mark. I realized then what must have happened. It appears that after the second shot misfired, I must have instinctively repeated chambering a round, not realizing the misfired bullet had already been ejected. Therefore I had ejected a perfectly good round, and had consequently faced the charging buck with an empty rifle. I shook my head at the thought. I had been acting automatically, and my actions were quicker than my thinking.

Gary arrived with the truck shortly after I returned to my tree, and I waved him over to show him the evidence of everything that had happened. "Holy shit, what happened here?" he exclaimed as he walked over and saw blood all over my clothes, the tree, and the snow. I explained the harrowing experience to him, and he stared at me in wide-eyed disbelief. Together we dragged the massive animal back to the truck. Since my experience with that crazed buck, I have a much better understanding of the term "buck fever."

CHAPTER 28

Coming Full Circle

I WAS VERY PROUD OF ALL MY HUNTING accomplishments, and often thought of my parents as I grew older and reflected on all the interesting turns my life had taken. I was saddened that I couldn't share my adventures with my father, and wished that for just a moment he could see how far I had come with my own business. Almost three decades after his passing, I decided to make another trip to Poland, and this time I would focus on visiting my ancestral homelands in Lubocheń. I had not been back to Poland since the Iron Curtain fell, and I was eager to experience what a democratic Poland felt like. It was almost hard to imagine that the corrupt, oppressive system I had known my entire life was now gone. I decided to take the trip without my family, because I wanted to mainly spend time hunting in the same region where my father was employed as head forester over half a century earlier. I hadn't spent any significant time in these woods since I was a boy, and now that Communism had ended, I felt I could possibly reclaim a part of my father's memory by spending a few weeks trekking through the forests he loved his whole life.

A few days after arriving and visiting with my sister Henrietta, who still lives in a nearby village, I made my way to an old mansion deep in the forest that had belonged to one of the neighboring estates. This estate had bordered Lady Rose's and, like most great estates, had been nationalized by the Communists after the war. The mansion had now been restored by the Polish government, and had been converted into a lodge to accommodate foreign hunters who came to the region (mainly to hunt roe deer). The building also served as the offices of the regional forestry administrator, and I made an appointment to meet with him in anticipation of my hunt in those woods. As a foreign citizen, I had to register before I could hunt, but in truth I also wanted to make the acquaintance of the man who essentially took my father's place as caretaker of these lands.

The day of my appointment I introduced myself and explained my background. I told the young man that my father had been head forester in this area before and during the war. He eyed me curiously as I spoke, and when he realized that I was a bit confused as to why he was staring at me blankly, he blurted out, "You look very familiar to me. Have you ever been on TV?" It was at this moment that I remembered that TV Polonia, one of the biggest TV networks in Poland, had done a piece on my leopard hunt in Africa. The interview had aired a few years before on what is the equivalent of one of the largest news channels in the country. I had provided TVP with pictures and footage of the hunt, and they had interviewed me on national TV about my experiences.

The Polish-American community in Chicago always maintained close ties with Poland, and I had come to the attention of some Polish television producers thanks to my various involvements in the hunting world and in the Polish community in Chicago. I had long ago forgotten about the show, but apparently it made quite an impression on this man. He remembered that the hunter in the video was from this very region of Poland—and it was in fact me. At the same time, there was also a major article in a Polish hunting magazine about my trips to Africa, and I think many of the people in this part of Poland took a special interest because I was their "hometown boy" who had gone on to have a successful life in America.

I confirmed that I was the very man from Luboched who was featured in those hunting stories, and that broke the ice between us. He became very accommodating and agreed to arrange a carriage drawn by two horses to take us on a tour of the forests where I grew up. As we explored the forests in the carriage, we came upon another forester who was out walking the woods as we were being given a tour. Immediately upon being introduced to the man, I felt a sense of recognition. Although we had never met, we quickly realized that our families had been good friends before the war, and a bond of kinship was established. This young man's grandfather was actually a good friend of my father's, and I remembered his grandfather well. My father and his grandfather had worked this land together, for Lady Rose. It was like being reunited with old family. It's amazing what recognition of simple family names can mean to two people when they meet. The two young foresters took me on a beautiful excursion through the woods, showing me places that even I didn't recall from all my years spent there.

We paused at a tall embankment where old Norwegian spruce trees grew, and we could see the Wda River flowing gently below. I had spent countless hours swimming, playing, and fishing in this river. In the distance, a few hundred yards away, we could see the river bend to the left, and I remembered that just above this bend was the place where the old forester's house had been. This was the last home my family occupied before they moved into Lady Rose's manor itself. It had been a large, gorgeous manor with a peaked roof and several fireplaces. Unfortunately, the Nazis burned it down in 1939, and there was no trace left of it. Yet this place was so rich with natural beauty, and it captured perfectly the serenity and grandeur of the Tuchola forests I loved. I stood there, surveying the land.

"You know," the young forester began gently. "Everyone still calls this 'Swiderski's Place,'" he said, using the Polish phrase "Leśniczówka Swiderskiego." The young men had brought me here just to show me this, even though it had been over fifty years since my father left Poland. I became very emotional in that moment. To see my father's memory being honored here so many years after he had gone was a powerful moment for me. I was honored that even the third generation of young foresters after the war, like the young men before me, knew my father's name and legacy, and I felt there could be no better testament to a man's character than that.

As I walked those old stomping grounds of my father's, I realized I was now older than he was the last time he was here. He had been gone from this earth for over thirty years now, but with every step in those woods I thought of him, and of everything our family had been through both in Lubocheń and while forging our new life in America. At a ripe age, when most men would be settling into retirement and complacency, my father chose to start a completely new life for himself when he moved to America at age sixty, without any knowledge of English. I was now over sixty myself and had a new understanding of the great sacrifices my parents had to make in those years. It must have been incredibly difficult and painful for them to leave Poland at the time, and it just goes to show how bad the conditions must have been to drive them to make such a decision after years of struggling under the weight of Communism. In my youth, Communism was all I knew, and so at the time I simply didn't know any better. It was only in my later years, as I started to reflect on the changing world, that I was truly able to comprehend what it all must have meant for my father, to see his homeland torn apart from the inside. The old world order where honor and dignity ruled was turned upside down during his lifetime, and the fabric of social cohesion and common decency was ripped to shreds while he watched, helpless to do anything about it. That was why we left.

I loved this place dearly—the very leaves on the trees reminded me of home, and of my youth. Just as Anton Plehn, Lady Rose's father, had fallen in love with the gentle fields of flowers and ancient trees over 150 years ago, so had all who had ever called this part of Poland home. I realized that the last custodian of this land's rich history was my father, Bruno Swiderski. When this land was the privately held property of an aristocratic German family for almost one hundred years, my father was the last one left standing to watch over it. More than a job, I believe my father loved his work, and performed his duties with diligence and integrity. How fitting that the locals called this beautiful spot Swiderski's Place, because I believe part of the reason he couldn't bear to continue living here was that Poland had become a twisted horror of a country, even after they fought on the winning side in World War II. My father understood in his heart that people were basically good by nature. Lady Rose had protected our family when she could have easily looked the other way, when the Nazis wanted to ship us off. My father defended her, and he defended his helpless countrymen as well. In those days, nationalities and borders mattered less to us than how decent your neighbors were as people. It's true that even honest people get taken advantage of or are betrayed at times. It happened to Lady Rose, to my father, and even to me, but these disappointments seemed a small price to pay for living as a respectable and decent human being. My father showed me long ago that a life lived in such a way will never be filled with regrets. It was clear to me then what my father must have seen in the 1950s, that the only thing that can really tear a society apart from the inside is a twisted and corrupt government that oppresses its citizens and robs them of their basic dignity. This is what began happening in Poland in those postwar years.

The greatest joy and deepest fulfillment that a man can have is to see the fruits of his labor passed on to the next generation, for there to be some legacy that will last beyond the epitaph on a tombstone. I think every man yearns for this to some degree, and for years my father toiled in Poland trying to achieve many things that may have been possible before the war, but were no longer. In the end, America was the only light at the end of the tunnel that could redeem the ideas my father had about the proper way to live. He worked hard even in his advanced years, and I learned from his example. If there was opportunity before you, it was wrong to let it go to waste, and America provided constant opportunities for even penniless immigrants. It was such a stark contrast to Communist Poland, where there was nothing except quicksand that trapped every honest, hardworking man that was left.

Life in America wasn't easy, but things of value never come without effort. America had many things of value to offer people who were willing to work hard. Sadly, I don't know whether that is the case anymore. I'm not sure what America today is offering the young and hungry, but it certainly isn't the same things that it offered me over fifty years ago. I have lived through times when humanity was going through more rapid changes than ever before. A new world order was being implemented because of World War II, and the golden age of America was upon us. I had parents who were smart and adaptive, and at the time, America still had open arms for immigrants from around the world. The tired and hungry and poor could come to America's shores and get a fair shot at life. In the 1950s and '60s my siblings and extended family and I were able to build good lives for ourselves in the city of Chicago just by starting off working in a factory. We earned a decent wage for honest work. I'm not sure whether the same could be said of America today. There are few opportunities for immigrants who arrive in the same kind of circumstances that we did back then.

The Cold War was a fascinating time to live through, even though it certainly didn't feel that way at the time. I always felt I straddled the great world divide—Communism versus freedom—more than almost anybody I knew. In my life, I came to know both systems intimately. For a while, when I was still young, I couldn't see beyond my nose as to what was really happening in the world. I had grown up saturated with Communist propaganda, yet after just a short time in America, I realized the Communist government had been forcing us to live a lie all those years. When I finally realized that what was really happening in Poland, all I could do was laugh at the exposed insecurity of the socialists compared to America's great capitalist success. I had escaped from behind the Iron Curtain at a time when few people had such opportunities, and I owe it to my father for seizing the chance when he could.

It was from an American vantage point that I could enjoy some of the greatest achievements of human civilization—like landing a man on the moon. As a matter of fact, one of the great American icons of the Cold War era became one of my clients. Captain James Lovell became famous after he successfully piloted *Apollo 13* back to Earth after a disastrous onboard explosion robbed the vessel of most of its oxygen and electrical power. He was played by Tom Hanks in the 1995 Oscar-winning film *Apollo 13*. In the years after the 1970 mission, Captain Lovell became one of the most famous men in America for safely bringing the vessel back to Earth using manual navigation. He was on all the talk shows, gave speeches around the world, and was frequently present on national media outlets.

Imagine my surprise when, in the early years of my business, Captain Lovell became one of my clients! His family had settled in the Chicago area, and it turned out he was an avid hunter and fisherman. One time, he asked me to deliver a fish mount I did for him to his house, a request I gladly obliged. I walked into the study of his large home in Lake Forest, Illinois, and found myself surrounded by an invaluable collection of national memorabilia from his various Apollo missions. The pictures and awards, many from the president of the United States, that lined his wall were simply overwhelming, and here I was mounting a piece of my own work alongside his treasured memories. It turned out Jim was a regular and friendly guy, and he gladly obliged when I asked him to sign an autograph for my daughter, Krystyna.

I would sometimes dine at the restaurant he owned in Lake Forest, and he would always make a point of coming over to say hello when he saw me. In Poland, it would have been unthinkable for an average person like me to have the opportunity and privilege to be on a personal, friendly, first-name basis with a man of his status. Here I was, an immigrant from Poland, and I was rubbing elbows with some of the greatest Americans of the twentieth century. It was an honor and an experience that I never expected, but it spoke to the true democracy that is at the heart of America.

What I experienced in America was so much better, and was actually closer to the ideal of equality that socialism and Communism pretended to advocate for. It was only in capitalist America that everyone truly was treated as equal, and if you had a skill or something of value to trade, you were as important as the next guy, whether he was a national hero or not. In Poland the class divisions were so stark, with a ruling elite of privileged party cronies and everybody else beneath them. They acted like royalty, and average citizens were treated as though they weren't good enough to lick the boot of a Communist VIP. Those same socialist bigwigs, who preached to no end about how the average person was exploited under a capitalist system, couldn't see the reality that they were the ones doing the oppressing. My interactions with true members of the American elite only solidified this point in my mind. It was an opportunity I would have never had in Poland.

Another notable person I had the pleasure to befriend in my years as a taxidermist was a man named Dale Brooks. In the 1980s, Dale worked for Northrop Grumman and was a key player in developing the "Star Wars" Strategic Defense Initiative that President Reagan had initiated to fend off the Soviet threat. In those days, the Star Wars program was in the news all the time. It was considered a major approach to winning the arms race against the Soviets. Dale's business card said he was a "director" in the electronics division, and he always traveled with three large, burly men who I presumed were his bodyguards. In those days he would have been a key kidnapping target by Soviet agents, who would have tried to pry US state secrets out of him. Nonetheless, he always had time to visit my shop, and he brought me dozens of deer from his hunts over the years. We would banter about his work bringing down the Soviet Empire, and once again I was amazed that just because of my line of work, the movers and shakers of the day would come to my studio just as regular people would, and pay me for my services. All these interactions over the years showed me how America truly is a country of no limitations. Anything you wanted to become, you could achieve it in this country. Here I was, a foreigner, and I realized that anything I wanted to dream, America could provide. In the system of forced "equality" that the Communists tried to implement, there was no such chance for the average person. No matter how famous, wealthy, or important the people whom I crossed paths with were, they always treated me like just another American, and it was one of the best feelings in the world.

Of course, the peaceful downfall of Communism was among the greatest and most profound changes and triumphs I witnessed in my life. The relief and joy Sława and I felt when it happened was simply beyond measure. I thought of my parents often during that time, and although they had been gone for over a decade when it happened, I wished so deeply that they could have lived to see that day. The battle between Communism and the free, capitalistic system of the West was the defining geopolitical conflict of my entire life. Looking back on it now, I realize that the life I led was defined by the moments that not only shaped the globe but also shaped my own life down to the smallest level, with the choices our family would make in the years that followed the end of a free Poland in 1939.

When I watched the collapse of the "Evil Empire," I felt it was in a way a culmination and affirmation of all the ideas I had known and internalized as right and good in my life. When the Berlin Wall fell, it was a confirmation of all the choices my parents had made, and I had made decades before. In my mind nothing had ever been in doubt, but now the whole world knew it. I knew the Communists were full of lies, only out to line their own pockets. I saw how the same good, honest, hardworking people who didn't stand a chance in Poland had flourished beyond their wildest imaginations in America. I was not an unusual case—I was surrounded by successful immigrant-entrepreneurs, and to me this was the great legacy of capitalism and democracy that I learned firsthand.

I was thinking about these things as I enjoyed my last visit to Lubocheń. The Polish people finally regained independence after fifty years of war and oppression, but despite all the healing that came with the fall of Communism, this place was still only a shadow of its former self. So much in the very psyche of the Polish people had been damaged or erased by Soviet rule. Together, the Nazis and Soviets had killed the majority of the Polish elite—the doctors, academics, lawyers, and clergy, and of course the majority of military officers, in order to subjugate the Polish nation to slavery. A generation was lost to death and deportation, and those who remained suffered the worst of those Cold War years. Polish culture was greatly damaged because of it.

Men like my father, who did business on a handshake and for whom their word was their bond, were once common. Now, cynicism invaded the hearts of many Poles, thanks to the ever-present corruption of the Communist system that they were forced to live under. So many lessons of Polish tradition were lost, and it was obvious to me that the only reason I was able to escape that fate was because I moved to America. Even with my father's strong character, after fifteen years of Communism he had lost his will to live in a system that kept honest men down. If we had stayed in Poland, I don't know that he could have taught me the same lessons, with the same energy, as he did when we moved to America when I was only nineteen years old. America gave my father a new lease on life. Once again the values that were so cherished in prewar Poland mattered and were valued in an open and democratic society. He was able to be himself, to work hard, to work honestly, and to make a decent life—just like he had before the war.

Walking around those woods, I felt I was possibly one of the few people still around who knew all of what happened there, to whom this land had once belonged and about all the illustrious European personalities that had come here when this was a grand estate at the turn of the century. The Plehns had lived a life full of rich adventure and meaningful work, and I felt strongly tied to that influence as I retraced the footsteps of my boyhood. It was almost as if in a dream that I recalled those heads of exotic African animals lining the long, tall corridors of Lady Rose's home, the home where I was born. I would never in a million years have dreamed that one hundred years after the Plehns traveled to Africa to explore exotic new frontiers and hunt wild game, I would be doing the same. It was a full-circle moment for me, to be walking around the grounds of "Swiderski's Place," knowing I was one of the few people who straddled the divide between the old world, full of memories and traditions, and the new, which had been torn down and rebuilt again, with mixed results.

A strange thing started happening at the turn of this last century, however. America, which had long been the golden knight on the world stage and the envy and object of admiration of everyone, began to change. I had seen America's magnificent rise in the postwar era, and now I watched with a saddened heart, as it seemed we were turning into a nation on the defense. I can't help but tie this decline to the rise of socialist tendencies when I see that society has made it harder for the average Joe to arrive and make something of himself through hard work. It seems the government has only tried to hamper the beautiful wings of freedom that allowed this country to flourish for so long. Now regulations and bureaucracy are at such a level that sometimes I wonder whether I'm living in a socialist country again.

As I grow older, it seems to me that America is being lured into a system that the Communists abandoned a long time ago. When I hear politicians spouting off empty promises about providing all requirements for living to anyone and everyone, regardless of whether they need it or are entitled to it, I am reminded of all the exact same promises the Communists made in Poland after WWII. Just as it was then, it sounds incredibly enticing, but as someone who has lived through it, I can tell for certain that no good will come of it. A nanny state government that serves its population's every possible whim only discourages people from working hard and maintaining their own dignity by following their vision for their own life. Industries tend to deteriorate because there are no incentives, the job market shrinks, and unemployment rises. This is clearly what is happening today in

America. There are constantly more laws, and more regulations, and things are not moving in the direction of freedom.

Worst of all, I see that youth are not being properly educated about history. I suppose that anyone who has lived through history himself will always say that the history books and the media are wrong. I see a political correctness that leads our society to obscuring the truth about the subtle horrors of living in a socialist system, mainly because we fear offending anybody with a different opinion. Today, it seems that even when we defend American values we are in danger of being labeled a bigot. I've seen the rising antagonism towards patriotic groups like my esteemed Safari Club International. We speak freely and openly about defending American values—honor, liberty, freedom from oppression—and for some reason these words have in some circles become synonymous with bigotry or extremism by portions of the US culture. In some ways I think not much has changed. When I arrived in America in 1960, no one here really knew what Communism was. They had some ideas, but it was largely guesses, and all that Americans had to go on was the firsthand accounts of the few witnesses like me, who had lived through it. Today, it seems people still don't understand what Communism is, and don't realize that some of the policies they are implementing are very much akin to that horrible way of life. Back then it took a generation or two for the truth to really come out, and now it seems in the last generation since the Cold War wound down that we are forgetting again.

As I walked through the Tuchola forests, which had seen so much carnage and mayhem this century, I was overcome with a realization that all the sacrifices of the freedom fighters of WWII are already being forgotten. Men like my brother Henry, who were drafted against their will—and on threat of death to their entire families—into the German army, are fading from public memory. He had seen so much horror, but he escaped the Nazi machine and joined the free Polish army as soon as he could. My father did the same at home, working to keep whatever he could to keep the family and neighbors alive. Then, of course, there were my uncles, who perhaps suffered the worst kind of trauma of all, because they were betrayed by their own countrymen after the war. The way Communism could turn one brother against another is indescribable. The torture and beating of so many Polish WWII heroes at the hands of the paranoid Communists, who were afraid of American hegemony, is a dark black mark on Polish history. Today those sacrifices seem to mean less and less, and I see America consistently implement policies that move us in the direction of hamstringing the individual, and giving more power to the state.

I spent the remainder of my two weeks in Poland hunting, and I bagged a nice roe deer and also shot a wild boar. Unfortunately, the boar ran away. I was sure my shot had been well placed, and I knew the animal would not be hard to find, but the local guide I hired did not want to track him, as he didn't think I had even hit the animal. I was frustrated because I knew I had hit him, but there was nothing I could do. The law in Poland requires that a foreign hunter be accompanied by a registered hunting guide at all times, and since the guide didn't want to track the animal, my hands were tied. I tried arguing with him, but he just brushed me off and assured me I hadn't hit the animal and that he got away clean. I don't think this man knew what an experienced hunter

I was, but he was the one who held the power in this situation, and so my hunt came to an abrupt end. Three days later some local lumber workers found my boar. He had been shot and had died, but by the time we found him, the skin had already been badly damaged by scavengers. The local guide was very apologetic because it turned out I was right. My shot was good, and if we had just tracked the animal that day, we probably would have found him. It was doubly upsetting that I had to leave this animal behind because this was a sentimental hunt in the forests where my father first taught me to hunt. For him, as for me, it would be extremely unethical not to look for the game he shot. I was frustrated by these nonsensical rules and regulations, and I was very sorry that my hunt in the woods of my youth ended in such a way. Luckily, I was also able to bag a local roe deer, and to this day he is mounted full size and stands proudly in my trophy room as one of my most prized possessions.

As the son of a European forester, I always considered the hunting culture to be one that cultivates a great appreciation for nature and for camaraderie among fellow citizens to support the natural wonder. I grew up with the values that encompassed that great era, and I rarely saw those values held in high esteem by the society around me. I was sad when I realized that if any of these young Polish people I met wanted to immigrate to America today, in 2014, they would not be able to accomplish what I had accomplished, in as little time. I remembered buying my first brand-new Thunderbird on a factory worker's salary when I was only twenty-two years old. Life was simple, and those opportunities for earning through hard work are largely gone.

In the 1960s, if you were a hardworking person, you would have a real chance. You could be judged by your work ethic, and you would be rewarded for it. You would have decent earnings for honest work, and you would get promoted when you paid your dues. Now there are no such guarantees, and people's values are all askew because of this situation. My father became the biggest American patriot I knew, even though America didn't become his adopted home until he was almost sixty years old. He wholeheartedly embraced everything that America stood for.

All hope is not lost, however. There is still more opportunity in America than almost anywhere else in the world, for the time being. There are small enclaves of freedom and hope, like the American Polonia in Chicago, which is over one million strong and works to maintain those values. The artists' community here is also very important, and is largely composed of political refugees from Communism who had to flee Poland because of their involvement with the pro-freedom Solidarity movement. Many of these people were famous movie, stage, and television stars in Poland before they had to escape to the US. These people would rather start over from scratch in a free America and fight for the true Polish culture from abroad than succumb to the oppression and persecution they were subjected to in Communist Poland. Sława and I have done all that we can to support these communities of artists and immigrants, usually in the form of hosting events and fundraisers for their causes. That we are able to support two of our most important values—freedom and Polish culture—thanks to more than fifty years of hard work in America, is one of the greatest and most fulfilling accomplishments that Sława and I enjoy in this lifetime.

Compared to other places, America is still the land of opportunity and freedom, but we must be vigilant. There is still a group of people who cherish the freedom that they know the warriors of this century won at a heavy price. There are still young men and women today who work to fight for freedom, and who understand what it means. I do the best I can to mentor young people who come into my shop, although their numbers are much smaller now than they were a few years ago. In the 1980s the ideas of hunting and roaming the wilderness of the American frontiers were still very popular and romantic notions. Young men would ride their bikes to my studio after work just to ask whether they could sit, watch, and learn. I took many of them under my wing, and mentored them for years. That era may be gone, but I believe that if we remain vigilant, all hope will not be lost.

One of the brightest lights I see for the future of America is the first-generation children of immigrants—those like my own daughter, Krystyna. This generation of young people did not have the same barriers that we did as foreigners, but luckily they still have all of the same values. When Krystyna was growing up, she was always proud to report at school that her father was an immigrant and had his own business. Even her teacher told her then, in the 1980s, that it was a big deal. I also loved my job because I worked out of the studio in my home, so I was always there when she came home from school, and we got to spend a lot of time together while she was growing up. I can't describe how proud I am of her today, that she is also running her own business, and takes pride in her work.

I share a deep love of nature and animals with my daughter, and I even took her to Africa once. She wowed not only me but also the local trackers with her ability to track animals. In just a few days of being on the ground she got the hang of it and was almost as good as they were. To be a tracker you have to have immense ability to pay attention to details. A single blade of grass broken in one direction gives you a clue about the direction the animal went. I was amazed that I had my own Sherlock Holmes with me, and was so proud of her talents.

While Krystyna was at the university, she complained that some of her professors who taught political science were preaching theories that were just the opposite of what she had been taught at home. I tried my best to advise her to not take them too seriously, but to listen and take it all in knowing what she knew from her own family's experience. I always told her the most important thing was getting good grades, and trying to learn something along the way, even if your teachers were seriously misguided. Secretly, though, I was so proud that I had raised a daughter with such wise judgment and solid character. I knew she was in no danger of being brainwashed by deluded academics.

When I look around me, I see that immigrants pay close attention to what philosophical road their children are being led down. Today, the business Krystyna built from scratch is blooming, and she is very talented and hardworking, and is earning fitting rewards for her dedication. Sława and I couldn't be more proud. Like many young people who are the children of immigrants from behind the Iron Curtain, she is excelling despite the obstacles our present system is throwing at her. I see this same set of values and work ethic in the children of my friends, and know that America still has a chance. I'm reminded of a wise saying that goes, "Those who do not know history, do not have a future." When we raise our children with the weight of history behind us, and show them how American democracy and capitalism are the truest forces for good and decency in the world, then we have a chance to keep creating opportunities for the American dream for generations to come.

ACKNOWLEDGMENTS

WE WOULD LIKE TO THANK OUR CO-WRITER AND editor, Aleksandra Corwin, affectionately known as Ola, for her outstanding work on bringing this manuscript to life. Without her, this book would probably have never materialized. We are grateful to our good friends and Ola's parents, Kasia and Janusz Kulczuga, for making this important introduction. Ola was a tremendous asset to us throughout the entire process, and she helped me convey in beautiful words my life experiences and my thoughts. She is also the daughter of immigrants, and we are indebted to her hard work, perspective, and guidance in helping us fulfill the dream of seeing this book completed.

I extend my deepest gratitude to my brother Henry Swiderski, his wife, Margaret Swiderski, my sister Henrietta Pruszynowska, and my brother Kazimierz (Casey) Swiderski for sharing with me and with Ola their recollections of the troubled times of our youth. Without them the details in this book would not have been so rich.

I deeply regret that my sister Halina Hoyner did not live to read this book. I did not remember her much from my childhood; she left Lubocheń when I was a small child, but after we reunited in the US, we become very close. She passed away June 5, 2013, and I still miss her.

I am grateful to my friend Dr. Richard Markuszewski for his support and encouragement to pursue writing this book. He motivated and inspired me to get my ideas down on paper, and provided valuable feedback along the way, for which we are eternally grateful. I would like to extend the same gratitude to Dr. Marian Olpinski and his wife, Barbara Olpinski—their support and encouragement has been very valuable, and we appreciate their early reading of this manuscript.

I am thankful to our friends Jola Kowalik and Wojciech Zalog, owners of Art Vision, for their friendship, help, support, and encouragement during the process of creating this book.

I would like to thank Polish historian Krzysztof Kufel for all the late-night talks we shared about the history of Lubocheń. Both he and my friend Piotr Rothegel, who did extensive research and translation for me from Berlin, Germany, were key to making this manuscript as historically accurate as possible.

In my personal life there are many people who have helped me to get to where I am today, and without them this book would never have been possible.

I will never forget the kindness Frank Huschitt showed me when I was just starting off, and for all the valuable business guidance he provided. Without him, Old World Taxidermy probably wouldn't have gotten off the ground as well as it did. I also extend a special thanks to my friend Dale Rimkus.

My eternal gratitude and appreciation also goes out to my talented and dedicated friends in the Chicago Polish art community. These people inspired me to keep my ethnic culture alive in my heart, nourishing it while we are all so far from home.

Most of these people are Polish immigrants, just like Sława and me. Many of them, in fact, are political refugees, having arrived in the US during the early days of martial law in Poland, when Solidarity members were being persecuted. These people were the artists and intellectuals advocating for change and democracy in Poland during the troubled years of the early 1980s. Many of them were well-known stage and screen actors, who abandoned their successful careers in favor of a chance at freedom in America. In Chicago they established performing arts groups, which have created a thriving cultural sphere for immigrants, and all who know them are grateful for their vibrant contributions to our lives in our home away from home. Our good friend, actress Elzbieta Kochanowska-Michalik, was instrumental in introducing us to this community of Polish stars. Among them are Krzysztof Arsenowicz, Zbigniew Bernolak, Mich Bochnak, Ryszard Gajewski-Gebka, Andrzej Krukowski, Julita Mroczkowska, Wojciech Malec, Agata Paleczny, Liliana Piekarski, Andrzej Piekarski, Andrzej Slabiak, Kasia Sobczyk, Miroslawa Sojka-Topor, the performing group Goranie, Ewa Staniszewska, and Alicja Szymankiewicz. Many of them often risked their lives in their contributions to Solidarity.

We have had the honor and privilege of hosting many of these great artists in our home for theatrical and musical events and fundraisers. I would like to acknowledge all the artists who have performed in our residence for both private and public events, especially Barbara Bilszta, director of the Polish Symphony Orchestra, and Wojciech Niewrzol, conductor. I would like to express my admiration for their talents, their sacrifices, and their tireless work to promote Polish culture far away from their homeland. They have contributed immensely to their adopted country with their talents and their efforts. Some of them came as political refugees, often taking on menial jobs, and yet they are above all full of appreciation for the refuge and safety America has provided.

I would like to extend a special thank-you to our friends Bogdan Lanko and his wife, Ewa Milde. Both of them graduated from a prestigious acting school in Kraków and were successful actors in Poland, yet they had to leave their country during Communist-imposed martial law because they were being persecuted for their involvement in the Solidarity movement. They devoted their talents to promoting Polish culture in America—they produced many theatrical plays and regularly entertain the public with live theater productions in Chicago, which employ dozens of Polish-American artists.

Our dear friend Elzbieta Kochanowska-Michalik also abandoned her successful acting career and arrived in the US as a political refugee seeking liberty and freedom of speech. She is now doing a tremendous job as an ambassador for Polish culture and art. She is tireless in her determined contributions to cultural causes among the Polish community.

We greatly appreciate the friendship of Zbigniew and Helen Karaś and admire their continuous promotion of Polish culture and for their support of the Polish religious community.

Also, we would like to express our admiration to Walter Kotaba, one of my friends from my early days in America for his contributions and his support for Polish culture and arts trough the TV and radio stations which he owns.

I would like to express my appreciation to Bozena Jankowska, who is an art critic for the Polish daily newspaper *Dziennik Związkowy*, for writing kind words about our contributions in promoting Polish culture.

We are proud that like us, all of our friends have worked hard, and actively contributed to American civil society. They have never been a burden on the system, and have always stood up for the ideas they believed in, earning their right to do so in America through hard work, paying taxes, and participating in the democratic process—something none of us who come from Communist Poland will ever take for granted.

THE END

Game viewing on our first safari in the Kalahari

Me, Dr. Don Kettlekamp, Dr. Wally
Zollman and his wife Brenda

Sława and a friend

Sława and I with the staff at the camp in the Kalahari

A Baobab tree

Sława with Adam, our Professional Hunter 1991

The wounded baby Eland we nursed back to health

Getting settled in our accommodations in the Transvaal Province

Africa in our blood

Baobab Tree

Sława and a termite mound

Sława with an adopted pet, a Rhodesian Ridgeback

Gemsbok antelope

Sława with her PH Timmy

Wildebeest

The dried up Sand River

Our PH Adam, and the Land
Rover we financed for him

Our plane to Bazaruto

Game viewing platform

Bobyjan

Setting up to hunt in Thabazimbi

The view from our lodge in Thabazimbi

Sława with the women who believed she
was a witch after she treated their child
with a "magical" antibiotic ointment

With a sail fish in Bazaruto

With Stella's son George, the
owner of Thabazimbi Safaris

Sława with an impala antelope

With friends in Bazaruto

Sława and Stella in Thabazimbi

Sława in Bazaruto

The leopard

The sleeping doberman

Sława with African artists we worked with

The leadwood bar I designed

Cape Buffalo carved out of
Leadwood, also by Robert Nzali

Carvings by Robert Nzali, an artist of the Shona Tribe
in Zimbabewe, Leadwood carved with wildebeests

Bazaruto at low tide, where you can
walk three miles into the ocean

Ancient bushman paintings

One of our good friends and a phenomenal artist, David Mudede with one of his carvings

Butter Jade bust by artist Moses Chikumbirike

Butter jade sculpture, also by Moses Chikumbirike

Buck Fever

Tuchola Forest 1998

Lady Plehn's estate 1998

Lubocheń 1998

OUR HOME

Here are some pictures of our home—the place we have worked hard to build with our own hands. Here we are surround by a beautiful garden where we planted every tree, shrub, and flower and cared for them for over 40 years. This is where bird build nests and wake us up with their serenades. This is where Krysia grew up, and where my mother instilled in her a love of flowers while she played under the watchful eyes of my father. This is the place where we spent countless memorable moments with our family and friends—moments of joy and happiness that we will cherish for the rest of our lives.

From left Casey, Halina, Henrietta, Me, Henry 1978

EVENTS AT OUR PALATINE HOME

Henry, Casey, and I

With Henry Sept 2014

Me, Sława's Mother, Krysia, Sława 2008

Sława in Belize with another adopted "pet"

Krysia and I in Gdansk

With Krysia Belize 1988

Jamaica 1980s

Krystyna in Sun City, South Africa

2002 Zimbabwe Sława with kids
on Mark Russo's property

Krysia and I on Safari 2007

Zimbabewe 2002

Fishing in Acapulco

Traveling goats in Zimbabewe 2002

Natives village Zimbabwe 2002

Mozambique 2002

South Africa with Krysia

Zimbabwe 2002 with Craig Bone, world renowned wildlife painter.
From left Me, Craig Bone, Sława, and Mark Russo—our host

OUR TROPHY ROOM

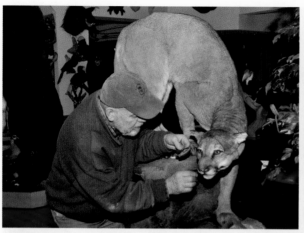